Allies or Adversaries

Governments throughout the developing world have witnessed a proliferation of nongovernmental, nonprofit organizations (NGOs) providing services like education, healthcare and piped drinking water in their territory. In *Allies or Adversaries*, Jennifer N. Brass explains how these NGOs have changed the nature of service provision, governance, and state development in the early twenty-first century.

Analysing original surveys as well as interviews with public officials, NGOs and citizens, Brass traces street-level government–NGO and state–society relations in rural, town, and city settings of Kenya. She examines several case studies of NGOs within Africa in order to demonstrate how the boundary between purely "state" and "nonstate" actors blurs, resulting in a very slow turn toward more accountable and democratic public service administration. Ideal for scholars, international development practitioners, and students interested in global or international affairs, this detailed analysis provides rich data about NGO–government and citizen–state interactions in an accessible and original manner.

Jennifer N. Brass is a professor at the School of Public and Environmental Affairs at Indiana University, Bloomington. Brass was a 2015 recipient of the Indiana University-wide Outstanding Junior Faculty Award, and has received awards from the African Politics Conference Group at the American Political Science Association and from the International Society for Third-Sector Research. Brass has completed field research in Senegal, Kenya, Djibouti and Uganda, and has conducted trainings for the US State Department, the US armed services, and the private sector.

Allies or Adversaries

NGOs *and the State in Africa*

JENNIFER N. BRASS
Indiana University

CAMBRIDGE
UNIVERSITY PRESS

CAMBRIDGE
UNIVERSITY PRESS

One Liberty Plaza, New York NY 10006, USA

Cambridge University Press is part of the University of Cambridge.

It furthers the University's mission by disseminating knowledge in the pursuit of education, learning, and research at the highest international levels of excellence.

www.cambridge.org
Information on this title: www.cambridge.org/9781107162983

First published 2016

A catalog record for this publication is available from the British Library

Library of Congress Cataloging in Publication data
Names: Brass, Jennifer N., author.
Title: Allies or adversaries : NGOs and the state in Africa / Jennifer N. Brass, Indiana University.
Description: New York NY : Cambridge University Press, 2016. | Includes bibliographical references and index.
Identifiers: LCCN 2016019085 | ISBN 9781107162983 (alk. paper)
Subjects: LCSH: Non-governmental organizations – Kenya. | Economic development projects – Kenya. | Non-governmental organizations – Political aspects – Kenya. | Kenya – Politics and government – 2002–
Classification: LCC HC865.Z9 E4426   2016 | DDC 338.91096762 – dc23
LC record available at https://lccn.loc.gov/2016019085

ISBN 978-1-107-16298-3 Hardback

For Betty

Contents

Figures and tables

Figures

Tables

Preface

In 2002, at the age of 24, I moved to Nairobi, Kenya to work for a small local NGO. Africa was not completely new to me: as an undergraduate, I spent a year studying abroad in Dakar, Senegal, where I lived with a local family, took classes at the university, interned with the US Peace Corps, and traveled in nearby countries. Afterwards, I graduated with a degree focused on African Studies, then worked for an international development-focused NGO in Washington, DC. I felt it was time to try working in Africa. An opportunity arose in Nairobi and off I went.

The NGO where I worked was located in one of the city's industrial-area slums – "informal settlements," as they are known in the development industry, or "villages," as local residents call them. In these areas, large factories stand interspersed with unauthorized neighborhoods where residents live in makeshift houses of corrugated iron sheets, wood, plastic, and sometimes cardboard; open sewage and muddy laneways create a hopscotch pattern of solid land to negotiate during the rains; and microentrepreneurs sell shoes, clothes, household goods, and foodstuffs along each path.

In the midst of these conditions, a young Kenyan woman started the organization in the early 1990s. She wanted to help address the lack of schools in the area, where only nine government schools served approximately 140,000 children. As the program grew, she also aimed to assist members of the community in dealing with the HIV/AIDS epidemic. To do so, the NGO operated a nonformal primary school, eventually serving more than 950 children, 40 staff members, and the nearby community. At the school, pupils were taught the government curriculum, participated in extra-curricular activities, and ate a nutritious meal each day. Alongside the school services, the NGO also provided financial support, counseling by a trained social worker, nutrition training, and enterprise development for a women's group whose members were HIV-positive.

Armed with only a primary school teaching certificate and a healthy supply of gumption, the founder began by hiring four other teachers at a wage of about $10/month, and coordinating with a local church to use their hall for classrooms. Not long after, a European NGO looking for projects to fund in the slums noticed the informal school and offered aid. The European organization helped the school settle onto unclaimed land, build corrugated iron and wood structures to serve as classrooms, and register with the government – as a "testing center" for the Kenya Certificate of Primary Education, the exam required for students to enter secondary school.[1] The school's international funder also paid teacher salaries and administrative costs, and managed the NGO's accounts and hiring.

After a few years, the European NGO was unable to continue its support. It helped the fledgling Kenyan organization find a second international NGO supporter, this time an American one, which funded nearly all of the school's annual budget of $80,000 for the next five years. At that point, however, the American NGOs' headquarters announced global priority changes, and it stopped supporting the Kenyan NGO after only three months. The founder then sent out an SOS to every foreigner who had been involved with the NGO, asking for assistance. Two colleagues of mine and I obtained financial support to cover our expenses, and headed to Kenya.

Over the next eight months, we successfully implemented a financial management plan, accounting system, and human resources manual, and we worked to find cost-cutting measures and new donors. Today, the NGO is funded in part by three different European NGOs, an American NGO, several individuals from around the world, and school fees from the students. Some summers, it hosts 10–12 European volunteers who act as teaching assistants and run training seminars for the staff and students. To our surprise, the Kenyan government has at times embraced the NGO as a "showcase" nonformal school, visited and displayed by Ministers of Education as a success story in the slum. Yet it still receives almost no money from the Kenyan government – though Ministry of Education

---

[1] The school registered as a testing center, and not a primary school, because of its informal nature and the lack of official training by much of the staff. At the same time, the Head Teacher was invited to Head Teachers' meetings at the local Division and District Education Office, and the pupils were invited to participate in extra-curricular events at the Division, District, Provincial and National level with government and formal private schools.

officials have been in very slow-moving talks with the NGO for several years regarding partial public funding for teacher salaries.

The story of this NGO is not unique. Wherever I traveled in Kenya during 2002, I noticed signs for this NGO and that one, met people working for big international NGOs and small local ones, and witnessed vehicles emblazoned with NGO logos driving up and down the country. Prosperous suburbs of Nairobi were full of foreign and local NGO workers and offices, and have become known as "NGO centers." Traveling back and forth to the slum by local minibus *matatu* transport, pop or hip-hop music blaring and diesel fumes filling my head, I reflected on the state of affairs. Where was the government in this situation? What had brought all of these organizations to Kenya? What were they achieving? Wasn't a lot of what they did supposed to be done by the government, particularly the core service of education – which even Adam Smith, granddaddy of the free market, believed the "watchman state" should provide? Were NGOs letting the government off the hook in their duty to provide? And were they making service provision decisions that might normally reside in the realm of the state? Did any of this matter to regular people – did it change how they viewed their government?

During 2002, and many times in the years since, Kenyans have told me that NGOs have been a blessing to the country, providing things that they could not rely upon the government to deliver, helping out when they did not trust the government to come through. In 2002, people seemed to view NGOs with hope; the government, with disillusionment. But what does it mean when people drop their expectations of their government? Does it lower government legitimacy in their eyes to see these other nonstate actors – often foreigners – provide basic services? And how has the situation changed since 2002, when the country experienced its first multi-party elections in decades?

These are the settings, experiences, and thought processes that formed the impetus for this book. The idea for this research came out of an enriching personal experience in Kenya, yet one that left me frustrated and disappointed with the Kenyan government. Over the course of conducting this research, however, I've discovered that – as is often the case – there are two sides to the story. In many ways, NGOs have actually had a positive impact on government, and their existence helped to make the Kenyan state stronger. Despite the conclusions of many recent books on African politics proclaiming the weakening of the state in Africa, I came to believe that NGOs helped support, encourage, and bolster a more able state in Kenya.

Acknowledgments

As anyone who has written one knows, a book cannot be finished without the advice, encouragement, and empathy of a team of colleagues and friends. I began the formal process of writing this book as a doctoral student of Political Science at the University of California, Berkeley. I am grateful to my dissertation committee members, David Leonard, Leo Arriola, Chris Ansell, and Michael Watts. David was a dedicated chair and advisor, closely reviewing chapter drafts and pushing me to do a bit more "heavy mental lifting" to make my points clear. Where David gave me the blueprint for a long career in academia, Leo became my role model for the next generation of African politics scholars. Talking to him always reinvigorated my interest in research; his love of learning is infectious. Chris proved that scholarship on comparative politics and public administration could be successfully interwoven and respected. Michael provided the perspective from outside Political Science that ensured my topics were broadly relevant to social scientists, and helped me develop my voice as a scholar.

At key points in my graduate school experience, Berkeley faculty Ann Swidler, Ted Miguel, Todd LaPorte, Kiren Chaudhry, Steve Vogel, and Paul Pierson also provided advice and mentoring, for which I am grateful. My student cohort was likewise an excellent extended family; special thanks are due to my dissertation-writing partners, Jennifer Dixon, Sam Handlin, Jon Hassid, Rachel Stern, and Susanne Wengle, as well as Martha Johnson, Robin Turner, Kristin Reed, Chris Blattman, Jody LaPorte, and Dann Naseemullah.

I am also indebted to colleagues, mentors, and friends at Indiana University (IU), where I am faculty in the School of Public and Environmental

Affairs (SPEA). Crucial to improving this book was a day-long manuscript review hosted by the Workshop in Political Theory and Policy Analysis, during which I received invaluable feedback from special guest Aili Tripp, who generously donated her time and energies for the event, alongside Elinor Ostrom, Lauren MacLean, Matt Auer, Todd Beer, Ashley Bowers, Sergio Fernandez, Kirsten Gronbjerg, Tim Hellwig, Maria Grosz-Ngate, and Anh Tran, each of whom provided detailed comments on at least one chapter of the manuscript. Lisa Amsler, Beth Buggenhagen, Sumit Ganguly, Beth Gazley, John Graham, Jeffrey Hart, Michael McGuire, Mike McGinnis, Sam Obeng, Justin Ross, and Allison Schnable also provided feedback that improved the manuscript at key junctures. Additional mentoring from Michael and Lisa helped me keep my eye on the finish line. I received excellent research support from graduate students Liz Baldwin, Kirk Harris, Susan Wambugu, and Shannon Lea Watkins. At IU, I owe a particular debt of gratitude to Lauren MacLean, who has helped move this book along in too many ways to count. I am extraordinarily lucky to count her as a mentor, co-author, and friend.

For many of us, a book spawned from a doctoral dissertation is intensely tied to the author's self-identity – and those identities are tested during the rougher moments of the research and writing process. In addition to the aforementioned people and institutions, I recognize several support networks and well-timed external reminders that the work was good, the challenges were surmountable, and the course was worth staying. During my first year of graduate school, I received a National Science Foundation multi-year fellowship that funded most of my field research in Kenya. My application for that grant was the first time the ideas that became this book were put to paper in an organized form. Later, during my first years on the Indiana University faculty, I was equally fortuitous to receive accolades from the African Politics Conference Group (APCG) and the International Society for Third-Sector Research (ISTR), which again quieted my inner critic. The APCG has become an intergenerational community of individuals I value for collegiality and generosity of time – many individuals I met through APCG have given me thoughtful feedback on drafts of this book. Likewise, my colleagues at the Midwest Working Group on Political Economy (MGAPE) and an informal group of ladies who study Africa have provided professional-personal support. From these groups, I especially thank Claire Adida, Marc Bellemare, Ryan Briggs, Karisa Cloward, Jeff Conroy-Krutz, Kim Yi Dionne, John Harbeson, Frank Holmquist, Adrienne LeBas, Ashley Leinweber, Gina Lambright, Rachel Beatty Riedl, Laura Seay, Ryan Sheely, and Nic van de Walle for their feedback. I also thank others in the broader academic community for formal and informal support along the way, including Tim Buthe, Melani Cammett, Mary Kay Gugerty, Martin Lodge, Johanna Mair, Woody Powell, Aseem Prakash, Kenneth Prewitt, Rachel Robinson, Monique Segarra, and David Suarez.

People have also supported me outside of the office during this long process. I owe my largest thanks to my family. My husband (and colleague), Matthew Baggetta, has been my biggest cheerleader. He provides unwavering support, whether by commenting on drafts, brainstorming solutions to writing problems, or volunteering to cook me dinner and take care of our home when I am single-mindedly focused on writing. Our son, meanwhile, provides the daily small joys that remind me why I work on "big questions" – I hope to help find answers for future generations. When I was myself a child, I learned from my mom to take risks and dream big, even when the likelihood of failure was high. My dad, on the other hand, taught me the importance of hard work and attention to detail – and the proper place of both in a life that is also full of play. During years of going back and forth to Kenya, it was big sister who always pulled me back home, and who demonstrated the most pride in my work as a scholar of Africa. Friends have acted similarly; happily, there are too many to name. Without the early influence of the Concordia Language Villages – Dahveed and Zuwenna in particular – I might never have gone to Africa.

Of course, this book could not have been completed without considerable and generous time, thought and energy put in by hundreds of Kenyans, most of whom remain nameless for confidentiality reasons. At the Institute for Development Studies (IDS) at the University of Nairobi, scholars Karuti Kanyinga and Winnie Mitullah helped me navigate the Kenyan political landscape, as well as its bureaucracy. Tom Wolf, likewise, opened his network of Kenya scholars to me, and facilitated my survey research in many ways. From Mbeere District, a very special thank you is owed to Mwaniki, who volunteered many days of his time to bring me into the back roads and small villages of the district to speak with NGOs I may not have found myself. And in Nairobi, I cannot thank Betty Nyagoha and Joseph Ngigi enough. Betty, along with Joseph Oloo and the entire Gatoto family, including Lucy Karuri, Scholastica Muasya, Winnie Mutua, Rhoda Mutua, and many others, inspired this book. Joseph Ngigi made the research a logistic reality, not only finding me places to live when in Nairobi, but also providing Gold Mine transportation wherever I needed to go. (And I wouldn't have been in Kenya at all if it weren't for Colman Farrell.) They have become true, lifelong friends.

I owe appreciation to several publishers for permission to reprint material that has already been published. Chapter 4 of this book is based on "Why Do NGOs Go Where They Go? Evidence from Kenya," originally published in *World Development*, Vol. 40, Issue 2 (2012), pp. 387–401. Some material from Chapters 5 and 6 draw from material published in "Blurring Boundaries: The Integration of NGOs into Kenyan Governance," from *Governance: An International Journal of Policy, Administration, and Institutions*, Vol. 25, Issue 2 (2012), pp. 209–235, and "Blurring the Boundaries: NGOs and Government in Kenyan Service Provision," which is Chapter 5 of Melani Cammet and Lauren M. Maclean (eds.) *The Politics of Non-State Social Welfare in the Global South*, Cornell University Press (2014).

Lastly, I am grateful to my publisher, Cambridge University Press, particularly editor Robert Dreesen, along with the production team at Cambridge. With their help and that of Elizabeth Andrews, Peter Dimock, and two anonymous reviewers, this book has improved immensely. All remaining errors and omissions are my own.

I

NGOs and state development

Joseph Mukani, the manager of Mbeere Community Development Programme (MCDP), hurries into the small, cluttered office where I am waiting to interview him.[1] The office is located among the row of brightly painted, single-story shops, hair salons, and cafés that briefly line one side of a dusty dirt road, arising abruptly after miles of sparsely inhabited farmland and quickly disappearing again into fields punctuated by mud buildings with roofs made of thatch or iron sheeting. I have come to learn about NGO programming in the rural district of Mbeere, Kenya from this small organization, which is the local implementing partner of a large US-based nonprofit active in thirty countries around the world.[2]

Mukani tells me about the NGO's activities, including training programs in agriculture, health, finance, and business development. He describes one training seminar the organization conducted on improving livelihoods through goat rearing, attended by self-help groups from around the district, as well as Ministry of Livestock officers eager to learn new techniques to pass on to others during their extension service activities. As he speaks, I wonder how effective the training – one of very many I heard about or witnessed – would be in changing habits on the ground, and whether paying for the government officials' time and transportation to the seminar was worth the expense.

[1] To protect their identity, the names of the NGO and its manager, as well as identifying information about the organization's location, have been changed.
[2] The office I visited has three employees, and there is a larger office in nearby Embu town, which is staffed by employees of both the Kenyan-based NGO and the US-based one.

Mukani also describes a deworming program the organization conducted in the district to help the Ministry of Health. The deworming drugs, meant to be distributed to schoolchildren across Mbeere, were donated by a Scandinavian government aid agency and brought to the district office of the Ministry months earlier. The pills had not been distributed, however, as the Ministry office had neither a vehicle nor the funds to transport a staff member to schools throughout the district. MCDP stepped in to provide transportation and an allowance for a government officer to administer the pills to schoolchildren. "The government has the drugs, but they just expire if they don't get facilitation. So we add that," he tells me. He is pleased with the interaction with the ministry. "It's a true partnership," he says.

In addition, the organization works to support schoolchildren through a child sponsorship program for primary and secondary school students and early childhood development programs, and by rehabilitating and furnishing existing public school buildings. MCDP's goal is to provide a safety net for disadvantaged families in the area, and they rehabilitate three to six government schools each year. They have also improved government water services by extending pipeline several kilometers to reach a village that had not been connected to the public service previously.

When I ask explicitly about the organization's interactions with the government, the response is complex. Mukani states that MCDP makes its programmatic decisions independently from the government, but then says that he works closely with the Ministries of Agriculture, Livestock, Education, Health, and Public Works, and that he is a member of the District Development Committee, a government-led group that is meant to manage development activities in the district as a whole. He complains weakly about government inefficiencies, saying, "Government doesn't move that far the way we do. It takes them so much time [to do things]." But he then suggests that things are changing, since, "Service contracts are new in government, but are old at NGOs." And he insists that, "NGOs also need government. They have certain institutions enabling [NGOs] to do their jobs." At the end of the interview, he explains that most people in Kenya are more concerned about whether or not they get goods and services than about the type of organization the resources come from. He opines that government is needed for the long term. "NGOs came [to Kenya] when donors wouldn't give to government. If government worked, NGOs wouldn't be needed.

NGOs know they're short term. Government should continue," he concludes.

Much of the academic work on NGO–government interactions describes a hostile, conflictual relationship and asserts that NGOs often undermine developing states.[3] This view is encapsulated in Fernando and Heston's claim that "NGO activity presents the most serious challenges to the imperatives of statehood in the realms of territorial integrity, security, autonomy and revenue" (2011, 8). The interview just described and most others I conducted in Kenya between 2002 and 2012, however, point to changes in this relationship and to a more complex reality on the ground. Rather than threatening the state, nongovernmental organizations have come to comprise part of the de facto organizational makeup of the state in many developing countries of the world. Under the right conditions, they have become part and parcel of public service administration through interpenetration with government. NGOs support state capacity and along the way enhance state legitimacy in the eyes of the citizens, who maintain both a pragmatic and wary view of the state and those who control it. Such a change is significant for weakly institutionalized states and their citizens, with both positive and negative implications.

This book traces the interactions between states, NGOs, and citizens to bring to light this emerging pattern of governance in developing countries. In doing so, it provides detailed answers to a number of important and related questions about NGOs, service provision, and state development. The book also addresses key questions about four "elements of stateness" – territoriality, governance, administrative capacity, and legitimacy:

- What does NGO provision of services look like on the ground – what factors draw NGOs to work in particular locations, and what implications does NGO location have for *territoriality*?
- How has the *governance* of service provision changed with the growth of NGOs over time? What changes do we see, not only in the way decisions are made and implemented, but also in the relationships

---

[3] In a 2012 review article, Watkins, Swidler, and Hannan agree that whether NGOs pose a threat to states in poor countries has been one of two key debates among NGO scholars. (The other debate, largely among anthropologists, concerns whether or not NGOs actually fulfill their promises to the poor.)

between NGOs and governments? Under what conditions do we see collaboration or conflict in these relationships?

- Does (or to what extent does) the provision of services by NGOs allow a government to shirk its duty to provide for the people? How has *administrative capacity* been affected?
- Do citizens respond differently to provision of services by NGOs than they do to those provided by governments? Specifically, does NGO service provision undermine citizen perceptions of the state, or could it instead bolster state *legitimacy*?

The book draws on extensive evidence from in-country research in one developing country, Kenya, supplemented with data from Latin America, the Middle East, the former Soviet Union, and South, Central, and East Asia. It provides the reader with interrelated arguments about the changing nature of NGO–government relationships, the governance of service provision, state–society relations, and state development, which are outlined in this brief introduction.

WHAT ARE NGOS?

A considerable literature has developed in order to conceptualize NGOs and related organizations (Salamon 1994, Uphoff 1993, Vakil 1997, Werker and Ahmed 2008). Most scholars agree that NGOs are private, not-for-profit organizations that seek to improve society in some way. Variation among organizations can be found in: where the organization first developed or is headquartered in the world; how it obtains funding; the scope of its activities (local, national, cross-national, international); whether it is a locally-formed, grassroots initiative of the poor or an elite-formed organization; whether it is a membership association or a professionalized organization; and whether it is secular or religious. NGOs are usually secular organizations, though they are sometimes registered in association with a church or other religious organization, making the *strict* characterization of NGOs as "secular organizations" inaccurate.[4] In

---

[4] Indeed, over the course of research for this project, the use of the term FBO, or "faith-based organization," also grew, partially in response to the US funding of FBOs during the George W. Bush administration. The line between church-based development activities (not registered as NGOs) and NGO activities, like the line between CBOs and NGOs, is incredibly fuzzy. Often, individual churches or national-level church organizations run development programs, clinics, etc. Usually, these are not registered as NGOs, but sometimes they are. Clearly, the messy reality of registration choice makes perfect interpretation of the impact of NGOs difficult.

Kenya, NGOs register with the NGO Coordination Board (NGO Board) of the government.

This book employs the definition of NGOs used by the Kenyan government at the time of research. The government defines NGOs as

A private voluntary grouping of individuals or associations not operated for profit or for other commercial purposes but which have organized themselves nationally or internationally for the benefit of the public at large and for the promotion of social welfare, development, charity or research in the areas inclusive but not restricted to health, relief, agricultural, education, industry, and supply of amenities and services.

(Republic of Kenya 1992)

I use this definition since most of the data in the book comes from Kenya, and the definition guided my data collection. In Kenya, it is also a useful definition because the government draws legal, regulatory, and registration distinctions between professionalized, formal NGOs and their Community-Based Organization (CBO) cousins. Most foreign-based, other-oriented charity groups and organizations are classified as NGOs, along with similar Kenya-based organizations.

WHY ARE THERE SO MANY NGOS NOW?

For the past 25 years, states around the world have witnessed the rapid growth of nonprofit, nongovernmental organizations providing goods and services in their territories. NGOs can be global players like Oxfam[5] and CARE[6] that are headquartered in the West and have offices in nearly 100 countries; organizations like BRAC,[7] which began as a home-grown organization in Bangladesh and spread throughout the world; regionally important actors like Kenya-based AMREF[8] in Africa; large,

[5] Oxfam began in the UK in 1942 to fight hunger during World War II and by 2016 had programs in 96 countries. See: http://www.oxfam.org/.
[6] CARE began in 1945 as an American network of organizations delivering care packages to survivors of World War II, and has grown to an organization that was working in 84 countries by the mid-2010s. See: http://care.org/.
[7] Like Oxfam and CARE, BRAC (formerly Bangladesh Rural Advancement Committee) began as a relief organization, serving Bangladesh, in 1972. It now claims to be the largest development organization in the world with more than 90,000 staff in about 15 countries. See: http://www.brac.net/. ActionAid is a similar organization. Although founded in the UK in 1972, it is now headquartered in South Africa, and the organization was working in 45 countries of Africa, Latin America, and Asia by the mid-2010. See: http://www.actionaid.org/.
[8] AMREF was founded in Kenya in 1957 to provide mobile medical services to remote populations. By 2014, the organization was working in seven African countries. See: http://amref.org/.

single-country organizations; or small but formalized organizations working in one country or community. All NGOs undertake not-for-profit
programming that aims to better the lives of individuals and societies.
NGO work usually falls into the areas of healthcare, education, agriculture, the environment, humanitarian relief, and basic water and sanitation
infrastructure.

Estimates vary widely on the present number of NGOs. According to
the World Bank, international development NGOs based in rich countries
grew from 6,000 to 26,000 between 1990 and 1999.[9] By 2010, thousands
of NGOs were employing millions of people in Nigeria (Smith 2010);
nearly 8,000 NGOs were operating in Kyrgyzstan (Pugachev nd); tens of
thousands of NGOs were in Bangladesh, with at least one in nearly 80
percent of villages (Rahman 2006); and more than one million organizations were operating in India (McGann and Johnstone 2006). Regardless
of the exact number of NGOs, the position of these nongovernmental
organizations has shifted from that of minor and little-discussed players
focusing on the welfare of the poor to major, central actors on the world
stage of development, receiving, in some cases, more donor funds than
their state counterparts (Chege 1999, Doyle and Patel 2008, Batley 2006,
Mayhew 2005).

NGOs rose to the forefront of discussion in international development
conversations as part of a paradigm shift from a belief in government-
led development to dedication to private-led development (Kamat 2004).
While the particulars differ, the historical patterns are similar in developing countries around the world. In the years following World War II,
post-colonial states promised to improve basic services such as education,
infrastructure, and security for their citizens. Initially, states were able to
make good on these promises. From the 1940s through the 1970s the
consensus among not only national policymakers, but also international
economists and development banks, was that the state was *the* actor
capable of developing an economy due to the many market imperfections
in poor countries (Bates 1989, Hirschman 1981). Young "developmental
state" (Johnson 1982) governments therefore became pervasive, involved
in all elements of the economy, service provision, and welfare (Mkandawire 2001). In much of sub-Saharan Africa, states quickly became
the largest employers, creating thousands of new jobs in the civil service, state-owned enterprises (SOEs), schools, clinics, and infrastructure

---

[9] World Bank website, "Defining Civil Society," at http://go.worldbank.org/
4CE7W046K0 (accessed April 11, 2006 and August 10, 2009).

projects.[10] In many poor countries, growing numbers of university-educated students saw the civil service as their future employer (Prewitt 1971, Barkan 1975), and were actually guaranteed employment (van de Walle 2001). With governments focused on import-substituting industrialization, state-owned factories and manufacturing plants absorbed many graduates.

For many states this period of easy expansion was short-lived. Patronage-based systems resulted in politically – not economically – rational policies (Bates 1981). Goods and services were distributed to loyal clients in exchange for votes and support. Over time, these patterns created economic problems and perverse incentives within organizations (Ekeh 1975). In many countries, farmers withdrew from commercial markets, reducing tax revenues (Bates 1981). Added to these challenges were a series of economic disasters in the 1970s and early 1980s: oil shocks, plunging world market commodity prices, truncated industrial capability due to the increasing relative costs of imports, and a string of debilitating droughts.

By the late 1980s, most of the developing world had experienced prolonged economic stagnation. Meanwhile, an ideology of liberalization had gained strength in the West, where policymakers promoted deregulation, privatization, and reduced trade barriers as pathways to economic growth. International financial institutions and other donors quickly began to insist on economic liberalization as a precondition to loans and grants for developing countries. States were often required to liberalize exchange rates and financial markets, privatize or outsource public services, reduce trade barriers, trim national budgets, and maintain sustainable monetary policies in order to receive aid.[11]

The role of the government in service provision changed dramatically over this period. Governments retreated from welfare and public good provision in order to reduce public expenditure and comply with the donor push for privatization. For example, Tanzanian social services as a percentage of government expenditure halved between 1981 and 1986,

---

[10] Thus, for example, by 1979, 15 years after independence, 42 percent of formal employment in Kenya was in the government (Hazlewood 1979). Similarly, in Nigeria, the number of SOEs grew from 250 to more than 800 in the 1970s (Lewis 1994, 443), and the Nigerian government grew 50 percent in the first five years after independence (van de Walle 2001).

[11] Most states did not actually implement all policies; in general, they implemented stabilization measures, but not real structural change (van de Walle 2001). Consequently, the IFIs withheld funds for noncompliance, as in Kenya, for much of the 1990s.

at the same time as fees for public services increased dramatically (Tripp 1994). In Kenya, spending on education dropped from 18 percent of the budget in 1980 to 7.1 percent in 1996, and in the health sector, government spending decreased from $9.82 million in 1980 to $6.2 million in 1993 and $3.61 million in 1996 (Katumanga 2004, 48). By the end of the 1980s, political scientist Michael Bratton could write, "especially in the remotest regions of the African countryside, governments often have had little choice but to cede responsibility for the provision of basic services" (1989, 569).

Throughout the developing world, "the 'roll-back of the state' was accompanied by a growth in NGO service provision and the replacement of government structures by informal, nongovernmental arrangements" (Campbell 1996, 2–3 citing Farrington 1993, 189 and Bennet 1995, xii). Donors, armed with the norms of world society, strongly supported the growth of NGOs, and associations proliferated as these norms made headway (Schofer and Longhofer 2011). In the 1990s, for example, official development assistance (ODA) to NGOs increased 34 percent (Epstein and Gang 2006), and by 1999, most of USAID's $711 million in aid to Africa went to NGOs (Chege 1999).[12] By contrast, in Kenya, ODA to the government halved between 1990 and 1994, and it halved again by 1999 (Organization for Economic Cooperation and Development 2013), as donors maintained distrustful relationships with the government (Mosley and Abrar 2006). In such places, donors bypassed states with low capacity for governance, giving money to NGOs when they believed doing so would enable their support to achieve their intended outcomes (Dietrich 2013). At the same time, many governments continued to channel monies, including aid, into maintaining patronage networks and procuring votes (Jablonski 2014).

More recently, in the mid-2000s almost 50 percent of funds from the Global Fund to Fight AIDS, Tuberculosis and Malaria (Global Fund) and nearly 45 percent of funding for the US President's Emergency Plan for AIDS Relief (PEPFAR) was directed toward NGOs around the world (Doyle and Patel 2008). In the 2010s, countries like Cambodia received as much as 20 percent of their international aid via NGOs (Suárez and Marshall 2014). Nonprofits have been touted as more efficient, effective,

---

[12] More precise statistics on funding to NGOs is not available for the 1990s and is of limited quality for the 2000s. For a discussion of the limitations of existing African statistics, see Jervin (2013).

flexible, participatory, democratic, accountable, and transparent than their government bureaucracy counterparts.[13]

Over the years, NGOs have moved from providing supplemental charity and relief work to being increasingly involved in basic development and service provision based on a participatory approach (Brodhead 1987). For example, in the Kenyan health services sector alone, NGOs now run nearly 90 percent of clinics and as many hospitals as the government (World Resources Institute 2003, 87). Alongside ministries of health, education, agriculture, and public works, we now see NGOs providing education, healthcare, child and women's assistance, agricultural extension services, employment, and even, in some cases, roads, wells, and other infrastructure. Thus, many of the goods and services that are today provided by NGOs were traditionally associated with states and governments; these services form part of the social contract between a state and its citizens (Campbell 1996, 9; Cannon 1996; Whaites 1998; Heurlin 2010). Because of this overlap, many governments – especially those dependent on the distribution of patronage goods – exert strategies to maintain control over NGOs working in their territory (Bratton 1989). Despite these government efforts to maintain leverage over NGOs, we have come to see significant changes in the nature of NGO–government relationships, the governance of service provision, and state–society relations due to NGO activity.

WHAT CHANGES HAVE RESULTED FROM NGOS?

The changing nature of NGO–government relationships

Comparative historical analysis of NGO–government relationships in Kenya and other countries reveals an increase in collaborative working relationships between NGOs and governments over the past 25 years. Where NGO–government interactions in developing countries were once dominated by mutual suspicion, distrust, conflict, and governmental control, over time they have become more cooperative, even positive and, in some cases, actively collaborative. This trend is not universal, but tends to be true in the presence of certain conditions: high-performing NGOs that focus on service provision rather than politics, human rights or corruption; stable government regulations, actions, and policy that demonstrate

---

[13] The perception of benefits to funding NGOs was one reason for shifts in donor funding, although there were other reasons as well.

commitment to development and grant space for organizational autonomy; lack of competition for funding between NGOs and governments;
and both types of organizations deliberately striving to create positive
working relationships. Where these conditions are wholly absent or on
the decline, however, conflictual relations become more common or even
the norm.

In most parts of the world, however, collaboration and the conditions that facilitate it are driven by two factors. First, donor and funding
organizations – not only multi- and bilateral donors, but also dominant
philanthropic organizations – started requiring collaboration as a condition of funding (Ndegwa 1996). As specific examples, the percentage
of World Bank projects that require active civil society organization participation increased from approximately 20 percent at the start of the
1990s to greater than 80 percent by 2010.[14] Likewise, the Global Fund,
which disbursed US$2.5 to 3.5 billion annually between 2009 and 2012,
requires recipients to work in partnerships of government, NGO, community, and private sector actors.[15] Governments and NGOs have had
no choice but to work together, at least on a surface level.

Yet even in the absence of consistent donor presence, government
and NGO relationships have tended to become more positive over time.
This trend points to the importance of a second factor: social learning.
Representatives from both NGOs and government agencies have grown
over time to understand that it is in their mutual interest to work together.
Through repeated interactions that facilitate the slow development of
trust, leaders and managers in both types of organizations come to realize
that there are win–win outcomes of engagement with the other sector. As
Clark reminded us two decades ago, "Even 'bad' governments often have
'good' departments with which NGOs can work" (Clark 1992, 153).

A limited number of academic articles have begun to document such
changes across a range of countries and contexts, suggesting a generalizable phenomenon. Comparing West Africa's Gambia to Ecuador
and Guatemala in Latin America, for example, Segarra (1997) and
Brautigam and Segarra (2007) show that in all three countries, NGOs and

---

[14] The World Bank includes NGOs among many types of nongovernmental organizations
it considers as part of "civil society," such as community-based organizations, social
movements, labor unions, faith-based groups, and foundations. See: http://go.worldbank
.org/Q4JHC82S8o

[15] The Global Fund is registered as a nonprofit foundation in Switzerland, and refers to
their multisectoral model as their "Partnership Strategy." See: www.theglobalfund.org/
en/about/fundingspending/

governments failed in their first attempts at donor-encouraged partnerships in the 1980s and 1990s. By the 2000s, however, NGOs and their government counterparts were engaged in the collaborative implementation of programs and creation of policy to a great extent in Gambia and Ecuador, and to a lesser but apparent degree in Guatemala (ibid.). Segarra and Brautigam argue that these changes stem from the creation of trust during repeated iterations of interactions over many years, which allowed both governments and NGOs to learn that working together was in their mutual interest (ibid.). They cite a Gambian government official as saying "ten years ago ... NGOs were seen as interfering, but we have now seen that they have strategic advantages" (Brautigam and Segarra 2007, 160). Like researchers working in other areas of the world (Rose 2011, Pugachev nd), Brautigam and Segarra also credit donor requirements for collaboration as a crucial impetus for beginning interactions, and seeing partnerships as mutually beneficial (ibid.).

Elsewhere in Africa and Latin America, we find comparable stories. In Ghana, Atibil (2012) documents a similar trend spanning Rawlings's transition from a military regime to an electoral system. She argues that psychological factors – specifically mutual perceptions of civil society organizations and the government – changed over time, creating space for positive relationships as well as political opening.

These trends are likewise visible in Asia. In a survey of Cambodian NGOs, nearly 60 percent of respondents reported positive working relations with government, and 40 percent shared complaints that they heard from community members with the government (Suárez and Marshall 2014). In the health sector in Pakistan, moreover, governments increasingly recognize the boost that they receive from collaboration with NGOs to increase service provision (Ejaz, Shaikh, and Rizvi 2011). Over time, the Government of Pakistan has learned that working with NGOs allows it to do things that it could not have done by itself (ibid.) and it has changed some of its policies accordingly to increase complementarity of service provision (Campos, Khan, and Tessendorf 2004). As a result, collaboration between the government and NGOs has grown over the past two decades. Similar trends are occurring in the health sector in Bangladesh, although relationships can still become hostile (Zafar Ullah et al. 2006). Governmental policy and regulation have changed over time to facilitate these more collaborative relationships (ibid.). Although tensions between NGOs and governments persist in both countries and in India, "the policies of partnership have not only come to stay but are also becoming increasingly institutionalized" due to donor pressures and changing socio-political environments (Nair 2011, 253).

Even in China, local governments are increasingly collaborating with charities and nonprofits to deliver services like education and health-care (Teets 2012). Although these relationships generally take the form of contracting rather than co-production, they are still signs of growing government willingness to work with nongovernmental organizations. These collaborations reflect movement away from direct control of the society by the state, and instead toward state supervision of the market and society, integrating civil society into a more pluralistic policy environment (ibid.).

The governance of service provision

These collaborative NGO–government interactions have led to significant changes in the governance of service delivery, both in the implementation of services among public and nongovernmental organizations and in decision-making around public service provision. In both domains, increased collaboration has resulted in a blurring of the boundaries between government and nongovernmental organizations and programs, as NGOs gain de facto or "practical" authority (Abers and Keck 2013) alongside government actors in the country. At times, it is difficult to tell where the government ends and the NGO begins.

On the implementation side of governance, NGOs and governments have increasingly worked together to provide services. In Kenya, NGOs and line ministries pool resources for joint projects, NGOs pay for activities that allow the government to fulfill its mandate, experts from government ministries are seconded to NGOs to oversee the implementation of technical programs, and NGOs rent office space within government ministry buildings, physically co-locating. NGOs raise the capacity of the state to provide services by extending the reach of government some degree farther than it could go in the NGOs' absence – sometimes quite literally, as when an NGO provides petrol to power a Ministry of Agriculture vehicle to a remote village to work with farmers. Rather than letting governments "off the hook" in their promise of service provision, NGOs supplement government activities. Individual civil servants involved in joint programs – especially extension officers – report doing more of the work they were trained to do, not less. In most parts of the country, government organizations of service administration remain the primary provider of services. Yet in far-flung places that are remote or difficult to reach, NGOs often play the part of government, broadcasting public service provision to a greater swath of the territory.

On the decision-making side of governance, similar patterns emerge. In most places, governments take the lead in service delivery decision-making. Yet rather than dictate what NGOs are to do, the government now invites NGOs to sit on national and local policymaking committees and integrates NGO plans and budgets into national and local planning. As a representative example, one district of Kenya proposed 149 service delivery projects in its five-year planning document (2008–2012); of these, 44, or just less than 30 percent, were to be funded or implemented by NGOs working in the area, based on the NGOs' own plans.

One important result of collaborative service provision comes in the form of a very slow movement toward greater transparency and accountability within the civil service in Kenya. In essence, we see a process of institutional isomorphism within agencies of government, as they very slowly adopt the practices of their NGO partner organizations. This shift gradually raises the administrative capacity of the state. It must be stressed that these changes are small and slow, and that the quality of service provision and of government accountability still remain extremely low in places like Kenya.

Still, we should not dismiss movement toward democratic governance, however slight. Some of these changes come from deliberate strategies that government agencies use to obtain capacity-building training programs from NGOs or bring successful NGO leaders into prominent government positions. Others changes appear to be less intentional outcomes of social learning (Segarra 1997); government workers see the praise NGOs providing services get, and they mimic NGO activities. As Ndegwa (1996) has shown, even NGOs' "mundane activities" of everyday service provision can empower grassroots communities to engage their government.

Despite small signs of such changes, however, NGOs' methods of service implementation make it difficult to clearly or objectively measure the impact of NGO programs. This measurement challenge is due in part to collaborative working relations, in which indirect NGO funding makes it impossible to tease out causality in increases or decreases in service provision. Yet it is also difficult to measure impact because NGOs are not always particularly effective or efficient organizations. They do not, for example, necessarily spend their funds in the most cost-effective manner – sometimes, this inefficiency is due to their own donors' conditions or requirements, but on other occasions it is because there is "a lot of cheating done by NGOs" with money (2007–1[16]). Many of the funds that NGOs bring to programs must be used for one-time expenses on durable goods, such as vaccines, school buildings, or boreholes, or on educational training programs, most of which end up being short-term seminars. Many NGOs (and the public or private donors behind them) are rightly criticized for favoring short-term, financially sustainable programming, such as single-day trainings on any number of topics, rather than long-term investments in human capital via health or education programs' staff salaries, or intensive, long-term education for promising individuals.

On the flip side, NGOs do tend to have the resources and the flexibility to experiment with new types of programs in a way that governments do not. Much as US states are seen as a testing ground for US federal policy, NGOs can be seen as testing grounds for national policy in developing countries. Several clear programmatic successes have come from these experiments, most notably forms of conditional cash transfers.

Service provision, the social contract, and state–society relations

How do such changes to service provision and governance affect the people receiving services? More specifically, how does NGO provision of services affect perceptions of the state? It has been argued elsewhere that nonstate service provision can sever the social contract between state and society: as people receive services from nonstate actors rather than from their government, their loyalty to the state declines as their loyalty to the NGOs increases. NGO provision of services can, therefore, threaten a state's legitimacy (Bratton 1989, Jelinek 2006, Doyle and Patel 2008, Batley and McLoughlin 2010, McLoughlin 2011). With such logic in mind, authoritarian governments throughout the world have clamped down on NGO activities, even those that are explicitly apolitical and do not seek social change. At various times in the past decade, for example, governments in Russia, Uzbekistan, Venezuela, Ethiopia, Zimbabwe, Swaziland, Kenya, India, Sri Lanka, China, and Afghanistan have reacted by banning some or all NGOs and their funding sources.

Evidence reveals that such action is unnecessary. Rather than reflecting poorly on the government, receiving services from NGOs has either

---

[16] Citations in this format refer to interview sources. This reference is to the first interview conducted in 2007.

no effect on or in fact improves Kenyans' perceptions of the state. The strongest explanation for this phenomenon is somewhat paradoxical: Kenyan expectations of their government are exceedingly low; as such, the provision of services – regardless of their origins – is seen in positive terms, and credit for service provision is diffuse. Government actors, especially politicians, often slyly claim credit for the work done by NGOs, but Kenyans also appear to be willing to give government agents credit. This attribution is not due to people confusing NGOs with the government; Kenyans generally know the origins of services they receive. Most Kenyans do not link NGO service provision with government failure to fulfill the social contract because they seem to understand and even accept the limitations of their government.

Implications for state development

The foregoing arguments have crucial, yet mixed implications for developing states, whose very nature is changing because of NGO penetration. For decades in many of these states, the modal form of the state has been neopatrimonialism (Bratton and Walle 1997) or "personal rule" (Jackson and Rosberg 1984b, Leonard and Strauss 2003). These states are characterized by highly concentrated power and extremely high levels of patronage, largely arising in many countries as a legacy of colonialism (Ekeh 1975). As NGOs gain salience, the manner of governing in these patrimonial states may also change, albeit very gradually.

The growth of NGOs and the mindset they put forth encourage more equitable, participatory, and a politically motivated distribution of resources and services, since private actors, and international nonprofits in particular, tend to be less subject to clientelistic demands. Governments, seeing the positive response NGOs get from the people, mimic these strategies. As a result, the growth of NGOs providing a range of services within developing countries allows more to be done. On the whole, even when many NGOs are not particularly effective or efficient organizations, more services are provided to more people where NGO engagement is high than would occur in their absence. As NGOs and governments work together, moreover, government actors, especially civil servants in public administration, learn from their NGO counterparts, who have experimented with a range of program options. Improved accountability trickles into the public service, raising the level of public administrative capacity.

NGOs do more than run parallel programs or train civil servants, however. NGO presence can change the nature of the state in the twenty-first century, as NGOs become part and parcel of public service delivery – in essence, part of the institutionalized, organizational form of the state in development. In territorially far-flung places in particular, NGOs act as the state in service provision. They have gained "practical authority" alongside state actors, as they demonstrate problem-solving capacity and gain recognition for doing so (Abers and Keck 2013). In bringing services, they also bring hope for the future to people with few expectations that their government will provide, despite its rhetoric.

In an age where scholars have asserted the "erosion of stateness" in Africa (Young 2004) and have famously declared traditional forms of development aid to be noxious and "dead" (Moyo 2009), this study provides an important empirical assessment of both aid via NGOs and the developing state. It shows that where states are relatively weak, NGOs bolster public services and governance.

Thus the state has not been supplanted by NGOs; rather, it has been supplemented by them. This is not without potential downsides, however. Although there is currently a clear role for private nonprofit organizations in governance, the long-term viability of relying on NGOs for the governance of service provision is questionable. First, funding for NGOs fluctuates considerably, leaving recipient countries that depend on them in a precarious position. Second, reliance on NGOs often puts some degree of decision-making in the hands of foreign actors, including NGOs' donors (Morfit 2011), which may be objectionable if we believe in home-grown solutions. Even if we accept foreign-originating ideas, relying on donor-funded NGOs is only a tenable state of affairs as long as the donors are benevolent. Third, although NGOs do tend to have the interests of recipient communities in mind, they are not democratically accountable to citizens of developing countries, and are financially accountable only to their donors. Fourth, NGOs, unlike governments, can pull out of a country or a community without notice or explanation. Citizens of such communities rarely have recourse when this occurs, since NGO programs tend to exist on a voluntary basis.

Governments of developing countries, unlike NGOs, are in a country for the long haul, and they are, at least in principle, accountable to their citizens. Because of this status, investing in government development, meaning the development of purely public agency capacity, may be a more fruitful means of ensuring service provision over the long term.

The question is not only one of reliance on NGOs or governments, however; negative implications of NGO activities can be more complex. In many developing countries, governments do not seem to have the interests of their citizens at the forefront of their minds. Many governments are corrupt, if not downright predatory. In such cases, NGOs providing services to the population may actually prolong the tenure of a bad government. By providing services that lend legitimacy to the state, NGOs run the risk of propping up such regimes. In some cases, NGOs cannot prevent governments from taking credit for their work, but if their services are placating the populace, such action may not be in a country's long-term interests. NGO work certainly can and has been co-opted on many occasions as well – sometimes governments engage with NGOs for precisely that purpose. It is thus imperative that we think critically about the proper role for NGO engagement in service provision in developing countries.

RESEARCH DESIGN: MULTIPLE FORMS OF ANALYSIS; MULTIPLE SOURCES OF DATA

This book is about the effects of NGOs on the developing state. To assess these outcomes, I use an "effects of causes" design (Goertz and Mahoney 2012, 41): rather than beginning with an outcome, Y, and determining how that outcome came to be, I begin with a causal factor, X, and examine how it has affected Y. In concrete terms, I begin with an empirical phenomenon, the proliferation of NGOs in the global South (X), and analyze how it has affected the state (Y).[17]

The analysis in this book employs a mixed-method approach that weaves quantitative evaluation of original datasets and survey work together with qualitative analysis of the cross-national literature on NGOs, in-depth interviews, case studies, and other information gathered during twenty-two months spent in Kenya.[18] Secondary source materials

---

[17] Although this approach may be less common than one in which a puzzling outcome is explained, it is necessary because of the extremely rapid growth of NGOs in developing countries around the world and our collective lack of knowledge about their effects.

[18] Research and analysis were conducted in an iterative fashion; I lived in Kenya for eight months in 2002, when the seed for this book was planted, and then conducted field research May to August 2005, September to November 2006, January to June 2007,

from a range of government ministries, independent think tanks, NGOs, and donor organizations supplement primary source evidence.[19]

The quantitative analyses employ three original datasets, one of which combines existing data in novel ways and two of which stem from surveys created for this research.[20] The first, used in the chapter on Territoriality (Chapter 4), contains information on NGOs, development indicators, and service provision levels across seventy administrative districts.[21] Data from government censuses, UNDP Human Development Reports, and seven different Kenyan government agencies and ministries were collected and combined with a complete database from the Government of Kenya's NGO Coordination Bureau (NGO Board), the government agency responsible for registering, monitoring, and assessing NGOs' work in the country. The database not only lists each of the 4,210 NGOs operating in Kenya at the time of research, but also provides information on the areas of the country in which they work, facilitating analysis of territorial implications throughout the country.

The second dataset, used in Chapter 7, compares data from the early post-independence period of the late 1960s to the present day. Specifically, it uses my 2008 replication of a survey of secondary school students in Eastern Province first conducted in 1966–1967.[22] The survey asked questions about citizenship, nation building, and the state in Kenya.

July to November 2008, and in June 2012. Kenya was purposively selected (Gerring 2008) as representative of developing countries in order to facilitate generalizing from it, making use of significant subnational variation at the district or individual unit of analysis. I compare across approximately 70 districts and two sets of 500 individuals within the country, as well as dozens of organizations. As such, I avoid the common criticism that much of the scholarship on NGOs to date lacks rigorous, systematic data collection and analysis.

[19] Using multiple sources of data and multiple means of analysis draws on the strengths of each. Interview data often help to make sense of the trends found by analyzing the survey research. In particular, they help to draw out the mechanisms by which variables interact. Methodologically, quantitative statistical and regression analysis complements qualitative interview analysis. The combination of these methodological strategies means that results from one type of data can not only verify those from another type, but also compensate for the weaknesses of individual methods (Small 2011).

[20] Additional details on these datasets and how they were assembled are found in the relevant chapters.

[21] At the time of data collection there were 72 districts in Kenya, although comprehensive data were only available for 70.

[22] The 1960s survey was conducted by George von der Muhll under the direction of Kenneth Prewitt, who later became director of the US Census.

Comparing the two iterations of survey responses helps measure the causes of changes in perceptions of state legitimacy over time.[23]

The final dataset, used in Chapter 8, comes from an original survey of 500 adults and determines current perceptions of the state, linking state legitimacy to governmental and nongovernment service provision more concretely. Respondents were asked from whom they receive the core state services of education, healthcare, and policing, the extent of their familiarity and interactions with NGOs, their views on NGOs and the government, and their level of political participation.[24] Some of the questions in this survey were modeled on Afrobarometer questions (see www.afrobarometer.org), facilitating comparison to Afrobarometer's national samples from the same year on particular questions, but most were original.

These statistical analyses are complemented by qualitative assessment of NGOs' impact.[25] The book draws on semi-structured interviews I

---

[23] In the 2008 replication, half of the 500 respondents, randomly assigned, received questions identical to those asked in the 1960s, while the other half received a questionnaire in which some prompts were modified to include NGOs in the questions or answers. This allows for a comparison over time that includes information about NGOs in the present time period.

[24] Respondents were randomly selected from across the full districts of Machakos and Mbeere, as well as a separate random sample from urban Machakos town and long-standing neighborhoods in the capital, Nairobi. This strategy facilitates rural, town, and urban experience comparison. As a result of these choices, 52 percent of survey respondents identified Kamba as their mother tongue, and 19 percent Mbeere, Meru, or Embu although these languages were spoken by 9 percent and 8 percent respectively in national surveys from the same year (Afrobarometer 2008). The Nairobi subsample is closer to a representative sample of the country than the full sample, although it over-represents the Kikuyu and Luo ethnicities and under-represents the Kalenjin and Luhya most notably. In the Nairobi sample, Kikuyu account for 45 percent of responses, followed by 21 percent Luo, 12 percent Kamba, 11 percent Luhya, 4 percent Kisii, 4 percent Mbeere/Embu/Meru, and 4 percent from other groups. This distribution compares to the national-level breakdown, according to Afrobarometer, of 18 percent Kikuyu, 13 percent Luo, 9 percent Kamba, 14 percent Luhya, 7 percent Kisii, 8 percent Mbeere/Embu/Meru, 12 percent Kalenjin, and 19 percent from other groups (Afrobarometer 2008).

[25] Qualitative work is particularly important for the study of less-developed countries like Kenya, since statistical data can be unreliable – government statistics offices are often sorely underfunded. Moreover, comprehensive and reliable data on nongovernmental service provision is in severely short supply, not only from past decades, but also for the present time period. In addition, research touching even tangentially on issues of government legitimacy was stymied in Kenya by the government during much, if not all of the Moi administration, which stretched 24 years from 1978 to 2002, making for a large gap in cross-temporal analysis. Supplementing quantitative data with qualitative research provides weight to and flexibility in the use of the findings, since qualitative

conducted with more than one hundred governmental and nongovernmental workers, government officials, and Kenyan citizens. Interviews
covered such topics as the programs offered by NGOs and government
respectively, organizations' goals and motivations, funding sources, and
relationships with local and national government offices and officers.
They also probed the relationship between NGOs, Kenyans, and the
state. I selected respondents from registries of NGOs working in the
three primary districts as well as through snowball sampling.[26]

These interviews provided much of the understanding that allows
meaningful interpretation of statistical results in the manuscript. In particular, information gleaned from interviews facilitates understanding of
causal mechanisms, and also provides data on the NGO sector in Kenya,
NGO–government interactions historically and in the present time, service provision methods, and administrative processes.

I complement data from Kenya, a typical-case (Gerring 2001) study,
with review of existing scholarship on NGOs, service provision, and
governance in South America, Africa, the Middle East, the former Soviet
Union, and Asia. I reviewed hundreds of academic articles on NGOs,
in addition to work on state capacity, governance, and legitimacy. This
secondary research facilitates statements on the generalizability of the
Kenyan experience, which strengthens the validity of the results.[27]

---

        understandings that support numbers-driven findings increase our confidence in their
        validity.
[26]   Interviews were semi-structured and lasted between twenty minutes and three hours,
        with an average interview length of approximately one hour. The substantive areas of
        involvement of the NGO interviewees roughly parallel those at the national level. Specif-
        ically, the national percentage of organizations by sector and the percentage of my inter-
        views in that sector are as follows, where the first number is the percent at the national
        level and the second in my interviews: general development (40:38), governance (4:5),
        health (14:18), relief (2:0), disadvantaged groups (17:10), agriculture (4:12), education
        (8:5), environment (6:7), other (5:5). Thus my interviews are slightly biased toward
        NGOs working in health and agriculture, and I under-represent NGOs focused on relief
        and disadvantaged groups. Interviewees were asked whether they or anyone at their orga-
        nization had previously worked in government (for NGO respondents) or in an NGO
        (if government respondents), as such a history could bias their views of and experiences
        working with the other type of organization. Only one respondent answered positively,
        suggesting that personnel movement between NGOs and government is not the primary
        cause of increased collaboration between the sectors. One respondent worked for nine
        years as a social services officer before joining an NGO working on education, HIV,
        and enterprise development programs (2008–32). Her views of government were more
        positive than most of the NGO interviewees, but her organization did not appear to
        work with government in a significantly different manner than others.
[27]   Likewise, the country case study adds insights beyond what would be possible with only
        the cross-national comparison. It captures the benefits of single-country case studies,

A TYPICAL CASE WITH TEMPORAL AND
SUBNATIONAL VARIATION

Kenya is an important country of focus for research on NGOs and the state for a variety of reasons. Kenya is representative of many developing countries, and not only those in Africa. While Kenya is a fairly strong state by African standards, it falls near the middle of less-developed countries internationally: Kenya ranked 128th out of 169 countries in the 2010 Human Development Index (UNDP 2010), putting it at the very top of the "low human development" category, but below such "medium human development" countries as Cambodia (ranked 126), Equatorial Guinea (119), Honduras (108), and Turkmenistan (83). Likewise, Freedom House scored Kenya an average "partly free" 3.5 out of 7 in its annual Freedom in the World index (Freedom House 2011), placing it squarely in the middle of the range of countries. Unlike some extremely poor or weak African countries, moreover, Kenya has a developed manufacturing and export sector, as well as a growing information technology sector, making it comparable with many of the countries of Latin America and Asia.

The Kenyan government has worked to track the development of the NGO sector in the country, and has made this and other statistical information available to researchers, allowing a general picture of the NGO sector in the country to be drawn. The Kenyan government allows foreign researchers to work in the country, provided they have the necessary, easily obtained research clearance and it does not limit research topics to any observable degree. Given these conditions, studying Kenya is pragmatic as well as representative.

The country also facilitates study of temporal and subnational variation. As Chapter 3 will detail in earnest, Kenya, like many states in Latin America, Africa, and Asia (Atibil 2012; Brautigam and Segarra 2007; Nair 2011), has experienced changes in NGO–state interactions over time. It shifted from highly conflictual to much more collaborative state–society relations. Analyzing this case allows us, therefore, to understand the conditions that undergird both conflictual and collaborative NGO–state relations, as well as the factors that facilitate the change from the former to the latter.

most notably that they allow for a depth of understanding of mechanisms that is difficult to otherwise achieve. As Dietrich Rueschemeyer points out, "Quite a few single-case studies rank among the most powerful and influential works in social and political analysis" (2003, 307), and can be used to test our causal theories. Second, as Rueschemeyer and others make clear, a single case does not imply a single observation (Rueschemeyer 2003; Wittenberg 2007).

In addition to interesting temporal variation, Kenya is a diverse country with significant subnational differences, which shed light on important trends related to NGOs. The number and per capita density of NGOs at the district level, for example, varied significantly across Kenya's 72 districts at the time of research, which facilitates an analysis of the ecological conditions that draw NGOs to locate their programs in particular places at the subnational level (see Chapter 4).[28] Subnational variation also comes in the form of level of urbanization, which can shape NGOs' effects. In particular, the rural–town–urban divide is important in shaping how citizens view the state in relation to their interactions with NGOs. In studies of NGOs, street-level interactions in rural districts are often overlooked, yet NGOs have a greater capacity to address governance at the local level than they do at the national horizon (Clayton 1998). Individuals, moreover, are affected by the everyday acts of low-level civil servants and local politicians and not just by decisions made by elites in the capital city.

Subnational districts of interest

Original research for this manuscript was conducted primarily in urban Nairobi, the capital city; in a large town, Machakos town; and across two rural districts, Machakos and Mbeere. Supplemental interviews in the Naivasha, Nakuru, Kisii, Migori, and Narok districts of Rift Valley and Nyanza Provinces confirmed the validity of the findings.

Machakos and Mbeere districts were chosen because they were similar in many regards during field research, but different in an important way, following Mills' method of difference (see Table 1.1). The districts were approximately equidistant from the capital in terms of the time it took to reach them, and they had similar voting records in presidential elections, comparable infant mortality, literacy, HIV and malaria rates, and

---

[28] Here, note that at the time of most data collection, a district was the third-level administrative unit: below the national and provincial levels, and above the division, location, and sublocation levels. A district was an administrative unit, and most districts overlapped with several subnational political units (constituencies) and local political units (counties). Each constituency voted for its own Member of Parliament (MP), meaning that most districts were served by several MPs, who were the highest political officials in the district unless the district was fortunate enough to claim a Minister or Assistant Minister. In 2009, the number of districts grew to more than 200, largely overlapping with the country's 210 political constituencies and MPs. After a new constitution passed in 2010, however, 47 counties replaced these districts. For the sake of consistency and to flag the time period of research, I use the term "district" throughout the book, since the reorganization into counties was still ongoing at the end of the research period.

TABLE 1.1. *Characteristics of Machakos and Mbeere districts*

Indicator	Machakos	Mbeere
Distance of district HQ to Nairobi (km)[29][+]	63	163
Percentage of 1997 presidential vote for Moi (%)[#]	33	35
Infant mortality per 1,000 live births (1989)[*]	43.9	42.0
Adult literacy rate (%) (1989)[*]	80	77
Malaria rate (%) (1994)[**]	11	13
Life expectancy (years) (1989)[*]	68	70
HIV rate (%) (2005)[**]	4.3	3.5
# of NGOs (2005)[^]	120	31
# of NGOs (2006)[~]	292	213
Population (2000)[++]	907,000	171,000
Population density (2000)[++]	143	81
Km of paved roads per 1,000km²[+]	60.0	14.8

Sources:
[+] Republic of Kenya (2007).
[#] Arriola (2013).
[*] Government of Kenya Census (1989).
[**] UNDP (2006).
[^] National Council of NGOs (2005).
[~] NGO Coordination Bureau (2006).
[++] Government of Kenya Census (1999).

approximately the same life expectancy. At the time of research the two full districts had approximately the same level of NGOs per capita.[30]

The districts vary, however, in terms of level of urbanization. Machakos is more urban, with more towns – including an important commercial center, higher population density, and a higher proportion

[29] While the distance of Machakos' District Headquarters is significantly closer to Nairobi than that of Mbeere, this difference is mitigated by the fact that the road to Machakos was in far worse condition than that to Mbeere at the time of research, making the time it takes to travel to each quite similar. Moreover, many of the NGOs that work in Mbeere district have offices in Embu town rather than in Siakago, where Mbeere's District Headquarters was located. Embu town is thirty kilometers closer to Nairobi, and sits on the border between Mbeere and Embu districts.

[30] It is worth noting that the population level in Machakos is higher than in Mbeere, which likely accounts for much of the difference in the number of NGOs. GDP per capita in Mbeere, however, is significantly higher than in Machakos. This advantage could be due to increasing khat growth in Mbeere (Government of Kenya Ministry of State for the Development of Northern Kenya and Other Arid Lands 2008). Khat is a mild stimulant chewed throughout the countries of the Red Sea. Cultivation and trade has grown in recent years in Kenya, as the demand and prices for khat are more reliable than those for the other commonly grown stimulants, coffee and tea. Standards of living in Mbeere, however, do not seem to be positively impacted by this higher GDP.

of paved roads than Mbeere. The districts' headquarters were representative of these differences. Machakos town is a bustling, vibrant small city (municipal population of approximately 150,000) on the Nairobi–Mombasa highway, the overland artery of the country. Machakos town is also the seat of the County Council and the town with the greatest concentration of NGO offices, facilitating NGO–government interactions.

Siakago town, however, is very small, lacking both municipal status and a paved access road, which made travel to Mbeere's seat of government costly. It is about an hour's drive from the nearest city of Machakos town's size, Embu town. Mbeere district split from Embu district in 1996, but much of the activity in Mbeere still gravitates toward Embu town rather than Siakago.

The selection of these districts of focus reflect one significant trade-off (Gerring 2001) made in designing the research for this book – in data gathered in 2008, I controlled for political alignment and post-election violence, which partially limited variation in ethnicity and patronage. This was a conscious and necessary decision. On theoretical grounds, controlling for these other political factors allows us to isolate the generalizable effects of NGOs in service provision, rather than of ethnic patronage politics, which may be collinear. Politically, both Machakos and Mbeere and their majority ethnicities were aligned with the Kibaki administration during the time of research, but neither area was considered strongly supportive or strongly critical of Moi during his long tenure as president. In both districts, Moi earned about one-third of votes cast in 1997.

On practical grounds, much of the data collection for this book occurred in late 2008, not long after post-election ethnic violence wracked several parts of Kenya, resulting in the death of more than 1,000 people and the displacement of half a million others (Cheeseman 2008). The focus on Machakos and Mbeere controls for this violence, since there was limited or no violent conflict in them.[31] Note that most districts of Kenya experienced very little electoral violence (see http://legacy.ushahidi .com/ for a map of electoral violence in 2008), so the selection of districts without violence represents the norm. Most interviews and survey respondents identified as ethnically Kamba or Mbeere, but in Nairobi and the

---

[31] Ethnically, Machakos is majority Kamba, while those of the Mbeere ethnicity populate Mbeere, which is sometimes included in the larger Embu grouping to the East of Mount Kenya.

follow-up interviews, I also spoke with individuals from the Kikuyu, Kisii, Luo, and Maasai communities.

A ROADMAP OF THE CHAPTERS AHEAD

The analysis of NGOs and state development proceeds as follows. Chapter 2 provides conceptualizations of key terms used throughout the book, and it theorizes the relationship between NGOs and the state, specifically looking at four "elements of stateness": territoriality, governance, administrative capacity, and legitimacy. In so doing, it introduces important scholarly theories that help the reader to understand changes occurring around the world related to NGOs, including those on civil society, governance and privatization, institutional isomorphism, and the social contract between a state and its people. It also provides the reader with an analysis of the various conditions under which NGOs and their government counterparts either collaborate or conflict with one another. These concepts, theories and conditions are then applied throughout the remaining chapters of the book.

Chapter 3 comprises a contextual background of the country case study, Kenya. The chapter provides the reader with a brief overview of the Kenyan political economy, followed by a detailed history of non-state actors providing social services, and of NGO–government relationships within the country. Here, it primarily chronicles the transition from hostile NGO–government interactions during the Moi administration (1978–2002) to largely collaborative relationships during the Kibaki administration (2002–2012). The final section of the chapter turns to an overview of the NGO sector in contemporary times. It details the types of organizations present in Kenya, activities done, and the ways in which citizens engaged with NGOs in the early years of the twenty-first century.

Chapters 4 through 8 address the four elements of stateness, analyzing NGO implications for territoriality, governance, capacity, and legitimacy by turn. Chapter 4 examines the interplay between NGOs and territory, probing the factors that determine how NGOs choose the locations in which they work, and the impact that locational variation has on the territoriality of the state as a whole. It is worth noting that data from Kenya demonstrate that NGO placement is not determined by patronage politics, unlike most other service provision, but instead by a combination of need and convenience factors. On a per capita basis, moreover, data reveal that NGOs contribute to the territoriality of the state by locating in places where the state is weak and assisting the state to broadcast governing presence.

Chapter 5 probes the issue of governance, investigating how NGO involvement in service provision is changing patterns of both policymaking and policy implementation. The chapter demonstrates that NGOs have become intertwined with their government counterparts in service provision, resulting in increasingly robust overall provision. This change reflects a move toward polycentric governance, in which roles are shared and boundaries are blurred; NGOs become part of the organizational form of the state in service provision. At the same time, such changes are not without exception and limitations, which are analyzed in the latter half of the chapter. The chapter ends with a discussion of areas of continued tension between NGOs and government officials and potential downsides to NGO integration.

Chapter 6 moves inside the bureaucracy to examine changes to administrative capacity resulting from the proliferation of NGOs. Data from Kenya reveal that the blurring of boundaries and activities described in Chapter 5 resulted in increased capacity, as government actors learned the benefits of collaboration with NGOs and mimicked successful NGO strategies. At the local level, service-providing agencies became increasingly transparent, accountable, and participatory – a very slow movement toward more democratic governance of service provision. Overall levels of administrative capacity remained extremely low, however. Concerns exist, moreover, about how participatory, efficient or effective NGOs actually are.

Chapters 7 and 8 investigate NGOs' impacts on state legitimacy. They use two different original survey instruments, Afrobarometer data, and in-depth interviews, to understand whether popular support for government changes in the presence of NGO activity, and to explain variation in such support. Chapter 7 investigates whether the legitimacy of the Kenyan state decreased in the face of NGO proliferation, comparing survey data from 1966, before NGOs, to replicated results in 2008, after NGO numbers surged. The data reveal that legitimacy levels in the 2000s were nearly identical to those in the early post-independence era. Endemic insecurity and corruption are negatively associated with state legitimacy levels, but NGOs are not.

Chapter 8 reveals that NGOs did not undermine state legitimacy in the early twenty-first century in Kenya. Although most Kenyans had more positive opinions about NGOs than they did about the government, NGO presence improved perceptions of government or had little effect. Support for NGOs clearly did not translate into a distaste for government. Qualitative analysis of interview data explains the main reason for this finding: the people of Kenya expected exceedingly little from their government, so they tended to be pleased to receive any services at all, regardless of the source.

The concluding chapter, Chapter 9, ties the threads together in an analysis of how our understanding of the state has changed as nonstate actors gain salience in many of the world's least-developed countries. In addition to synthesizing the findings of the empirical chapters, I draw on research from Latin America, Africa, the Middle East, the former Soviet Union, and South, Central and East Asia, to show the applicability of my findings in Kenya to the situation in the wider world. The chapter concludes with discussion of remaining questions and implications for state development in the future.

2

Theorizing NGOs and the state

Territoriality, governance, capacity, legitimacy

> *Like any other group or organization, the state is constructed and recon-*
> *structed, invented and reinvented, through its interaction as a whole and of*
> *its parts with others. It is not a fixed entity; its organization, goals, means,*
> *partners, and operative rules change as it allies with and opposes others*
> *inside and outside its territory. The state continually morphs.*
>
> (Migdal 2001, 23)

> *A veritable 'associational revolution' now seems underway at the global*
> *level that may constitute as significant a social and political development of*
> *the latter twentieth century as the rise of the nation state was of the latter*
> *nineteenth century.*
>
> (Salamon 1993, 1)

This chapter provides the conceptualizations and theories that form the foundation for the arguments contained in the book. It addresses NGOs' effects on the state as a whole, as well as on four component "elements of stateness" – territoriality, governance, administrative capacity, and legitimacy. Existing theories of organizational placement, governance and privatization, civil society, and the social contract between a state and society each help explain the role NGOs play in state building, and the organizational and institutional change we have witnessed over time.

A large body of literature has emerged to address NGOs and their impact. Detailed research on NGOs began in earnest around 1990. This initial research tended to focus on describing or conceptualizing NGOs (Vakil 1997; Uphoff 1993), and on explaining the growth of the sector (Salamon 1994), particularly as a response to state and economic crisis (Bratton 1989; Sandberg 1994; Tripp 1997; Kioko, Mute, and Akivaga

2002). Articles at the time also provided broad analyses of state–society or state–NGO relations (Bebbington et al. 1993; Bratton 1989, 1990; Clark 1995; Kameri-Mbote 2000; Clark 1993; Whaites 1998; Sen 1999; Sanyal 1994; Cannon 1996; Campbell 1996) and issues of donors and accountability (Ebrahim 2003; Edwards and Hulme 1996b; Van Der Heijden 1987).

Starting in the 2000s, studies began to disaggregate the effects in particular sectors. They have looked, for example, at the role NGOs play specifically in the health sector (Wamai 2004; Palmer 2006; Ejaz, Shaikh, and Rizvi 2011; Pugachev nd; Pick, Givaudan, and Reich 2008; Pfeiffer 2003; Leonard and Leonard 2004), in the fight against HIV/AIDS (Parkhurst 2005; Doyle and Patel 2008; Swidler and Watkins 2009; Chikwendu 2004), in education (Rose 2011; Seay 2010; Leinweber 2011), in water service provision (Rusca and Schwartz 2012), in agriculture (Puplampu and Tettey 2000; Igoe 2003), and in municipal government (Keese and Argudo 2006), including slum upgrading (Otiso 2003) and sanitation (Carrard et al. 2009).[1] Importantly, academic studies have also shifted toward assessing NGOs' role in directly political outcomes like governance (Grindle 2004; Mercer 2003; Swidler 2007; Brass 2012a), regulation (Gugerty 2008; Gugerty and Prakash 2010), policymaking (Batley 2011; Wamai 2004), local politics (Boulding 2014), and collective or cooperative action (Fearon, Humphreys, and Weinstein 2011; Desai and Joshi 2011).

Although these studies explored different aspects of NGOs' effects in the political sphere, very little research has measured the real feedback effects of NGO provision of services on state development.[2] Scholarship on NGOs has been rife with assertions that such organizations undermine, threaten, or regularly conflict with the state in developing countries. While there are circumstances in which adversarial relationships occur, which are discussed later in this chapter, in many places there has also been a change in the relationship between the state and society. The relationship has become more complex than common arguments suggest, as NGOs

---

[1] Interestingly, agriculture was the only sector frequently studied in depth before the 2000s (Poole 1994; Bebbington et al. 1993).

[2] Notable exceptions include the works of Obiyan, who asks, "Will the state die as the NGOs thrive?" in Nigeria (2005, 301); Fernando (2011), who critiques the role of NGOs in state formation in Sri Lanka and Bangladesh; de Waal, who examines the role of famine relief – including that by NGOs in Ethiopia, Sudan, Somalia, and Zaire – on political development (de Waal 1997); and Jelinek (2006), who examines whether NGOs undermine or build government capacity in wartime Afghanistan.

and their government counterparts have learned that it is in their mutual interest to work together, collaboratively, most of the time.

As a result of this collaboration, NGOs have become part of the organizational makeup of the state in many developing countries. NGOs and government agencies share complex interactions, resulting in a blurring of the boundaries between the two sectors.

CONCEPTUALIZING THE STATE

What is a state? Research focusing on the state has long been a core component of the study of politics, which we can trace back to the writings of the earliest philosophers. From Hobbes to Weber, Smith to Marx, Durkheim to Gramsci, much of the canon in the field examines the nature of the state. Though some periods of research have dismissed the importance of focusing on the state, eventually the state is "brought back in" to the discussion (Evans, Rueschemeyer, and Skocpol 1985), because an analysis of political life without it would be impossible.

Research approaches to the state have varied, however. Sometimes, our focus has been on considering the state as an autonomous operator or set of players, acting on its own accord (Allison 1971; Skocpol 1979; Johnson 1982; Haggard 1990); at other times, research has focused on the "embedded" nature of the "state in society" (Migdal 1988, 2001) or the societal actors in the state (Evans 1995). We have also looked at the state through the lenses of its formal rules, function, behavior, and institutions. Those researchers focused on the international arena have historically examined states' actions vis-à-vis other states. Others are interested in relations between states and markets. Whenever we study democracy, law, economic regulation, ethnic minorities, human rights, or civil society, we are analyzing some elements of the state.

More recently, many political scientists have debated whether or not the state still matters; whether it is weakening in relation to private enterprises, international organizations, or certain strong philanthropic organizations; and how it fits into a networked political economy characterized by global interactions and exchanges (Keohane 1984; Ohmae 1990; Strange 1996).[3] Looking at Africa in particular, scholars question the

---

[3] The literature on Africa differs on several levels from what has been written about globalization's impact on the state in general: first, the Africanist perspective focuses on the detrimental role of personal rule that has characterized most African states since independence; second, it tends to place less emphasis on economic globalization, since

very "stateness" of African states (Migdal 1988; Doornbos 1990; Sandberg 1994, 7; Herbst 2000; Young 1994; 2004; Callaghy 1987; Jackson 1990; Widner 1995; Herbst 1996–97). My research, however, demonstrates that the state *is* important and questions this pessimistic bent, opting to view states not as static, ideal-type Weberian institutions, but as mutable, diverse, and ever changing. I elucidate the ways in which the state has changed and is changing in response to an important new set of actors gaining strength in many areas of the world.

"The state" is nonetheless a difficult concept – understandable in common parlance, but slippery when one attempts to grasp it firmly and pin it down for dissection. Part of the reason for this difficulty is that the state is not one-dimensional, but complex and multifaceted, making pithy definitions inadequate (Turner and Young 1985, 12; Kjaer, Hansen, and Thomsen 2002). In "Politics as a Vocation" (1919), Weber famously argued that the state is "a human community that (successfully) claims the monopoly of the legitimate use of physical force within a given territory." In work published later, Weber elaborated on the formal characteristics of the modern state:

> It possesses an administrative and legal order subject to change by legislation, to which the organized corporate activity of the administrative staff, which is also regulated by legislation, is oriented. This system of order claims binding authority, not only over the members of the state, the citizens, most of whom have obtained membership by birth, but also to a very large extent, over all action taking place in the area of its jurisdiction. It is thus a compulsory association with a territorial basis. Furthermore, to-day, the use of force is regarded as legitimate only so far as it is permitted by the state or prescribed by it.
>
> (Parsons 1947, 156)

Yet Weber's definitions are incomplete because they fail to recognize that, in addition to the physical buildings, written laws, and administrative offices of the state, there exists the abstract *idea* or *image* of the state – the construct that we draw to mind when thinking about the state, as well as the *practices* of the state – or the processes by which the state acts day-to-day (Young 1994; Weber 1919; Migdal 2001; Englebert 2000).[4]

Africa has tended to be less intertwined with the rest of the world; and third, it suggests that the impacts in Africa are much more severe, since African states have tended to be much less institutionalized than elsewhere in the world.

[4] David Easton's (1965) work on "political community" is also useful for this conceptualization, as I portray an expansive view of the state as the supreme community of organizations, rules, norms, and institutions that order society within a particular territorial entity.

In general, our image of the state is the Weberian archetype, but very few states have ever achieved a perfect resemblance to this bureaucratic-rational ideal in their day-to-day activities or practices. As Migdal put it, "While the image of the state implies a singular morality, one standard way, indeed *right* way of doing things, practices denote multiple types of performance and, possibly, some contention over what is *the* right way to act" (2001, 19, emphasis in original). Recognizing the possibility of multiple practices and viewpoints in our definition of the state allows us to admit as states those entities whose image does not perfectly align with their actual practices. Where nongovernmental actors have become part of the de facto organizational makeup of the state, as in Kenya, such is the case.

A STATE WITH BLURRED BOUNDARIES: THEORIES ON NGOS AND THE ELEMENTS OF STATENESS

What does the state look like, when the line between NGOs and the government blurs? What social scientific theories help make sense of the changes? Four elements of stateness have been particularly affected by the growth of NGO activity, and are the foci of this book: territoriality, governance, capacity, and legitimacy.[5] Several key questions as well as pertinent theories arise when considering these components of the state. These elements are discussed by turn in this chapter and summarized in Table 2.1.

Territoriality

"The state, to begin with, is a territorially demarcated entity" (Turner and Young 1985, 12). Behaviorally, "The state seeks to uphold its hegemony over the territory it rules" (ibid., 15). *Territoriality* combines characteristic with practice, as it refers to the demarcation, occupation, and defense

---

[5] This section parallels the discussion in Fowler (1991), which employs a similar passage from Young (1988) to discuss NGOs and the state. In addition to the four elements discussed here in the text, Young and Turner (1985) also identify "the conception of the state as a legal system" (14) as part of the administrative behavior, as well as behavior that "seeks to uphold and advance [the state's] security" (15) and its "revenue imperative" (16). For my purposes, these elements are only tangentially relevant, since NGOs do not generally impinge on security or legal systems at all. NGOs do arguably add to the resources available to society as a whole (and therefore state revenue), and could have been appropriately included in this analysis. Revenue garnered by the state from NGOs, however, is often indirect.

TABLE 2.1. *Defining four elements of stateness*

Element	Definition	Key questions	Crucial theories
Territoriality	The demarcation, occupation, and defense of a fixed geographical territory by governing institutions. **Where states act.**	What factors draw NGOs to work in particular locations? What does the resulting distribution of organizations indicate for how the state broadcasts power over the territory it claims?	Organizational placement
Governance	The patterns or methods by which governing occurs within a state. **How states govern.**	What changes have occurred in the way decisions about service provision are made and implemented as a result of NGOs? How have the relationships between NGOs and governments shifted over time?	Collaborative governance, Co-production, Synergy
Capacity	The ability to implement stated objectives. **What states implement.**	How have NGOs affected administrative capacity? Do NGOs allow government officials to shirk responsibility to their citizens, as some claim? Or do they enhance the government's ability to do its job?	Civil society, Social learning, Institutional isomorphism
Legitimacy	A generalized perception that the state has a right to govern and its actions are desirable, proper, or appropriate in its cultural context. **How states are perceived.**	Do NGOs providing services undermine the legitimacy of the state, or does NGOs presence bolster the way people view their state? Do citizens respond to NGO or government service provision differently?	Social contract

of a geographical territory by governing institutions. It concerns the "broadcasting of power" throughout a geographical space (Herbst 2000), or what was referred to in the 1960s as the penetration of geographical territory by governing authorities (Herz 1968). Territorial boundaries demarcate the lines of hegemony along which public authorities and peoples can make demands on each other, such as taxation, defense, security, or accountability. States in many developing countries struggle with territoriality. Peru's government in Lima, for example, fought the *Sendero Luminoso* (Shining Path) in the 1980s and 1990s, and the government in Pakistan today struggles to maintain territorial control over its own Northwest Frontier area (Naseemullah 2014).

What relationship exists between NGOs and territoriality, particularly in places with "geographically uneven patterns of state building" (Boone 2003, xi)? Some scholars argue that NGOs undermine the state by providing services in places where the state is weak on the ground. I find, however, that NGOs assist the state in creating organizational presence in remote areas by putting in place activities that locals associate with state jurisdiction. Instead of supplanting, NGOs supplement. Under the right conditions, NGOs impact the territoriality of the state by providing services in places that the government has been unable to reach, particularly in arid, sparsely populated areas where the NGOs-per-capita ratio is at its highest. In small market towns and villages, people expect *either* government or NGOs to be present, providing services, and see the two types of organizations as substitutes for one another. This finding accords with Foucaultian notions about shared authority and sovereignty, where non-state actors undertake governmental tasks in cooperation with the government (Foucault 1991, Sending and Neumann 2006, Biersteker 2012, 250).

Understanding this finding requires knowledge of the factors that draw organizations to work in particular locations. Because patron–client relationships dominate the distribution of public goods in many developing countries, it is logical to expect that national patrimonial chains of distribution would also sway NGOs' distribution of services. Clientelist distribution is therefore one possible pull factor for NGOs. The literature on nonprofit placement identifies two others as well: need and convenience (Bielefeld, Murdoch, and Waddell 1997, Joassart-Marcelli and Wolch 2003, Nemenoff 2008, Bielefeld and Murdoch 2004, Peck 2008, Büthe, Major, and de Mello e Souza 2012, Fruttero and Gauri 2005, Stirrat 2008).

In Kenya, NGO location is associated with both need for services and ease of accessing a particular location (Brass 2012b). On a per capita level, an objective need for services appears to be paramount – there are more NGOs per capita in outlying areas far from the capital, which tend to be poorer and to lack services. More importantly for our understanding of the politics of NGO placement, the organizations do not appear to be geographically distributed on the basis of national patrimonial dynamics: we are no more likely to find NGOs in the home region or support areas of powerful politicians than elsewhere. Instead, NGOs are relatively more prevalent in places where the state is weakly articulated. This observation aligns with recent evidence that donors bypass governments and channel money through NGOs in order to maximize the effect of aid (Dietrich 2013), which, in the past, was politically targeted in Kenya (Jablonski 2014, Briggs 2014).

It is important to remember, however, that NGO presence is not distributed evenly throughout the country, so NGO impacts are also uneven. Areas with high concentrations of well-funded and well-managed NGOs benefit more than others. Yet NGOs and government both see the role of NGOs as "gap-filling": that is, complementing the state.

Governance

Along with territoriality, a state is defined by issues of *governance*: the patterns or methods by which govern*ing* occurs. In formal language, governance is "the modes of social coordination by which actors engage in rulemaking and implementation and in the provision of collective goods" (Börzel and Risse 2010, 114). Behaviorally, the imperative for the state is to make decisions and to implement them independently of other organizations or authority (Turner and Young 1985, 15). For a state to truly have complete sovereignty, in principle, its representatives alone must make decisions about the presence, distribution, and operation of service provision in the society.

In weakly institutionalized states today, however, NGOs have begun to make governing decisions and to implement them. They often do so *alongside* their government counterparts, contrary to both the normative argument that government should "steer" the ship of state (make policy) while private actors "row" (implement policy) (Osborne and Gaebler 1992, see also discussion in Stoker 1998, Peters and Pierre 1998, 231) and the belief that government is eroding or becoming irrelevant to the governance process (Rhodes 1996, Rosenau and Czempiel 1992).[6] These latter opinions arose initially in the UK, Europe, and Australia following a neoliberal turn in the West, during which policymakers, scholars writing from the point of view of New Public Management in public administration, and international financial institutions on structural adjustment called for "new" and "good" governance. They sought the streamlining of public service provision, favoring third-party contracting and outsourcing to ostensibly more efficient and effective private organizations. Underpinning many of these calls was the notion that markets, freed from the oppressive hand of state intervention, would be able to supply goods and services faster, better, and cheaper than governments (Edwards and Hulme 1996b, 961). NGOs, for some, came to be "euphemisms for the private sector" (Puplampu and Tettey 2000),[7] considered more efficient, effective, flexible, and innovative than government (Bratton 1989, Fowler 1991, Owiti, Aluoka, and Oloo 2004, World Bank 1989). Although most writers and practitioners in this vein do not call for the complete removal of the government from all economic life, they do call for its role to be reduced to creating an "enabling environment" in which private organizations execute service delivery (World Bank 1989).

Such privatization may be fruitful in some contexts, yet in many developing countries we instead find that NGOs *join* public actors at many levels in making decisions and policy regarding service provision (Abers and Keck 2006). On the steering side, they sometimes sit on government planning boards; governments integrate NGO programs and budgets into local and national plans; and NGOs help to write state legislation. Additionally, on the rowing side, NGOs extend the service arm of the state to places and locations for which government counterparts lack sufficient funds; they also provide indirect services that the government is not able to provide. Often, NGOs work collaboratively with government actors on programs neither could run alone. Furthermore, by way of positive example, NGOs influence government offices and employees to improve

---

[6] Much of the writing on globalization has advanced the notion that changes in the global political economy are overwhelming the "retreating state" in a "race to the bottom," in which social welfare is sacrificed to the whims of global economic competition (Rodrik 1997, Strange 1996). While many states in Africa did constrict and even fail in the 1980s, more recent work specific to Africa in this broader literature makes some dramatic claims, arguing that African governments have entered a "permanent crisis" of the state and economy (van de Walle 2001), or are witnessing "the erosion of stateness" (Young 2004). Many scholars now debate about how best to "reconstruct" the African state.

[7] See also Besley and Maitreesh (2001), World Bank (1989), Pfeiffer (2003), Umali-Deininger and Schwartz (1994).

their quality of services. Governance under these conditions is not the removal of government, or "governance without government" (Rhodes 1996, Rosenau and Czempiel 1992), but the addition and acceptance of other actors, including NGOs, in the process.

Theories of collaborative governance, co-production, and synergies facilitate our understanding of these changes. Collaboration can be understood as the "process by which organizations with a stake in a problem seek a mutually determined solution [by pursuing] objectives they could not achieve working alone" (Sink 1998, 1188 cited in Gazley 2008). Scholarship on collaborative governance in developed countries points empirically to networks of public, private, and not-for-profit organizations proliferating to replace markets and hierarchies as problems become more complex. Such scholarship considers, for example, nonstate actors increasingly taking part in the policy decision-making process; a blurring of the boundaries between public and private actors or the advent of multi-centric, decentralized decision-making and authority; and more participatory governing processes (Cleveland 1972, Stoker 1998, Peters and Pierre 1998, Rhodes 2000, Rosenau 2000, Frederickson 2004, Bevir 2006). Here, governing patterns have moved from featuring government as *the* governing actor to incorporating government as the primary actor within a network that also includes nongovernmental actors (Kickert 1997, 736).

These relationships are sometimes discussed in terms of "co-production" and "synergy." The former involves outputs, services, or policies produced by individuals across a range of organizations – governmental and not – usually including citizens (Ostrom 1996). Programs are designed to integrate nongovernmental actors, and particularly those receiving the service, into the process (Ostrom 1996). Co-production, according to Ostrom (1996: 1083), is a form of synergy necessary for achieving higher levels of welfare in developing countries. Synergy, moreover, creates conditions not only in which civic engagement is more likely to develop and thrive, but also where bureaucratic organizations become stronger (Evans 1996, Lam 1996).

Two features stand out to support the idea that patterns in weakly institutionalized countries are more likely to reflect a merging of government and nonstate actors, rather than an "enabling" government that makes policy for nonstate contractors to implement. First, for a government to be able to effectively steer, it must be strong (Chaudhry 1993). The case of Kenya demonstrates that even countries with a mid-range level of development can lack this strength. In Kenya, Parliament has historically been captured by the executive presidency (McSherry and Brass 2007), and patronage politics impede a hands-off approach. The weakness of the steering capabilities on the government side has hampered the development of the ideal-type role distinction between an enabling state that delegates and the largely private actors who provide services. As Peters and Pierre observe, "For weaker states (or cities), joining forces with private sector actors has been an established strategy to increase their governing capacity" (1998, 233).

Second, the "hollowing" (Rhodes 1994) of the state in the Western context has involved intentional third-party contracting to nonstate actors, while the government retains control and provides funding. In many weakly institutionalized countries, however, the state has not deliberately contracted service provision to NGOs.[8] Instead, places like Kenya have witnessed "spontaneous privatization," in which nongovernmental actors try to fill the gaps left by the state without the state explicitly prompting them to do so (UN Habitat 2010, 14), sometimes following a government's inadequate response to crisis (Hershey 2013). Funding patterns accord with this description – analysis of the NGO Board's data from 2006 shows that only 1 percent of funding for NGOs in Kenya comes from Kenyan government sources. More recent figures are even lower: in 2009, only 0.25 percent of NGO funding originated with the Kenyan government (NGOs Co-ordination Board 2009, 32). Thus, while many developing country governments have come to rely on NGOs for some service provision, we should not assume that governments always initiate these relationships.

Administrative capacity

"[Thirdly] the state is ... a set of institutions of rule, an organizational expression of hegemony" (Turner and Young 1985, 13). Behaviorally, this characteristic expresses itself as *administrative capacity*, the state's ability to implement stated objectives and to realize goals (Evans 1995, Finegold and Skocpol 1995), often in opposition to powerful societal actors (Migdal 1988). Capacity is a slippery term, and is sometimes dismissed as tautological. It is true that it is easier to observe its consequences, such as levels of service provision or economic growth, than to

---

[8] In other developing countries, however, governments do contract out service provision like their Western counterparts, including South Africa, parts of Asia, and much of Latin America.

observe capacity itself (Kjaer, Hansen, and Thomsen 2002: 7), but we can still understand it as the ability to move from a written goal on paper to a vaccine provided, a road built, or a school opened. As Huntington puts it, capacity can be thought of as a country's "degree of government" – more government presence and output equals more capacity (1978, 1).

This definition is consistent with that of donor organizations, who see capacity as "the ability of people, institutions and societies to perform functions, solve problems and set and achieve objectives" (DFID 2008). Capacity acts in many ways as the interface between states and their peoples; people continually make demands on the state for greater standards of life, and states, *if* they have the ability to do so, respond to these demands, making for good state–society relations (Kjaer, Hansen, and Thomsen 2002).

In this book, the question addressed is whether NGOs enhance or undermine the state's administrative capacity to provide services. I find that when NGOs and governments work collaboratively, NGOs are able to influence government performance within public administration. Individuals and departments in government have learned from NGOs, and have begun to mimic the tools they have seen NGOs use successfully for years, calling for participatory development and civic education so that their agencies can better serve the community. This behavior facilitates accountability, therefore reflecting a very slow process of change toward democratic governance practices among civil servants.

NGOs act, therefore, as agents of civil society. Although some scholars critique the labeling of NGOs as "civil society" actors (Mercer 2002, Banks, Hulme, and Edwards 2015), NGOs display many civil society characteristics: most are autonomous from the state, undertake common or public goods activities, facilitate individual-level participation and group association, and emphasize citizen rights (Peterson and Van Til 2004). Autonomy is particularly crucial for civil society to achieve its goals, including pressing the government for change (Tripp 2001, 2000). Indeed, NGOs empower civic actors around the world – from the Balkan states (Grodeland 2006) to South Asia (Doyle and Patel 2008, Nair 2011), Africa (Atibil 2012, Heinrich 2001), and Latin America (Boulding 2010).[9]

---

[9] Looking specifically at Kenya, The International Center for Not-for-Profit Law, a promoter of civil society with programs in more than 100 countries, reports that NGOs are the most visible type of civil society organization in Kenya (ICNL 2010), and Kenyan scholars have been using the term interchangeably since at least the mid-1990s (Ndegwa 1996).

Two seminal texts on civil society, Alexis de Tocqueville's *Democracy in America* (1835) and Robert Putnam's *Making Democracy Work* (1993), help us to understand NGOs' role in capacity-building.

Tocqueville wrote about nineteenth-century America, where government administration was extremely weak, even "absent" (1835, 72), as it is in many developing countries today. Tocqueville observed that although the government acknowledged its obligations to society and had laws detailing service provision (Tocqueville 1835, 44–45), civic associations actually carried out many tasks:

> Americans of all ages, all stations in life, and all types of dispositions are forever forming associations.... Hospitals, prisons, and schools take shape in that way.... In every case, at the head of any new undertaking, where in France you would find the government or in England some territorial magnate, in the United States you are sure to find an association.
>
> (1835, 513)

In effect, Tocqueville perceived the nineteenth-century equivalent of NGOs as extending, or even composing, the social service wing of the state. As he saw it, nongovernmental provision of services in America allowed patriotism to spread through the new states of the West in churches, schools, and policing (1835, 293). Tocqueville thus witnessed in Antebellum America a blurring of state and civil society that nevertheless remained unrecognized in much of the literature that followed.

Putnam and his co-authors followed in Tocqueville's footsteps, arguing that the higher the degree of "civicness" in a society, the higher state performance will be (1993, 98). Although Putnam has been critiqued for not explaining the causal mechanism between civil society and government performance, scholars have argued that as horizontal relationships of trust and interdependence develop through membership in all types of associations, citizens become more involved in their larger society. These active democratic citizens insist on effective and responsive service delivery, and press their politicians to achieve it.[10] Thus, civil society "reinforces a strong state" (1993, 182), by increasing democratization and institutional accountability. This conclusion is echoed in later studies (Evans 1997). Clark, for example, argues that state–NGO interaction is important precisely *because* NGOs represent "genuinely participatory development" (Clark 1995, 600). Harbeson (1994, 1) asserts that civil

---

[10] Boix and Posner (1998) explicate this causal path, along with four other possible paths producing the correlation Putnam describes.

society is necessary for sustained political reform, state legitimacy, and improved governance, among other benefits. Civil society groups can act as a buffer, broker, symbol, agent, regulator, integrator, representative, or midwife between states and society (ibid., 24). Frank Holmquist's (1984) work on *harambee* groups in Kenya supports this idea, showing how the self-help groups enhanced state effectiveness.[11] Ndegwa (1996, 4) also shows that although NGOs don't always push for democratization directly, their "mundane activities" can clearly empower communities.

In more recent years, development practitioners, including those at the United Nations and the World Bank, frequently elide the use of the terms "civil society" and "NGOs" (United Nations Non-Governmental Liaison Service 2011, World Bank 2011, 1989, Hyden 1983). Brautigam and Segarra (2007) refer to this inclusion of NGOs as the "partnership norm" that the Bank first made explicit in staff guidelines in 1988. According to these researchers, staff members were told to encourage recipient governments to collaborate with NGOs (ibid., 152). Reflecting this faith in NGOs, the World Bank increased the percentage of its projects involving civil society organizations (CSOs), including NGOs, from 21 to 72 percent between 1990 and 2006, and to 81 percent by 2009.[12] The Bank highlights the role that nongovernmental actors play in public service provision in order to make them more democratic, accountable, and transparent.

This is not to say that service provision outcomes and administrative capacity have drastically improved as a result of NGO involvement. The fact remains that relative to the government, NGO resources are small and their impacts are often indirect. Civil society, moreover, is not without its limitations. Civil society groups in Africa fall victim to the same sorts of ethnic tensions and competition that exist within society as a whole (Kasfir 1998), and NGOs are generally run by elites in society, which can sway their activities toward elite interests (Ndegwa 1996). Neither are civil society groups, including NGOs, immune from corruption or patronage (Smith 2010). Many groups have grown dependent on their international donors, in some cases swaying from their civic intent in order to meet

[11] This argument relies on an assumption that NGOs and governments are not ultimately competing for the same resources.
[12] The World Bank's "overview" webpage on civil society explicitly says, "The World Bank consults and collaborates with thousands of members of Civil Society Organizations (CSOs) throughout the world, such as community-based organizations, *NGOs*, social movements, labor unions, faith-based groups, and foundations" (http://go.worldbank .org/PWRRFJ2QH0 (accessed April 11, 2011, emphasis added).

donor demands (Igoe 2003). NGOs are often not democratic organizations (Edwards and Hulme 1996b; Bebbington 1997; Edwards 2000), and are frequently more accountable to their donors than they are to the groups they aim to serve (Ebrahim 2003; Mercer 1999). Ironically, NGOs activities designed to "build capacity" through training of local government agents are often not efficacious (Swidler and Watkins 2009; Watkins, Swidler, and Hannan 2012; Barr, Marcel, and Trudy 2005).

Because NGOs are able to pay higher salaries, moreover, they can draw the most competent employees out of the public sector (Chege 1999; Schuller 2009).[13] Pfeiffer (2003) reveals this process at work in the health sector of Mozambique, where NGOs pulled government health workers out of important routine tasks. As a result, treatment quality decreased, as did the productivity and morale of staff remaining in government employ (Pfeiffer 2003).

Legitimacy

Finally, states are defined by their ties to citizens, ideally in "the supreme loyalty of the overwhelming majority of the people..." (Turner and Young 1985, 13). Such loyalty is needed for state *legitimacy*, a generalized acceptance of the state's authority to rule. Stated another way, legitimacy concerns a state's right to govern, based on the perception of its citizens that its actions are proper or appropriate in its cultural context (Suchman 1995).

I find that where citizens have contact with NGOs, state legitimacy is either unaffected or is actually higher than it is in the absence of these organizations. Likewise, having positive views of NGOs does not correlate with having negative perceptions of government. NGOs help the state to fulfill its end of the social contract, in which citizens give up freedoms in exchange for security and services.

Developing states have long predicated their legitimacy on the distribution of services and promises of economic development (Young 1988; Bratton 1989, 1989b; Fowler 1991; Kanyinga 1996, 71; Schatzberg 2001; Owiti, Aluoka, and Oloo 2004; Johnson 2015; Osodo and Matsvai 1997;

---

[13] Liberalization of exchange rates has meant lower real wages for civil service employees, who then compete for higher-paying NGO jobs. With exchange rate liberalization and devaluation, real wages for civil servants have fallen as much as 80 percent (van de Walle 2001), covering family food expenses for as little as three days per month (Tripp 1994). At the start of the twenty-first century, NGO salaries averaged five times as much as their government counterparts in Kenya (Chege 1999).

Jackson and Rosberg 1984a). As Julius Nyerere, the first president of Tanzania and a pan-African leader, said in 1961, "Freedom to many means immediate betterment, as if by magic. Unless I can meet at least some of these aspirations, my support will wane and my head will roll."

NGO presence also suggests to poor, rural people, who have great desires but little real expectations from government, that someone in the world outside their village cares about them – this improves their optimism about the future, and, by association, their support for government. People are thankful that services have been brought, and their thanks are diffuse. There exists variation in this effect, however: urbanites are more cynical than their rural counterparts. Even among city-dwellers, however, interactions with NGOs are not systematically associated with negative views of government.

These findings run counter to some of the dominant theories on NGOs, which assert that NGO provision of services can erode the social contract (Schuller 2009), thereby undermining government legitimacy. Fowler writes, "Of the five imperatives that are a constant source of political concern to African governments, legitimacy is potentially the one most susceptible to NGO expansion" (1991, 78). In a widely cited article, Michael Bratton explains that NGOs threaten legitimacy specifically *because* African governments rely on promises of service provision and economic development as their moral basis for holding power (1989). Legitimacy can suffer if NGOs offer services that the government cannot match (Martin 2004). In post-conflict countries, this is often the case – donors favor NGOs for service provision, with several unintended consequences for state building: low levels of capacity within local governments, unsustainable facilities, and insufficient upward and downward accountability among service providers (Batley and McLoughlin 2010, 132).[14]

Many of these arguments rely on an assumption that citizens in developing countries make comparisons between NGOs and the government, such that effective NGO action reflects poorly on the government. World Bank and UN development expert John Clark suggests NGOs themselves make this assumption; he writes that NGOs might not want to improve service delivery if it brings positive returns to the government by

---

[14] According to other researchers, however, NGOs sometimes use donor resources to deliberately compete with government for legitimacy (Obiyan 2005, 82), even publicly opposing politicians, questioning their credentials, or drawing attention to their mistakes (Sandberg 1994, 11).

increasing its popularity (Clark 1995, 596). Others assert that NGOs' participatory approach mobilizes people, encourages increased information sharing, fosters alternative political ideas, and empowers the disadvantaged, all of which can threaten extant political legitimacy, power, and order (Bratton 1989a, Fowler 1991, Boulding and Gibson 2009 citing Putnam 1993 and Putnam 2000, Martin 2004).

My findings, however, show that positive popular responses to NGOs do not equate to negative views of government, at least not in much of Kenya. Other recent research across Africa and in South Asia has come to the same conclusion (Sacks 2012, Dietrich and Winters 2015). If we consider NGOs to be part of the organizational form of the state, it is logical that NGOs do not undermine state legitimacy. Especially in rural areas, many people associate NGOs' good deeds with their local administrators or politicians, who are often credited with having brought the NGOs to the community. This makes sense in patrimonial societies, where "big men" who have access to the resources of the state (as civil servants or politicians) distribute these resources among their clients in exchange for decision-making authority.[15]

This finding may be a mixed blessing, however. In democratic polities, NGOs bolstering state legitimacy is probably beneficial for all concerned. In authoritarian regimes, however, NGOs may (inadvertently) placate demand for change. NGOs may provide an excuse for the government to withdraw from service provision (Campbell 1996) or to become dependent on nongovernmental and international actors (Englebert 2009). If NGOs leave, the short-term service provision benefits they brought can evaporate if there has not also been investment in local government officials (Doyle and Patel 2008).

ALLIES OR ADVERSARIES? CONDITIONS FACILITATING BLURRED BOUNDARIES

NGO–government relations provide the backdrop against which NGO activities affect these four elements of stateness within a country. Their interactions can range from deeply tense, conflictual relations to collaborative relationships between NGOs and public managers as allies.[16] Collaborative relationships are generally associated with several

---

[15] In economically poor societies, this distribution is not only strategically important for getting reelected; it is often morally required, as mutual exchange relations of patron–clientelism provide a kind of social insurance where no formal policies exist.

[16] I focus here on the dichotomy between generally collaborative and conflictual interactions deliberately, because I am interested in these broad categories, not in fine-grained

conditions, which are neither universal nor unwavering: high-performing, established NGOs that are focused primarily on service provision rather than human rights, democracy, or governance; a relatively open political climate, in which freedom of association is normally assured; a central government that is committed to development and grants autonomy to service providers; stable, predictable laws and regulations that provide positive incentives to the NGO sector; clear mechanisms for NGO–government engagement along multiple lines; deliberate efforts by NGO and government to create a positive working environment; and an alignment of interests among NGOs and government departments. These collaboration-promoting characteristics and their conflict-inducing counterparts can be discussed in four broad categories: (1) organizational attributes of both governments and NGOs; (2) characteristics of NGO regulation; (3) basis for and contours of NGO–government interaction; and (4) level of interest alignment between the organizations.[17] These categories are summarized in Table 2.2.

"Collaboration" and "conflict" are two ends of a spectrum that contains a range of possible interactions (Coston 1998). These relationships can be multifaceted as well – in some cases, an NGO and a government actor might collaborate even when each views the other as a "necessary evil" – what Bryant (2001) calls "critical engagement." Organizational pairings can also exist at multiple points on the spectrum simultaneously (Batley 2011, 317). For example, a Ministry of Health might have a conflictual relationship with a particular organization, yet the Ministry of Water in the same country might engage that NGO in a collaborative partnership. This can be true of interactions among different parts of the same organizations, at different levels, or even in different interactions of the same actors over time (Fisher 1998, Najam 2000, McLoughlin 2011, Ramanath and Ebrahim 2010). Ergo, certain conditions are more likely to facilitate collaborative or synergistic partnering relationships between NGOs and governments, while other conditions are associated with adversarial, conflictual, or – at best – neutral relationships.

disaggregation of them, which other scholars have elaborated (cf. Clark 1991, Fisher 1998, Najam 2000). Coston (1998), for example, creates an eight-part typology ranging from repression to collaboration, with rivalry, competition, contracting, third-party government, cooperation, and complementarity in between.

[17] The classification scheme here may differ slightly from that of the authors I cite. I strive to remain true to the author's intent. It is worth noting that Ansell and Gash (2008) identify similar characteristics that lead to or are present in successful collaborative governance.

TABLE 2.2. *Determinants of NGO–government relationship*

Category	Description under collaboration	Description under conflict
Organizational Attributes	*NGOs* • Focus on service provision • Established over many years • High performing • Leaders connected to government • Government-funded or diverse funding sources *Government* • New leaders (honeymoon period) • Effective, skilled staff and capable organizations • Committed to social change • Space for organizational autonomy • Economically and politically liberal	*NGOs* • Seek political change • Seek strong policy role • Low capacity • Work with politically sensitive groups • Funded by distrusted (often foreign) donors *Government* • High bureaucratic red tape • Low-skilled workers • Weak commitment to poverty reduction • Highly centralized; command-and-control administration • Economically statist and politically authoritarian
Characteristics of NGO Regulation	• Stable, predictable laws and regulation • Straightforward; compliance is feasible • Policies provide incentives to NGOs • Goal is to facilitate NGO effectiveness • NGOs accept state right to regulate • NGO role in creating rules governing them	• Laws and regulation unclear, sometimes intentionally • Goal is to suppress NGO activity through rigidity, excessiveness, or interference in NGO activities • NGOs avoid compliance with regulations

TABLE 2.2. *(cont.)*

Category	Description under collaboration	Description under conflict
	Basis for Interaction	*Basis for Interaction*
	• Informal, trust-based relations that have developed over time	• Competition for resources
	• Donors require consultations and collaboration	• Very rapid growth in NGO sector combined with limited government capacity to regulate
	Strategies of Engagement	*Strategies of Engagement*
	• Deliberate efforts to create positive working relationship	• Deliberate efforts to avoid government regulation or monitoring
Basis for and Contours of Interaction	• Government recognizes NGO contribution	• Government does not recognize NGO contribution
	Features of Interaction	*Features of Interaction*
	• Multiple forms of interaction occur	• Political will for cooperation lacking
	• NGOs avoid politically sensitive issues	• NGOs unwilling to engage in dialogue
	• Mechanisms for engagement clearly defined	• NGOs deliberately not transparent
	• Both organizations play role in writing formal agreements	• Asymmetrical power relations
	• Some flexibility exists in relationship	• Rigid agreements, written by one side
Level of Interest Alignment	• High level of alignment	• Low alignment of interests
	• Mechanisms exist for accommodation when there is conflict or tension	• Low levels of trust

Organizational attributes of both governments and NGOs

A number of organizational characteristics affect the nature of NGO–government relationships. On the NGO side, these pertain to organizational mission and strategy, age and size, leadership, source of funding, and program performance. On the government side, leadership and organizational performance are also important, as are their structure, development strategy, and political regime type.

NGO *characteristics*

Both the mission and the strategies of NGOs affect their interactions with government (Ramanath and Ebrahim 2010). Where an NGO's mission is oriented toward service provision, relations tend to be less conflictual than where NGOs aim to bring about social change – promoting human rights, anti-corruption measures, and civil and political liberties (Bratton 1989a), or participation, empowerment, or democracy (Clark 1992, Sen 1999, Banks and Hulme 2012). This principle is especially applicable to non-controversial services, like immunizations, clean water, and agricultural extension services (Bratton 1989a, Sen 1999). Governments see these activities as non-threatening, whereas governance activities can be a direct challenge to their rule. The latter is particularly true where NGOs organize protests, legally challenge the state via the courts, join with opposition leaders, or use media and informal communications to oppose the state (Clark 1992, Sen 1999, Banks and Hulme 2012, Nair 2011).

Likewise, where NGOs do not seek to engage in development planning as a deliberate strategy, but instead see their role as "gap filling" for the government, relations tend to be collaborative (Clark 1992). The same is also seen to be true, however, when the NGO sector is very small or weak, offering few services (Bratton 1989a). In such cases, NGOs are more likely to defer to government policy and service provision decisions.

When NGOs perform these gap-filling activities well, displaying high capacity and professionalism, governments tend to appreciate them and want to work together (Brautigam and Segarra 2007, Clark 1993). Conversely, miscalculating what is feasible (Nurul Alam 2011) or demonstrating poor performance and low skills (Clark 1993) can lead to a more acrimonious relationship. Likewise, if NGOs wish to avoid conflict, they must be careful not to generate loyalty from the people that comes at the *expense* of loyalty to government (Bratton 1989a, Heurlin 2010).

Conflict tends to be the norm where NGOs compete to make policy (McLoughlin 2011) or are perceived as engaging in anti-governmental activities (Tripp 2001). State–NGO relations are more likely to be strained where the organizations' missions are to provide services in disputed territories, in sensitive security areas, in places where rebellion could occur, or in refugee camps and cross-border operations (Bratton 1989a, McLoughlin 2011, Sen 1999), since these are sensitive or unstable areas for the government. Even if unintentional, NGOs working with a very narrow constituency or marginalized group in a country can raise concerns for the government (Clark 1993) by threatening to disrupt power dynamics.

Often, these factors interact with other characteristics of NGOs. Where NGOs have been present in a country for a long period of time, relations tend to be more collaborative, as longevity means that a degree of trust has developed with government and community leaders (Rose 2011, Jelinek 2006). Long-standing, strong leaders within NGOs reinforce these trends, since the government will have gained familiarity with them over time (Rose 2011). Likewise, NGOs whose leaders previously worked in government, or who have moved repeatedly between government and NGOs, are likely to be able to work collaboratively with government offices, since they have personal connections to them (McLoughlin 2011). Conflict can arise, however, if strong, capable leaders use their skills to challenge the government (Heurlin 2010).

Finally, an NGO's source and type of funding can influence how it interacts with the government, including public agencies. Organizations that are funded through government contracts tend to have collaborative relationships with government (Rosenberg, Hartwig, and Merson 2008), especially where few other sources of funding exist – though this collaboration can easily turn into co-optation of the NGO. NGOs with diverse funding bases also tend to be able to develop partnerships with government – and on a more equal footing – since the funding diversity facilitates autonomy from public agencies (Rose 2011, Nair 2011). In such cases, organizations can take advantage of even minimal room to maneuver to create "constructive reciprocities" with public offices (Tripp 2001, 105). Where NGOs and the government compete for resources, or where they are perceived by the government to be funded by foreign states or organizations that are not allies of the government (Clark 1993), distrust and apprehension can develop.

Government attributes

Some of the same types of organizational characteristics that matter for NGOs are also significant on the government side of the equation, though they can be important in different ways. Whereas leaders that have managed nongovernmental organizations for long periods of time are able to develop trusting relationships with their government counterparts over the years, *new* leaders in government can also have a "honeymoon period" that facilitates collaboration (Brautigam and Segarra 2007, Brass 2012a, Atibil 2012). This honeymoon is most likely to occur if the new government leader is seen as a change-oriented individual, has previously worked in NGOs, or came to power due to a crisis where uncertainty opens a space for learning.

As with NGOs, collaborative relationships are more likely to develop where government agencies have effective structures (Clark 1992) and knowledgeable and capable staff (Jelinek 2006, Mayhew 2005), as well as the capacity to comply with donor partnership requirements (Brautigam and Segarra 2007). Such government organizations are more likely able to complement the skills of their NGO counterparts. When government staff employees have few skills and organizations lack capacity, relations tend to be tense (Jelinek 2006, Bratton 1989a, Clark 1993, McLoughlin 2011). In these situations, NGO workers often become frustrated by government ineffectiveness, and public employees can be threatened by their NGO counterparts – particularly when there is a high level of NGO performance. This tension can be exacerbated where state legitimacy is low (McLoughlin 2011), excessive bureaucratic red tape slows interactions between the organizations (Pugachev nd), or a dominant but ineffective central government agency tries to maintain control over the service sector (Rose 2006).

Just as NGOs' mission and strategy affects interactions with government, a government's development strategy – not only at the national political level, but also the strategies of line ministries and local administrations – strongly influences the relationship. Public organizations that have a positive social agenda will find partnering with NGOs easier than those whose commitment to poverty reduction is weak (Clark 1993). Likewise, government organizations that are open to institutional pluralism in general are more apt to create a space for NGOs in policy creation or implementation (Clark 1993, Mayhew 2005, Coston 1998) than those that are resistant to such pluralism. Oftentimes this openness corresponds to states with a liberal economic development strategy (Heurlin 2010, Bratton 1989a), since such governments are more prone to contracting out to private organizations and to exerting less centralized control than are those with statist or socialist economic development strategies (Heurlin 2010, Neal 2008). Openness to pluralism also corresponds to states with democratic governance (Brautigam and Segarra 2007, Clark 1992), meaning not only a multi-party political system and respect for civil liberties (Bratton 1989a), but also a focus on accountability in the public administration (Clark 1993). That said, stability in both the economy and the political system create space for collaboration with NGOs as well (Nair 2011, McLoughlin 2011), and this can occur in nondemocratic spaces.

Government leaders, including public administration leaders, who are focused on asserting authority or restricting organizational autonomy will generally have more conflict-laden relationships with NGOs (Atibil 2012, Clark 1992, Mayhew 2005) than their hands-off colleagues. This is true not only of military dictatorships and one-party states (Clark 1992), but also personalist authoritarian regimes (Heurlin 2010). In the latter case, leaders tend to have a shallow base of elite support and must rely on patronage to maintain the compliance of those outside their base. NGOs can be used in such regimes to challenge the ruler (ibid.). Authoritarian rulers can avoid such challenges, however, if they co-opt NGOs (Heurlin 2010, Mayhew 2005). Political actors in patronage systems can sometimes even grant NGO services to loyal clients (Bratton 1989a).

Characteristics of NGO regulation

In addition to public organization attributes in general, the manner in which governments regulate NGOs strongly shapes how public organizations and nongovernmental organizations interact. Just as stability in politics and the economy facilitate collaborative relationships, so too do stability and predictability in the regulatory and legal environment (McLoughlin 2011). NGOs are more interested in working with public agencies where registering as an NGO is straightforward and easy to accomplish (Batley 2006), reporting requirements are reasonable, and taxation policies provide incentives for activities that conform with development priorities (Clark 1993). Finally, the motives for regulation matter – where regulation seeks to promote effective operation of NGOs (Batley 2006, Clark 1993) or incorporation of NGOs into state strategies (Heurlin 2010), partnerships are likely.

The response to regulation is also important. Collaboration is more likely where NGOs broadly accept state control through laws and frameworks of collaboration, but remain unsubordinated to the state (Nair 2011). Involving NGOs in creating regulation and NGO–government agreements facilitates positive responses (McLoughlin 2011, Coston 1998, Gugerty 2010), although NGOs engage in self-regulation in a number of countries (Gugerty 2008).

Generally, the inverse is also true. NGOs and government officials are more likely to come into conflict where laws, regulation, and "rules of

engagement" are unclear or disrespected (Batley 2006) (including intentionally informal rules (Heurlin 2010)), which is more likely in highly centralized, command-and-control environments (McLoughlin 2011). The
same is true where regulation is designed to suppress NGO activity
(Gugerty 2008; Mayhew 2005), is excessive or rigid (Bratton 1989a),
or directly interferes in NGOs' activities (Mayhew 2005) – even when
the regulation is not applied or implemented (Batley 2006). In such cases,
governments and line ministries face NGO counterparts unwilling to
comply with the laws and regulations (Palmer et al. 2006). This conflict can be exacerbated further when NGOs and government sectors
hold different opinions about regulation and how it is used (Mayhew
2005).

Basis for and contours of NGO–government interaction

The reasons that NGOs and government interact, as well as the contours
of those interactions, together form a third factor affecting the likelihood
of collaboration or conflict. Here, several elements are important: the
basis or impetus for NGO–government interactions; strategies both types
of organizations use in engaging with the other; and features of the actual
interactions, such as the degree of formality and power dynamics.

Basis for interactions
One of the key ingredients for a collaborative relationship between NGOs
and government agencies is a slow buildup of interactions over time.
These processes allow personal, informal, and trust-based relationships
to develop between NGO workers or leaders and their government counterparts (Rose 2011; Batley 2011; Pick, Givaudan, and Reich 2008; Nair
2011; McLoughlin 2011). As several scholars have noted, even where
relationships were conflictual at some point in time, repeated interactions
can mellow tensions (Bratton 1989a) by creating familiarity and facilitating social learning, often through key bridging individuals (Brautigam
and Segarra 2007). The role of donors is often important in such interactions, since many donors require governments to partner with NGOs
in order to receive funds. Donors often facilitate interactions by insisting
that consultation and collaboration occur (Brautigam and Segarra 2007;
Pugachev nd; Nurul Alam 2011; Batley 2011), and by working to create an environment that encourages NGO entrepreneurialism (Bratton
1989a).

On the other hand, conflictual relationships are likely when the basis for interaction between NGOs and government agencies or officials is due to competition over resources, including donor resources or clients (Pugachev nd; Mayhew 2005). In particular, in weak states, governments often feel threatened by NGOs when donors direct resources to the NGOs (Brass 2012a). Similar tensions arise when the NGO sector in a country grows more rapidly than the government's capacity to regulate, monitor, or keep track of organizations in the sector (Bratton 1989a). Both of these bases for interaction are more likely in relatively closed political systems and those with a high degree of government corruption and low capacity. However, if organizations initially interacted during a period of political repression, where conflict is high, such tensions can remain, even if democracy later develops (McLoughlin 2011; Sen 1999).

Strategies of engagement

Whereas I discussed NGOs' mission and strategy generally in the section on organizational attributes, here I highlight the strategy and tactics NGOs use to engage the government specifically. When NGO leaders or workers prioritize positive working relationships with government, and vice versa, collaborative relationships become more likely. Putting in the effort to recognize and engage the other organizations produces results. NGOs often deliberately invest considerable time in relationships with their government counterparts to avoid tension (Rose 2011; Pick, Givaudan, and Reich 2008), confrontation, or conflict (Batley 2011; Bratton 1989a; Clark 1992). To promote positive working relationships, they: draw attention to the congruence between their goals and those of the government (Bratton 1989a); deliberately share information about plans, programs, activities, and results with government (Jelinek 2006); work to coordinate activities with those of government (Jelinek 2006; Clark 1992); position their work strategically vis-à-vis government, including helping government departments improve their services and strengthen their systems (Clark 1992); and share resources with their government counterparts (Coston 1998). NGOs also often invite government officials to their trainings, workshops, project inaugurations, and other events (Jelinek 2006). This inclusiveness is often a deliberate strategy for keeping relationships cordial.

On the government side of the coin, collaboration is more likely when government agencies or officials formally recognize the contributions that NGOs make (Rose 2011). In some cases, public actors merely become resigned to the presence and popularity of NGOs (Cannon 1996), while others explicitly create spaces for their mutual cooperation (Clark 1993; Mayhew 2005; Coston 1998). In co-production relationships, governments deliberately share responsibility and operation with other actors, including NGOs (Coston 1998).

Under certain conditions, however, governments are unlikely to recognize NGOs' role in service provision. If NGOs' role in a service area becomes very large, or if NGOs and the government hold divergent understandings of the proper role of NGOs (Atibil 2012), the government may see the organizations as a threat and may respond by increasing its efforts to exert control (Rose 2011). Likewise, NGOs are unlikely to take a deliberately collaborative approach where the government is restrictive and controlling.

Features of interactions

The manner in which government and NGO actors actually engage when they interact is also an important component of their relationship – both informally, and in formal contracts and agreements. Informally, interactions are more likely to be associated with partnership when NGOs and government are committed to working together (Pugachev nd, Mayhew 2005), and multiple forms of engagement occur between the organizations (Rose 2006; McLoughlin 2011). For example, an NGO that provides health services in a community alongside government health workers and is also invited to take part in creating policy or regulation in the health sector is more likely to work in collaboration with government actors. Over time, NGOs often learn what the political obstacles in their environment are – and how to avoid them (Brautigam and Segarra 2007; Clark 1992).

Tensions or outright conflict are more likely to appear, however, when the political will for cooperation is lacking on one or both sides (Mayhew 2005). Clashes can occur when NGOs are unwilling to engage in dialogue with the government (Clark 1993), when they are deliberately opaque regarding their activities or funding (Cannon 1996), or, more generally, when there are clearly asymmetrical power relations and the government holds more power (Coston 1998). Even when broad regional or countrywide conditions appear to be favorable (McLoughlin 2011), local-level informal political conditions can create tense interactions.

The character of formal contracts or agreements between NGOs and their government counterparts also shape the collaborative or conflictual nature of their relationships. Some scholars suggest that NGO–government relations are more likely to be collaborative where the mechanisms for engagement are clearly defined (Mayhew 2005) with each actor's role clearly delineated (McLoughlin 2011), and where both sides play a role in writing formal agreements (Rose 2011). Others, however, suggest that formal, contractual agreements can allow governments to subordinate NGOs (Batley 2011), particularly when the contractual relationship is rigid (Nurul Alam 2011) or designed by only one side (McLoughlin 2011). The degree of contractual formality may not matter as much (Coston 1998) as having a degree of flexibility or room to maneuver in the relationship (Rose 2011). NGOs, in particular, are more likely to take a collaborative stance when they maintain an ability to negotiate their position with the government (Nair 2011). NGOs maintaining a degree of informality (Batley 2011), or relationships growing out of informal relationships between NGOs and government officials, can facilitate such collaborative relationships (Rose 2011).

Level of interest alignment between the organizations

Finally, interest alignment among NGOs and their government counterparts is crucial for the establishment and maintenance of strongly collaborative relationships (Puplampu and Tettey 2000; Brautigam and Segarra 2007; Rosenberg, Hartwig, and Merson 2008; Clark 1992; McLoughlin 2011; Sen 1999). Alternatively, if their interests do conflict, collaborative relationships are also possible when mechanisms exist to accommodate both sides (Coston 1998). Such interest alignment is more likely to occur where NGOs and public officials share common beliefs or values (McLoughlin 2011), and where NGOs bring resources to the relationship that supplement those of government (Bratton 1989a). According to several scholars, many NGOs and governments have learned over time that it is in their interests to collaborate (Brautigam and Segarra 2007; Clark 1992).

On the other hand, discord between organizations is more common when their interests do not align (Brautigam and Segarra 2007; Najam 1996). This is more likely to happen when government leaders take steps to make sure donor resources remain in government hands (Brautigam and Segarra 2007), when NGOs subscribe to a development theory that is different from that of government (Clark 1992), or when NGOs demand greater participation in setting the agenda than the state would like (Sen 1999).

At the most basic level, NGO–government interactions are shaped by the perceptions that NGO workers hold of the government as a whole, or government actors in particular, and vice versa. In particular, as in any human relationship, trust matters. Government and NGO actors have difficulty engaging in collaborative relationships when they distrust one another (Bebbington et al. 1993; Clark 1993), or perceive the other to distrust them (Jelinek 2006). This distrust can occur at both the individual and organizational levels. Like distrust, resentment brings tension (Jelinek 2006, Nurul Alam 2011), as when governments resent NGOs' access to resources (Clark 1993).

Conflict is more likely to arise when distrust is combined with perceptions among government actors or agencies that NGOs are competing with them for resources (Gugerty 2008; Coston 1998), for clients (Pugachev nd), or for political support (Bratton 1989a). Likewise, when government actors think NGOs are tools of foreign donors trying to change state policy (Pugachev nd), the likelihood of struggles increase. These perceptions can lead government to feel threatened or challenged by NGOs, which hampers collaboration (Clark 1992; Mayhew 2005).

On the NGO side, the possibility for collaboration or partnership is strained when NGOs perceive government officials to be incapable of implementing projects and programs (Jelinek 2006), to deliberately obstruct or interfere in NGOs' work (Nurul Alam 2011), or to have too much red tape (Pugachev nd). On both sides, such discordant perceptions often grow out of a history of mistrust and accusations of corruption (Batley 2011), or out of simple misinformation (Jelinek 2006). Where NGOs and government perceive each other as having mutual goals and a similar understanding of the means for achieving goals (Pugachev nd, Clark 1993; Coston 1998), collaboration becomes much more likely.

NGO–GOVERNMENT ISOMORPHISM: MOVING TOWARD COLLABORATION THROUGH SOCIAL LEARNING

The characteristics described in this chapter provide an overview of the conditions likely to make allies or adversaries of NGOs and their government counterparts, yet it is crucial to remember that relations are not static, and that these conditions are not universal. As Batley (2011, 308) explains in a comparative article on Bangladesh, India, and Pakistan, "Governments' relationships with voluntary associations or NGOs have evolved historically and are affected by the institutional characteristics of states and by the practices of governments." Indeed, in most places around the world, there has been a thawing of interactions from generalized tension or outright hostility toward something more collaborative or at least neutral in tone. NGOs and states have come to more collab-orative arrangements over time through a process of social learning and isomorphism (cf. Rosenberg, Hartwig, and Merson 2008; Brautigam and Segarra 2007; Keese and Argudo 2006; Rose 2006; Zafar Ullah et al. 2006; Taylor 2006; Brinkerhoff 2002).

What is social learning? It is the process by which actors acquire new knowledge through interaction with other people, organizations, and institutions in an environment. Akin to socialization, social learning does not occur via deliberate education. Instead, as people are exposed to new ideas and are persuaded to adopt them, they slowly adapt their understanding of what makes sense, is appropriate, or is legitimate (Brautigam and Segarra 2007). These changes can be seen in the NGO-and-government context as government offices adopt strategies, tech-niques, and processes previously associated with NGOs, rather than with public administrations.

I am not the first to apply social learning theory to studies of NGO–government relations. Here, I draw on Segarra (1997) and Brautigam and Segarra (2007), whose study of Ecuador, Gambia, and Guatemala shows how collaboration between NGOs and government, initially rejected by both sets of actors alike, became a taken-for-granted, legitimate, nor-mative practice through strategic social learning processes that occurred during the 1990s and into the 2000s. Despite significant initial resistance, governments in all three countries learned that partnering with NGOs was beneficial to them. Like Brautigam and Segarra, I draw attention to the role played by donors in these processes in Kenya. Donors not only encourage collaboration between NGOs and the government, but also fund certain types of NGO activities, thereby reinforcing the norms they see and approve. At the same time, social learning can occur as NGOs exert influence on policy and practice by example and interaction, rather than through direct confrontation with the government (Batley 2011).

In many countries, social learning has initiated a process of institu-tional isomorphism on the part of government line ministries (DiMaggio and Powell 1983). According to DiMaggio and Powell's (1983, 149) highly cited theory, isomorphism is the process by which organizations change strategies and structure such that they resemble others in their field – a process of homogenization in organizational characteristics. These changes involve social learning, as "organizational decision mak-ers learn appropriate responses and adjust their behavior accordingly" (ibid., 149). Three means of isomorphism exist: coercive, in which pres-sure from other organizations and society causes change; mimetic, which involves modeling organizational behavior and structure on the example of other, successful organizations in a field; and normative, in which organizations change through professionalization and formal education (ibid.).

Government agencies in many developing countries have changed through mimetic isomorphism, in which they learn from and adopt models of programmatic behavior and organizational dynamics from NGOs. Government workers model – sometimes explicitly and other times unintentionally – their programs on those of NGOs, which they perceive to be more legitimate and successful, confirming DiMaggio and Powell's theory (DiMaggio and Powell 1983, 152). Public administrators are also affected by coercive isomorphism, stemming largely from donor governments and multilateral development institutions, as well as from NGOs. Here, administrative agencies have adjusted their internal processes in response to pressure from donor organizations and NGOs, on which they are dependent for resources. Following DiMaggio and Powell (1983, 150), I show that even when the changes made are largely ceremonial, they are still consequential, able to change dynamics in the long run.

Through these processes of social learning and institutional isomorphism, bureaucratic organizations of government line ministries begin to resemble NGOs in several key ways that suggest improvements in their administrative capacity. First, line ministries have increasingly taken participatory approaches, integrating the views of beneficiary communities into planning and decision-making processes. These "demand-driven" approaches reflect a new way of thinking for many civil servants. Second, government offices have increasingly focused on performance management approaches – holding annual performance reviews for employees, setting targets for provision of services, and evaluating their work against these targets.

CONCLUSION

This chapter has provided conceptualizations of key terms in this book, theories of the interplay between NGO service provision and the state, and conditions under which NGOs and their government counterparts collaborate or conflict. Four "elements of stateness" – territoriality, governance, administrative capacity and legitimacy – were explained, as well as how they have changed as a result of the proliferation of NGOs providing services around the world. Theories of civil society, governance, the social contract, and social learning help elucidate these changes.

Under the conditions detailed in the chapter, NGOs can comprise an integral component of the organizational form of the state in developing countries like Kenya. When NGOs and governments share largely positive working relationships, and when NGOs are given room to maneuver, NGOs expand the nature of state service provision in such a way that we can include nongovernmental as well as governmental actors under the aegis of "the state." As NGOs and government work hand in hand on programs and projects, the line between public agency and private NGOs blurs. NGOs help to reconstitute the state through the creation of networks of actors undertaking functions that had traditionally been associated with the state. Symbolically, NGOs suggest to people that organizations are looking out for them. With the addition of these private actors, government performance improves.

3

Kenya as case study

Historical portraits of NGOs and the state[1]

"NGOs have been very active here for decades."
(NGO program manager, Machakos town, 2008)

"The old way of doing things was, 'We tell you what to do! You MUST do it.' The new way is working together, partnership, new ideas are good."
(Health sector NGO manager, Nairobi, 2006)

"Government doesn't see [NGOs] as a competitor or rival, but [as] a partner."
(NGO leader, Nakuru district, 2012)

This chapter contextualizes NGOs in Kenya, an important country of focus for research on NGOs and the state. Kenya has a long history of nonstate actors providing social services, which is detailed in this chapter. Examining this history provides an example of the characteristics associated with collaborative versus conflictual relationships discussed in general terms in Chapter 2.

During the administration of Daniel arap Moi (1978 to 2002), tensions between NGOs and government were high. Several years later, however, there was a rapid warming of the relations between the government and service-providing NGOs. NGOs and the government took advantage of Kenya's political opening in the 2000s, the new leadership team's long history working with civil society leaders, President Kibaki's hands-off administrative approach, and donor financial support for collaboration. During the Kibaki administration (2002 to 2013), attitudes between

---

[1] The section of this chapter detailing changing NGO–government relations over time in Kenya draws from Brass (2012a).

government and NGOs became increasingly open, with individuals on both sides more willing to work together.

The chapter also provides a snapshot of the NGO sector in one country, during one time period. It answers common questions about national NGO sectors: How many NGOs exist? Where do they come from? What do they do? Do the people interact with them? In the early 2000s, NGOs played a prominent role in Kenyan society, and many Kenyans had contact with NGOs. The sector was involved in a diverse range of activities across the country, which varied across the city-town-rural spectrum.

THE KENYAN POLITICAL ECONOMY: AN OVERVIEW

Understanding the broader Kenyan political economy at a basic level may help the reader to grasp the role that NGOs and other nongovernmental actors have played in service provision in the country. Kenya gained independence from British colonialists in 1963 under the leadership of Jomo Kenyatta, who ruled until his death in 1978. Unlike in many young or weak states, public administration in the early years of independence was relatively strong, partially due to British settler demand for and commitment to it during colonial times. Agencies in the new country were professionalized and civil servants were treated as respected technocrats (Leonard 1991). Kenya produced tea, coffee, and other agricultural goods for export and developed a manufacturing sector that supplied much of the region; the economy grew rapidly.

Politically, however, the Kenyatta administration, and the Moi regime that followed it, maintained national cohesion and stability by balancing or manipulating pressures from the country's many ethnic groups, the largest of which comprised less than a quarter of the population. The highly centralized government strategically granted access to state resources, distributing patronage goods and services through the Provincial Administration (Tamarkin 1978, Barkan and Chege 1989, Leonard 1991) and via ethnoregional power brokers (LeBas 2011). This approach created strong demand for leaders to "nourish and provide for their followers," distributing services based on loyalty, since there was little incentive to provide truly national public goods (Arriola 2013, 13). Corruption became rampant, particularly as Moi used state resources, including donor aid monies and projects, to pit some ethnic groups against one another and to form loyal blocs among others (Widner 1992, LeBas 2011), all while claiming to eschew "tribalism" (Haugerud 1993). Ethnic violence preceded the 1992 and 1997 elections. At the same time, opposition, media, and civil society groups were silenced (Ndegwa 1996).

Eventually, the demands of ethnic power balancing overwhelmed the professionalized public administration, as decisions were made for political rather than economic or bureaucratic rationale (Bates 1981). The system led to deteriorating economic conditions and service provision throughout the 1970s, 1980s, and 1990s, as well as the emergence of a dominant party-state with limited executive turnover (van de Walle 2001). Donors clashed openly with the Moi administration in the 1990s, periodically withdrawing support to the government.

During the Kibaki administration, the country experienced more prolonged violent ethnic conflict in the aftermath of the disputed 2007 election than had occurred previously, and the fear of repeat violence was high in 2013, although it did not materialize to any great extent. At the same time, the economy rebounded considerably amid political and civil rights opening and improvements in donor relations in the 2000s. The Kenyan media, civil society, and opposition groups have become largely free and critique of the government became common.

This is the context in which nongovernmental service provision has developed in Kenya – the focus of this chapter. Ethnic-based patronage politics and corruption remain dominant features of the political economic landscape in the twenty-first century. Multi-party rule, however, has introduced volatility and shifting ethnic coalitions, as well as increased roles for nongovernmental actors in public decision-making.

Because of these changes, even if ethnicity is the vehicle through which politics is often mobilized, it offers neither a sufficient nor a necessary explanation for all political phenomena in Kenya. For example, research has suggested that ethnic bias is not a consistent or especially powerful determinant of government service delivery in Africa (Kramon and Posner 2013). Data have also shown that donor aid channeled through NGOs specifically is not associated with ethnicity (Dietrich 2013). Therefore, this book places ethnicity to one side in examining interactions between NGOs, the Kenyan state, and ordinary Kenyans.

NONSTATE SERVICE PROVISION IN KENYAN HISTORY

Colonialism and the post-independence years: *harambee* groups and missionaries

Although the acronym "NGO" is relatively new, nongovernmental service provision in Kenya is not. Local and international nongovernmental organizations have existed in the territory since before independence. Within the country, a spirit of *"harambee"* (a Swahili term meaning, "let's pull together") has long motivated national development through self-help organizations. *Harambee* groups, still in existence today, originated in pre-colonial cooperative work parties and rotating work teams (Hill 1991), as well as in the Independent Schools Movement, in which indigenous groups, primarily Kikuyu and Luo, opened their own schools during the colonial period (Wallis 1985, Rosberg and Nottingham 1966, Natsoulas 1998). The colonial British government exploited *harambee* groups for forced labor, and resisted the Independent Schools Movement until it became clear that independence was forthcoming. *"Harambee!"* was the rallying cry of Kenya's first President, Jomo Kenyatta, and it became the country's motto after independence in 1963.

Kenyatta recognized that the Kenyan people would have to contribute significantly to the country's development efforts for it to advance, and he formalized the role of *harambee* in Sessional Paper Number 10 of 1965. He called on local *harambee* groups to pull together to achieve what they could on their own, promising that the government would supplement local efforts. Although thirty-one different types of self-help projects were described in the first National Policy of Community Development (Republic of Kenya 1963), the most common manifestations were *harambee* schools and clinics, in which a local community gathered its own resources to provide collective goods (Barkan and Holmquist 1989). The government or other outsiders sometimes stepped in and provided teachers, administrators, nurses, and clinicians, and other support like supplies (Chieni 1997, Thomas-Slayter 1985).

These local organizations had a large impact on Kenyan lives, especially in rural areas. They contributed significantly to capital formation throughout the country as well; self-help schemes were valued at nearly UK£2 million only four years after Kenyan independence (Prosser 1969). By 1979, 60 percent of secondary school students attended these nonformal schools (Makau 1996).

Although this type of participatory development might sound ideal, many of the services provided by *harambee* schools have been inferior to those of government (Oyugi 1995), and contribution to *harambee* groups was often more akin to obligatory taxation at the local level than to voluntary action (Hill 1991). The relationship between *harambee* groups and the government, moreover, has been contentious. In colonial times, many independent schools were designed to train students to question British rule (Anderson 1970), leading British officials in 1952 to declare most of them "local cells of opposition" and close them down (Holmquist 1984, 75). Likewise, following independence, the *harambee* movement was largely co-opted by political motivations and patronage (Widner 1992), weakening its development effectiveness. Although the central government viewed *harambee* as development "on the cheap" (Holmquist 1979), government planners saw the mushrooming costs of *harambee* service providers as problematic for budgets, causing conflicts between groups and the government (Wallis 1985). Within a few years after independence, the number of *harambee* secondary schools unaided by the government surpassed the number of schools receiving government funding (Hill 1991, 218).

Harambee was meant to legitimate the regime by redistributing wealth from the rich to the poor (Thomas-Slayter 1985), and it did succeed in bringing developing initiatives to rural areas (Hill 1991, Mbithi and Rasmusson 1977). Yet, at the same time, *harambee* became a tool of control that strengthened the country's dependence on patronage politics (Thomas-Slayter 1985; Widner 1992), reinforced inequality (Leys 1975; Oyugi 1995; Holmquist 1979; Hill 1991, 293), and provided justification for administrative recentralization (Barkan, Geist, and Ng'ethe 2003), particularly during the Moi administration (Barkan and Chege 1989). Local administrators coerced their communities into donating in order to gain the favor of their superiors when promotions were due (Transparency International Kenya 2003). Effective *harambee* groups, at the same time, threatened the authority and power of bureaucrats who were nominally in control of development (Holmquist 1979).

These issues led the government to impose licensing requirements on *harambee* groups in 1974 (Widner 1992). By the mid-1980s, the State House used this licensing power, as well as temporal restrictions on *harambee* fundraising, to carefully manipulate political outcomes in Moi's favor (Widner 1992). Later, the Moi administration moved to take over many *harambee* projects; the government assumed control of all secondary schools in 1990 (Oyugi 1995).

In many ways, government–*harambee* tensions set the stage for interactions between the government and NGOs during the Moi period. Both presidents Moi and Kibaki used *harambee* fundraisers as an opportunity to manipulate and co-opt potential opposition (Gifford 2009). Members of Parliament (MPs) vocally broadcast their contributions to local self-help programs to win votes and gain political favor (Waiguru 2002) until 2004, when the Public Officers Ethics Act was enacted, limiting this possibility. *Harambee* organizations continue to exist, and are registered and often referred to as Community-Based Organizations (CBOs), distinguishing them from their more formal and professionalized NGO counterparts (discussed later in this chapter).

Missionaries

Along with the development of indigenous nongovernmental organizations, the country has a long tradition of largely well-intentioned outsiders providing social services at relatively low cost. In addition to a smattering of secular organizations, which arose in the post-World War II years and were viewed positively during early independence (Kameri-Mbote 2000),[2] religious missionaries have been most prevalent. Whereas NGOs are formal secular organizations, missionaries are religious organizations and individuals. There can be overlap between the two, since both are often led and staffed by highly educated, cosmopolitan people with resources and authority. During colonialism, European missionaries provided most of the modern healthcare in the country through both large hospitals and small clinics. Missionaries also brought formal Western schooling to Kenya beginning in the late 1800s. They remained the primary providers of Western education during the colonial period, and managed most of the *harambee* schools in the early post-independence years (Wallis 1985).[3]

Many of the colonial missionary-founded institutions still exist. Health clinics established by missionaries remained faith-based institutions, while most of the schools were taken over by the government as part of the 1968 Education Act. Whereas Tanzania's Nyerere invited NGOs and even bilateral donors to take charge of service provision in specific, assigned areas of the country, Kenyan leaders preferred aid for education to go through the government. Missionaries responded by opening low-cost polytechnic schools focused on practical skills as an alternative to the government curriculum (IDOC 1975). Clinics and hospitals, however, usually remained in the hands of the churches following independence.

Church groups and the state maintained an ambivalent relationship. Although they worked very closely during much of the colonial period, particularly on "community development" initiatives designed to placate the populace (Holmquist 1984), in the transition to independence, most missionaries distanced themselves from the government on ideological

---

[2] These early NGOs were peripheral actors until the 1980s in most developing countries, Kenya included (Ndegwa 1996).
[3] Christian missionaries followed the same pattern of education and health service provision in South Asia in the 1800s and early 1900s (Nair 2011).

grounds (Hughes 2013). Churches and the Kenyan government have clashed periodically ever since, as the liberal, social-oriented National Christian Council of Churches (NCCK), an umbrella organization of the sixteen largest church groupings in the country, drew attention to the systematic inequalities and exclusions experienced by most Kenyans (IDOC 1975). NCCK's liberal theology, with its emphasis on justice and its calls for a return to multi-party democracy, ran counter to the interests of President Moi in particular. He targeted certain religious groups and mission agencies he deemed threatening and subversive during the 1980s and into the 1990s (Kanyinga 1996, Ndegwa 1996, Gifford 2009).

Despite this antagonism, missionaries continued to establish new programs following Kenya's independence. Indeed, Kenya in the 1970s has been described as a "Mecca for Western missionaries" (Hearn 2003). Still today, missionaries work in Kenya, often through faith-based organizations, a religious subset of NGOs that are included in the analysis of NGOs in this book. When donors were wary of supporting the Moi regime in the 1990s, considerable funds went to these organizations (Gifford 2009). In the 2000s, the US government under George W. Bush placed particular emphasis on partnering with these organizations to achieve US government donor objectives (Hearn 2003).

Conflict and control during the Moi administration

Familiarity with the history of *harambee* groups and missionary organizations provides context for understanding NGOs in Kenya, particularly the history of NGO–government relations. In Kenya, as in most developing countries, NGO growth has been staggering. During the Moi presidency, NGOs grew nearly fifteen-fold. In 1974, there were only 125 NGOs in Kenya; by 1990, there were more than 400 registered with the government (Bratton 1989a), soaring to more than 2,200 in the early 2000s (Barkan, Geist, and Ng'ethe 2003). This number excludes *harambee* groups.

As discussed in Chapter 1, this NGO growth in the 1980s and 1990s can be attributed to the neoliberal swing in development thinking that occurred around 1980, as well as the erosion of the economy in Kenya. NGO numbers grew largely in response to the reduction in social services like education, healthcare, and infrastructure that came with donor-required economic restructuring and economic deterioration (Kameri-Mbote 2000).

As the economy faltered in the 1980s, Moi created many of the conditions associated with conflictual NGO–government interactions described

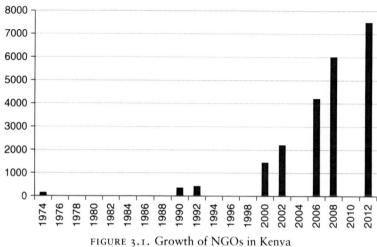

FIGURE 3.1. Growth of NGOs in Kenya

in Chapter 2. Moi consolidated power in the Office of the President, while actively neutralizing political and social "agents of agitation" and creating a one-party state (Ndegwa 1996, 26). Although he publicly proclaimed decentralization through programs like the District Focus for Rural Development (DFRD), Moi actually created upward-reporting requirements that made local administrators pawns of the center rather than being accountable to communities (Barkan, Geist, and Ng'ethe 2003). Within two years of taking office, he had retired six of the seven Provincial Commissioners (PCs), the administrative heads of the country's seven provinces, and moved about half of the District Commissioners – the administrators one step down from the PCs – out of the Provincial Administration and into line ministries, replacing them with more malleable, loyal individuals (Barkan and Chege 1989). Moi ruled largely through fear following a 1982 coup attempt. According to Jennifer Widner, he frequently reminded citizens in a number of ways "of the power he had to destroy the livelihoods of those who criticized the government" (Widner 1992, 168). State repression of ideologically minded politicians was swift, leading many political actors to instead focus on delivering services (Holmquist 1984, 80).

At the beginning of the 1980s, therefore, NGOs did not act in opposition to the government. Most NGOs provided development support apolitically, if sometimes coming into conflict with local-level politicians or administrators. Since independence, the Kenya National Council of Social Services (KNCSS) in the Ministry of Culture and Social Services had regulated NGOs. This ministry was focused on services for families, the youth, the elderly, and those with disabilities, and NGOs were initially seen as working in this space (Ng'ethe 1991). They provided, for example, approximately 40 percent of all healthcare services in Kenya by 1989 (Ndegwa 1996).

The implementation of increasing NGO regulation alongside rapidly deteriorating state–citizen relationships was what brought NGOs into increasing contestation with the government (Barkan, Geist, and Ng'ethe 2003, 89). In particular, a new type of professionalized and wealthier NGO arose in the latter half of the 1980s, with greater skill and interest in shaping Kenya's development trajectory than providing relief and welfare services (Ng'ethe 1991). Leadership of the sector shifted from a missionary and voluntary orientation to a professional, educated middle class (Kanyinga 1996), many of whom would have gone into the civil service in earlier decades (Ndegwa 1996). They saw NGO work as a welcome alternative to restrictive government employment.

Regulatory changes began in 1986, when NGOs were required to submit their plans and budgets to the government for approval and to channel funds through government. These new requirements were instigated by the permanent secretary in charge of internal security in retaliation for NCCK-led protests against the introduction of queue voting (Ndegwa 1996, 34). In 1988, KNCSS released the first directory of NGOs in Kenya, approximately one-quarter of which were internationally based.

In 1989, new legislation allowed the government to deregister NGOs and to set up a government agency based in the Office of the President, the NGO Coordination Board, to coordinate NGOs in the country (Kanyinga 1996). The NGO Board was to ensure that NGO activities accorded with national interests (Ndegwa 1996). At the same time, the Moi government integrated NGOs and their activities into the 1989–1993 National Development Plan. This inclusion simultaneously acknowledged the real welfare and poverty relief benefits that NGOs provided, particularly in rural areas, and served to maintain control over NGOs (Ndegwa 1996). NGOs lost many benefits they had received previously, such as duty-free imports and work permits for foreign nationals (Amutabi 2006). After extensive physical and legal confrontation with the Green Belt Movement NGO later that year, the Moi Government hurriedly passed a more restrictive NGO Bill in 1990 (Ndegwa 1996). Parliamentary discussions around the bill focused on the overwhelming need to control NGOs (ibid.).

In creating this legislation, the government reinforced the clear chain of command in the country's governance, which placed President Moi at the pinnacle of a steep pyramid of power. Government allowed little autonomy to civil society organizations, including NGOs. NGOs were expected to provided apolitical services, with the threat of deregistration for any activity that questioned the state (Ndegwa 1996). Although the act provided structure for a unified NGO sector, these changes were highly unpopular among the NGO community, particularly Nairobi-based NGO leaders. They understood that the government was deliberately working to stifle them (Kameri-Mbote 2000, Kanyinga 1996, Ndegwa 1996).

Several elements coalesced to provoke the State House to strengthen formal regulatory control over NGOs. First, Moi appeared threatened that NGOs that engaged independently in development activities infringed on its authority (Ng'ethe and Kanyinga 1992). In particular, Moi began to seem uneasy as the number of nongovernmental charitable organizations in the country grew rapidly. Although NGO numbers did not explode until the 1990s, they more than doubled during the first decade of his administration (ibid.). NGOs stepped in to help provide a national social safety net, yet the government had no systematic way to track what the organizations were doing.[4] The government argued that it had a right to monitor and regulate the activities of NGOs as a matter of sovereignty, especially since so many NGOs were foreign actors. By December 1986, Moi had become uncomfortable with NGOs, claiming they were involved in "subversive" activities to undermine the government (Amutabi 2006).

The absolute level of donor funding to NGOs was a second motivator for the Moi administration to introduce regulation. By 1990, as much as 18 percent of aid to Kenya was received by NGOs rather than the government (Ndegwa 1996, 20). Donors saw NGOs as a valuable alternative channel for aid (Mosley and Abrar 2006, 315). The government became concerned that donors favored NGOs (Chege 1999; Owiti, Aluoka, and Oloo 2004); many bi- and multilateral organizations explicitly shifted funds away from governments to NGOs in the 1980s (Amutabi 2006).

At the same time, donors pressured governments throughout Africa to allow nongovernmental actors to participate in state decision-making

---

[4] Scholars also lamented the lack of empirical information available on NGOs by the end of the 1980s (Ng'ethe, Mitullah, and Ngunyi 1990).

(Brautigam 1994, 59). The Moi government worried that this pressure could increase, threatening both its crucial donor funding and its power. Especially toward the end of the 1980s, the Moi administration faced growing questions regarding its use of donor resources, as its pro-Western Cold War stance declined in importance (Barkan, Geist, and Ng'ethe 2003). Relationships – and aid funding levels – between the Kenyan government and donors hit a nadir in the 1990s, as the Moi government refused donor conditionality and donors withheld or diverted their aid (Hornsby 2013, Organization for Economic Cooperation and Development 2013, Mosley and Abrar 2006).

The administration was also nervous that NGO activity reflected poorly on government in the eyes of "*wananchi,*" the people of Kenya. NGOs drew attention to problems that the state preferred not to highlight (Barkan, Geist, and Ng'ethe 2003), and were closer to the people than was the state (Amutabi 2006). Kenyan scholars writing at the time were not surprised that the state cracked down on NGOs since "NGOs were using donor funds to contest state legitimacy through delivery of services" (Kanyinga 1996). The government likely became concerned that NGOs threatened to become a strong and "separate political force" influencing partisan politics, as Fernando and Heston (1997, 13) and Sandberg (1994) identified elsewhere in the world. In Latin America and Eastern Europe, some political parties and their leaders are offshoots of NGOs, and Moi, who fought mightily against multi-party democracy, understood such could be possible in Kenya. Regulation allowed the government to "guard against the weakening of state legitimacy and the undesirable tendency of impinging on national sovereignty by NGOs" (Kameri-Mbote 2000, 7).

Finally, Moi began to experience considerable pressure for political liberalization from both the international community and local civil society, which he resisted. Partially due to their autonomy, NGOs in Kenya – as elsewhere – played a significant civil society role in the democratization of the 1990s (Ndegwa 1996). During this time they provided a "counterweight to state power" (Edwards and Hulme 1996b, 962). In fact, NGOs and churches have been the biggest promoters of civil rights and democracy in Kenya since the pre-multi-party election period (Kameri-Mbote 2000). As Tripp (2000, 191) points out, organizations like NGOs that are able to maintain autonomy from the state have been able to press for freedoms of association and expression because they do not gain from a continuation of politics as usual. Autonomous women's NGOs, for example, have facilitated an increase in women's rights in much of Africa

(Austin 2000). Although Moi worked throughout the 1980s to suppress independent organizations of all kinds, a small number maintained their autonomy (Ndegwa 1996).

The unified response by both national and international NGOs to the 1990 NGO Bill was unprecedented (Barkan, Geist, and Ng'ethe 2003). NGOs acted as civil society organizations to oppose the repressive state; they succeeded in pushing forth concessions between 1990 and 1992 (Ndegwa 1996). Thus, NCCK, the Law Society of Kenya, the International Commission of Jurists, the Greenbelt Movement, the Centre for Law and Research International (CLARION), and the Kenya Human Rights Commission all pressed the government, alongside other political opposition factions. Although these organizations were, even in aggregate, comparatively weak and incapable of protecting civil liberties in opposition to the Moi government (Widner 1992), through continuous engagement and opposition, they were able to secure some alterations to the 1990 Bill via regulations on the implementation of the act in 1992.

Throughout the ensuing decade until Moi left office, relations between NGOs and the government remained tense. In Kenya generally, citizens feared the government, which was thought to have coordinated political assassinations, disappearances, and torture, and known to have censored the media, compelled the provision of labor, unlawfully detained people, and restricted movement in the country, particularly in the lead-ups to both the 1992 and 1997 elections (Ndegwa 1998). According to Kenyan legal scholar Patricia Kameri-Mbote (2000), the government employed the NGO Act as justification for harassing NGOs in this climate.

Selective and inconsistent use of legislature to stifle dissent by limiting the freedoms of speech and assembly became common (Ndegwa 1998). After the first multi-party election of the Moi era, in 1992, failed to bring about political change, a number of prominent NGO-based civil society groups pushed for truly democratic reforms (Ndegwa 1998). Those that pressed for civil liberties, human rights, and environmental protection were particularly at risk, though poverty-relief organizations were not exempt. As an NGO leader in Mbeere said, "For a long time, lifting people out of poverty was seen as threatening" (2008–54). Activities with direct political implications were seen as aggressive: Moi described NGOs conducting civic education as "a threat to the security of the state" in 1997 (US Department of State 1998). The government deregistered several human rights NGOs in 1995, Nobel Prize winner Wangari Maathai's Green Belt Movement and CLARION in 1999 (Kameri-Mbote 2000), and the 304 and 340 NGOs (in 2002 and 2003 respectively) that were struck from the register for failing to adequately file paperwork (Republic of Kenya NGO Coordination Bureau).[5]

NGOs faced indirect obstacles as well. In the early 1990s, there was a perceptible, likely deliberate, slowdown in the process of registering an NGO with the government (Ng'ethe 1991). For example, the government took more than a year to process the registration of a Nairobi-based organization promoting public safety through collective action (2008–10). Its leader felt that the delay was due to government suspicion of NGOs as civil society.

As in other authoritarian states, the threat of punishment was sufficient to induce self-regulation in most NGOs. One NGO leader reported that during the Moi years she dared not stray from the government curriculum at her organization's primary school – the idea of introducing "civics" classes was particularly anathema to her. She believed the government rapidly shut down organizations whose programs taught students critical thinking skills (2007–26). NGO regulation acted as a deterrent to civic education.

The transition and beyond: collaborative relations during the Kibaki administration

NGO–government relations changed quickly following the 2002 presidential elections, in which an opposition coalition gained the presidency for the first time since Kenya's independence in 1963. In many cases, relations moved from conflict toward collaboration, in line with the theoretic descriptions from Chapter 2. As will be described in detail in subsequent chapters, in the arena of service provision, attitudes between government and NGOs became more open, with individuals on both sides more willing to work together. These improvements in relations occurred not only in pure service providing NGOs, but also in those delivering a combination of service provision and governance activities, making the changes more remarkable.

Why was the Kibaki administration less conflictual with NGOs than that of Moi? An answer commonly heard in Kenya, particularly among Kibaki supporters – even after the controversial 2007 elections and post-election violence, is, in the words of an informed observer, that "Kibaki is a technocrat who believes civil servants can do their jobs if you let them, and he welcomes any assistance we can get. He's a hands-off, learned president. Not like Moi – a primary school dropout!" (2008–43).

---

[5] Only twenty of these 644 organizations successfully appealed deregistration.

According to this line of thought, and consistent with scholarly theories outlined in Chapter 2, the new administration deliberately changed the nature of NGO–government relations, sensing that the benefits of positive interactions would outweigh the political threats. Decades of hierarchical control under Moi resulted in declining public service provision, a crumbling economy, and massive corruption. Taking advantage of the opening of Kenya's political system and the generalized feeling of goodwill, the Kibaki administration brought new nongovernmental voices into government – and pleased its donors in doing so. According to the leader of a health sector umbrella organization, the government realized how important NGOs were and tried to work together (2006–1).

For example, the Kibaki administration invited a number of prominent civil society leaders to direct government departments (2005–11). Integrating capable, demanding leaders into public administration meant that the "do-gooder" mentalities, participatory decision-making mechanisms, transparent spending practices (garnered through successfully navigating donor accountability requirements), and push for democratization common to NGOs were brought into government offices, sometimes for the first time (2005–6). Some informed observers suggested that this was a positive development; as one NGO leader said, "Civil society was all swallowed by government, so government is thinking like NGOs. Government employees are all from [NGOs]" (2008–33). Another NGO leader observed that the government understood there were real skills in the civil society sector and wanted those skills in the government (2006–2). Former thorns in the side of government were included in these efforts and encouraged to be vocal in their critiques, shaking up the government status quo. For example, Maina Kiai, former director of the nongovernmental Kenya Human Rights Commission, became head of its government counterpart and remained its active leader and a vocal critic of abuses until late 2008.

Still, there was some regression on this front: John Githongo, founder of Transparency International's Kenya office, became the government's "anti-corruption tsar," but left the country in 2005, fearing threats from those he exposed in his work (2005–11). One mid-level governance NGO respondent in Nairobi explained to me shortly after Githongo left Kenya that relationships between activist NGOs and the government had vacillated; immediately after Kibaki came to power, the administration drew in CSO leaders for their expertise and ideas, but by 2005, interactions became strained (2005–5). Among governance NGOs in this time period, there was concern that the government dealt with potential hostilities from civil society by deliberately "absorbing" prominent individuals into government (2005-4; 2005-11). One informed observer believed that instead of providing a platform for positive change, the power individuals gained once in government went to their heads and lowered their commitment to "the cause" (2005-7).

Another governance NGO respondent, however, reported that NGOs' approach had become one of "consultation not confrontation" with the Kibaki government (2005-9). A health NGO leader also said that there was considerable movement back and forth between NGOs and government employment (2006-2). This informed observer offered the nuanced view that the government did sometimes bring NGO leaders into government to silence them, but in other cases truly wanted the skills of the NGO sector to be present in the government as well (ibid.). He noted that it was easier for service providing NGOs to work with – and even critique – their government counterparts (ibid.). A USAID representative working in governance and democratization work in Kenya likewise opined that civil society leaders weren't so much co-opted as willingly went to help the new government, which recognized how helpful they could be (2007-8). Another nuanced perception was that the government had come to view NGOs as a "necessary evil" – it was better to work with NGOs than to get sued by them when they acted as vigilant watchdog organizations (2008-10).

In addition to changes in how the Kibaki administration chose to engage NGOs, a generational change in government began, bringing young people and new ideas to the civil service (2006-2, 2008-14). Members of the political opposition to Moi, many of whom had taken refuge in NGOs during Moi's rule, naturally aligned with the new government (Gifford 2009, 160). Although Kibaki opened a once-locked door to civil society, NGOs and civil society had consistently grown throughout the latter half of the Moi administration, pushing for better governance via political liberalization, economic development, improved service provision, and lower corruption. Even ardent Kibaki supporters agreed, saying that "education levels are also higher now; civil society has become stronger over time – growing out of the demonstrations during the Moi time... But it's true that Kibaki gives a bit more space" (2008-54).

Moreover, NGO involvement in governance was encouraged by donors, so Kibaki may have simply acted strategically to receive a better donor package than did his predecessor. And donors were quick to respond to Moi leaving office. Whereas total ODA to Kenya dropped from more than $1.8 billion in 1990 to $935 million in 1994 and as low as $430 million in 1999 (in constant 2013 dollars), it rose to $793 million the year after Kibaki came to power and returned to its 1990 level by 2009 (Organization for Economic Cooperation and Development 2013).[6] The Kibaki administration aimed to reduce its reliance on ODA as well and prepared annual budgets without it (Hornsby 2013).

Leading multinational institutions like the Global Fund to Fight AIDS, Tuberculosis and Malaria and the President's Emergency Plan for AIDS Relief (PEPFAR), moreover, required the government to work with NGOs in order to receive funding (2006–1). Officials throughout the government were thus likely influenced by a global pattern of change toward collaborative governance: as one senior NGO employee told me, "That's the new global approach – you must involve everyone now" (2008–26).

Even after the electoral violence of 2008, many people felt able to speak openly in a way that they couldn't in the past, saying "It's not like when it was a dictatorship!" (2008–19). One NGO worker said, "It's a plus, working with government" (2008–29). Many organizations explicitly spoke of positive working relationships with government offices (2006–2, 2006–4, 2007–17, 2008–11, 2008–24, 2008–29, 2008–32); informed observers in service provision reported an improvement in NGO–government interactions since the Moi administration (2006–1, 2008–14, 2008–18, 2008–20, 2008–24, 2008–26, 2008–33, 2008–54). That said, individuals working in governance organizations in Nairobi were less sanguine, as discussed earlier in this chapter.

In 2010, a popular referendum brought a new constitution to Kenya, paving the way for additional alterations to NGO–government interactions in the country. The participatory consultations leading to the new constitution, including the review of the prior constitution, were widely lauded. The implications of the new constitution are not fully known, as the document has not been entirely implemented as of 2016. The constitution does not explicitly discuss NGOs, but it does guarantee freedoms of expression, association, assembly, and public participation (Republic of Kenya 2010). Although relationships between NGOs and the government improved considerably during the ten years that Kibaki was in office, some tensions did remain. These are discussed in detail in Chapter 5, and include issues of mutual suspicious and lack of trust, poor communication between NGOs and the government, resentment over resource constraints, slow implementation of policy, and taking credit for others' work.

---

[6] Some of the increase was related to the electoral change of power in Kenya, but there was a concomitant shift toward general budget support among donors during the 2000s (Koeberke, Stavreski, and Walliser 2006).

Since Uhuru Kenyatta came to office in 2013, relationships have cooled somewhat between NGOs and the government, although it is too early into Kenyatta's tenure in office to comment extensively. The government passed the Public Benefit Organizations Act of 2013, but as of 2016, it had not yet been made operational, since a number of individuals and organizations are working to amend it. Should it go into effect, NGOs will be referred to as PBOs in Kenya. Items under consideration include limiting the amount of funding that PBOs can receive from foreign sources, granting high discretionary power to the government agency that regulates and monitors PBOs, and reducing the voice of civil society organizations on the board of the new government agency (ICNL 2015). Should such amendments pass, they are likely to push the country back toward more conflictual NGO–state relations. NGOs have been successfully campaigning against these amendments, but the government continues to propose more (ICNL 2016).

A SNAPSHOT OF THE NGO SECTOR IN THE EARLY TWENTY-FIRST CENTURY

At the start of the Kibaki administration, NGOs contributed 80 billion Kenyan shillings, or approximately US$1 billion, to the economy (NGOs Co-ordination Board 2009). The nonprofit sector, broadly conceived, employed more than 300,000 people fulltime, or about 2.1 percent of the economically active population, and a sizeable 16.3 percent of non-agricultural employment (Kanyinga 2004, 17).[7] NGOs specifically engaged approximately 105,000 workers, including volunteers (NGOs Co-ordination Board 2009, 36).

NGO numbers grew over the decade. There were 3,000 registered organizations in 2004 (The National Council of NGOs 2005), more than 4,200 by 2007 (Republic of Kenya NGO Coordination Bureau 2006), and nearly 7,500 in 2011 (Republic of Kenya NGO Coordination Bureau 2011a). According to its mission statement, the NGO Board registers NGOs in order to coordinate and monitor their activities and to avoid duplication of services. In addition to a legal registration requirement, a number of tax breaks, training seminars, and other coordinating activities offered by the NGO Board provide incentives for NGOs to register. Organizations are allowed to register as NGOs regardless of their origin,

---

[7] Nonprofits, according to Kanyinga's study, include NGOs as well as churches, professional associations like unions, advocacy organizations, and culture and recreation organizations.

size, revenue, or expenditure (Republic of Kenya NGO Coordination Bureau 2011a).[8]

This self-determination of status makes it sometimes difficult to distinguish between types of NGOs, or between NGOs and other organizations. Groups that might be better identified as *harambee* groups or Community-Based Organizations (CBOs) – less formal, smaller and less cosmopolitan than their NGO counterparts – often register as NGOs in Kenya. Since organizations are allowed to choose the classification (whether NGO or CBO), some register as NGOs in an attempt to attract resources (2008–16).

When conducting a survey of NGOs in the country between 2006 and 2008, the NGO Board itself determined that many of the NGO respondents they initially identified were actually CBOs (NGOs Coordination Board 2009, 24). By this the NGO Board perceived that these small NGOs more closely resembled *harambee* groups than stereotypical NGOs. Illustrating this point, some organizational leaders interviewed for this research merged the term when asked, saying, "I guess you could call it a Community-Based NGO" (2008–12). Numbering more than 220,000 (Kanyinga 2004), *harambee*s are required to register with the Ministry of Culture and Social Services under the Societies Act as Community-Based Organizations (CBOs).[9] They tend to be smaller than their NGO counterparts, established at the community level, and run by less-educated Kenyans in rural areas.

Professional NGOs in Kenya often implement their work through *harambee* groups or mobilize people into CBOs for their training programs (Otiso 2003). For example, one manager at a typical NGO at the time of research ran a livelihood program, in which it provided training to adults in agriculture, livestock rearing, and income generation. It organized the trainings through thirty-six CBOs across six geographic focal areas of Kenya (2008–18). NGO–CBO relations often appear in this nested form: a large foreign-based NGO will fund the programs of a Kenyan-based NGO, which will then distribute its funds via registered community groups (2008–44; 2008–52). Many *harambee* groups in the early 2000s were created to access the resources brought by NGOs.

The multidimensional nature of NGO work highlights the difficulty in determining when or whether NGOs in Kenya should be classified as

---

[8] Some organizations that have the characteristics of NGOs choose not to register as NGOs. For some, the cost of registration is prohibitive. Others want independence from government interference.

[9] Note that this ministry has had several names over time, as the number of ministries has changed repeatedly since independence.

international or domestic, foreign or local. Logically, we want to identify the differential impacts stemming from an organization's origins – whether they are locally based, with local decision-making; are based in another country, where high-level decisions are made; or, alternatively, are organizations with activities and decision-making across a range of countries. Such distinctions can be important because local and international organizations are often treated differently by donors (Kerlin 2006), and because the NGO sector can be fiercely competitive for resources (Cooley and Ron 2002). Ironically, local organizations often struggle to participate in development (Dill 2009) or to build indigenous capacity as a result (Barber and Bowie 2008, Patrick 2001).

Yet the strict dichotomy between "national" and "international" NGOs does not reflect the situation on the ground in Kenya (Ng'ethe 1991).[10] For example, it is not uncommon to find an NGO headquartered in Nairobi, staffed entirely by Kenyans, with offices throughout the country, that receives 80 percent of its funding from abroad, from donors spread across many different countries. Even in small towns, one finds local offices of European or American-based organizations, as well as NGOs that are local initiatives.

NGOs in Kenya – regardless of their origins – receive a majority of total funding via international sources.[11] Approximately 35 percent of the organizations that provided funding information to the NGO Board in 2005 received *all* of their funding from abroad, and more than 50 percent received 95 percent or more of their funding from international sources.[12] Among organizations that received a mix of local and international funds, the average NGO received 71 percent of their funds from abroad (Republic of Kenya NGO Coordination Bureau 2006). Indeed, 92 percent of all funds came from international sources. Most of these funds stem from private sources, not foreign governments. Most aid monies go to the Government of Kenya; at its peak, American aid through NGOs reached 13 percent.

---

[10] Ng'ethe (1991, 33) provides an extended discussion on this issue.
[11] The statistics in this and the next several paragraphs come from my analysis of the NGO Board's database at the end of 2006. Funding sources were listed in the database by numerical country code, but I was unable to obtain the codes from the government. Comparing the codes to other information in the database allowed me to confidently determine the code for Kenya, but not for other countries.
[12] These figures are provisional, as only 16 percent of registered NGOs submitted funding information on their returns for 2005. I am fairly confident with these estimates, however, since organizations submitting returns are likely the most robust organizations in the country, with the greatest funding sources.

The Kenyan government, however, provides minimal funding to NGOs. Looking again at the data from 2005, 8 percent of NGO funding came from within Kenya – 7 percent from local private sources, and at most 1 percent from the Kenyan government at the national or local level. According to more recent data from the NGO Board, only 0.25 percent of total NGO funding stemmed from the Kenyan government (NGOs Co-ordination Board 2009, 32). Organizations that are entirely funded by in-country sources accounted for less than 2.5 percent of total funding reported. These financial data provide evidence for claims that NGOs in Kenya maintain autonomy by remaining independent of the government with respect to funding.

At the same time, while the majority of funds come from the international community, most NGO leaders in Kenya are Kenyan nationals (Republic of Kenya NGO Coordination Bureau 2006), and at least one director of each NGO is required to be Kenyan. Of the 5,559 directors listed in the NGO Board database at the end of 2006, approximately 90 percent were Kenyan. Nearly all NGO staff members – over 99 percent – were Kenyan, even in the capital. NGOs sought work permits for only 530 expatriate individuals between 2004 and 2006 (NGOs Co-ordination Board 2009, 37–38). This national leadership and staffing mitigates the sway of foreign donors and overseas headquarters, since in-country staff members generally wield decision-making authority over local programs and projects. For the majority of NGOs, foreign funding releases a resource constraint and allows predominantly Kenyan organizations to achieve their civil society and development goals. While it is true that organizations "implanted" from the outside have been shown to have a high failure rate (Esman and Uphoff 1984), NGOs working in Kenya are almost entirely staffed by Kenyans.

Activities of NGOs

NGOs in Kenya focus on a broad range of activities – from improving agricultural techniques to providing scholarship programs to heightening the levels of civic engagement. Some of these activities, such as education, healthcare, and policing, are those traditionally associated with the state. Others focus on private sector development, whether through microfinance, agro-business development, or a variety of other skills-training activities. These activities can be broken down into several types of activities. Table 3.1 provides illustrative examples of NGO projects in each activity area.

TABLE 3.1. *NGO activity areas and types of programs involved*[13]

Activity	Types of project
Agriculture	• Introduction of nutritional or drought-resistant crops • Training on livestock-rearing technologies • Pastoralist support programs • Agro-business development
Education	• Maintenance or construction of school infrastructure • Sponsorship programs for education fees • Technology-in-schools programs • Adult education programs • General skills training for enterprise development (e.g., carpentry, dress-making, masonry, catering, welding, hairdressing)
Environment	• Water programs not specifically tied to agriculture • Forest, water, land, habitat, wildlife protection • Promotion of energy-saving devices (e.g., solar cookers, lighting)
General Development	• Poverty reduction programs • Social and economic improvement programs • NGOs with projects in multiple activity areas (e.g., education, health, environment, youth programs) • Business or development not specifically related to another activity area, such as business skills training programs or microfinance programs
Health	• Support for maintenance or construction of health facilities • HIV-related programs, whether educational, counseling, or purely medical • Malaria, TB, or other specific illness programs • Training for doctors, nurses, or community health workers
Marginalized Populations	• Support for women's groups • Children's programs outside schools (e.g., streetchildren's programs) • Programs targeting the youth (young adults between the age of 15 and 35) • Support for the disabled • Support for the elderly
Peace and Governance	• Anti-corruption, transparency, and accountability promotion • Support for civil education, voter registration, voter rights, democracy • Peace-building or conflict-reduction efforts

[13] Appendix A provides a complete list of the programs in Machakos (roman text) and Mbeere (italicized text) districts that were underway at the time of interviews in 2008.

TABLE 3.1. *(cont.)*

Activity	Types of project
	• Community policing initiatives • Programs promoting social justice and equity
Relief	• Refugee and internally displaced persons-related programs • Emergency assistance, including that caused by conflict in neighboring countries, natural disasters, and road accidents
Other	• Religious proselytizing • Art, sports, cultural exchange, or cultural preservation programs • Umbrella NGOs linking NGOs to donors or NGOs to each other • Housing and transportation-related programs • Ex-convict rehabilitation programs

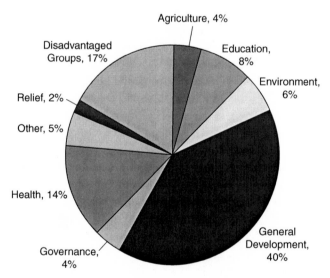

FIGURE 3.2. National Distribution of NGOs by Sector

The distribution of NGOs across these activity categories is shown in Figure 3.2.[14] Classifying the 4,211 organizations listed in the NGO Board database at the end of 2006 reveals that nearly half (40 percent) of

[14] I hand-coded the listings based on the names and mission statements of the 4,211 organizations. As a reliability check, a research assistant performed the same reading and classification steps. Without discussing our coding strategies beyond the set of categories used, the two distributions differed by less than 2 percent for any category.

the organizations were involved in "general development." These organizations often had broad, all-encompassing missions to do such things as "promote holistic development to enhance livelihood improvements for the disadvantaged" (Republic of Kenya NGO Coordination Bureau 2006). Others listed two or more activity areas in their mission, such as combining programming in ecology, food security, health, and nutrition in Kenya's arid and semi-arid lands.

The next most common type of organization made up 17 percent of all NGOs and focused on disadvantaged groups, such as women, children, the elderly, and the disabled. These NGOs were not sector-specific – for example, an NGO that provided support to the disabled might have included education, economic development, and health-related services. However, their specific focus on marginalized populations set them apart from "general development" NGOs.

Health-related missions accounted for 14 percent of NGOs, including organizations that focused on specific diseases like malaria and HIV, as well as those that provided medical facilities and training. A smaller percentage of NGOs focused on education, environment, agriculture, governance, or relief activities.

This distribution of NGO activities shows that the vast majority of registered NGOs in Kenya in 2006 focused primarily on poverty reduction. Income generation and livelihood support were a set of key activities undertaken by NGOs that crossed categories. Two of the in-vogue income generation programs at the time were microfinance and agricultural enterprise development such as beekeeping, fruit processing, and goat rearing. Microfinance programs ranged from the lending of small and medium sums of money at low interest to the creation of rotating saving and credit associations (ROSCAs) common in much of the developing world.[15] For example, a young NGO in Mbeere had a program providing emergency one-month loans of up to 2,000 KSH/- (about $30) at 10 percent interest and eight-month loans of up to 20,000/- (about $300) at 3 percent interest (2008–45). After a year of operation, the organization had made thirty-seven emergency loans totaling 92,000/- (about $1,375) and forty-seven normal loans for 557,000/- (about $8,325). Another NGO gave rotating loans to groups that self-formed into ROSCAs (2008–33).

Only 4 percent of registered NGOs engaged primarily in political activities – a fact likely to surprise scholars and practitioners who study or

---

[15] ROSCAs have existed in the developing world since before the explosive growth of NGOs – NGOs often facilitate the introduction of funds originating from outside the groups, however.

work for governance NGOs in Nairobi.[16] While human rights, democratization, and governance organizations in Nairobi are visible both nationally and internationally, they were and remain the exception rather than the rule. Governance NGOs often engage with a specific segment of the Kenyan government, such as the police force or politicians in the capital, which are agencies that are not representative of public administration as a whole as it exists throughout the country. Like most NGOs, most government ministries and civil servants are focused on service provision of some nature, and they concern themselves with issues of governance primarily as they relate to service provision.

Although governance was rarely an organization's primary activity, many NGOs worked on governance issues in the first decade of the twenty-first century. Not only did they monitor government spending, program implementation, and the use of taxes, but they also encouraged Kenyans to become engaged in this process. NGOs in Machakos, for example, had a wide range of responsibilities. These included: acting as watchdogs of government use of funds; serving as liaisons providing government information to the people and informing the government of people's needs; assisting Kenyans in protesting government mismanagement and holding government accountable; helping organize residents' associations; coordinating district-level participation in national human rights programs; conducting civic education; representing minority groups to government; and teaching people about the Kenyan tax system and their rights as taxpayers. The government was generally supportive of these activities, which encourage civic participation in a way that has seldom been seen in Kenya. In Mbeere as well, at least one NGO worked on governance issues, empowering people to understand that they have rights and can make demands of government (2008–54).

The distribution of NGO activities in four districts, shown in Figure 3.3, is virtually identical to the national distribution, suggesting that there are no particular regional, local, or ethnic-based patterns in the distribution of NGO activities. These four districts, Machakos, Mbeere, Taita Taveta, and Siaya, represent three different Kenyan

---

[16] My assessment is confirmed by the Government of Kenya, which estimates 9 percent of NGOs focus on advocacy, 39 percent on capacity building, and 53 percent on service provision (NGOs Co-ordination Board 2009, 29). Because their data is a year or two more recent than mine, the differences might be explained by post-electoral violence growth in governance and civic education NGOs responding to the 2007 elections. Among service provision organizations, the government also identifies health and education as very common, with 12 percent and 11 percent of activities, respectively (NGOs Co-ordination Board 2009, 30).

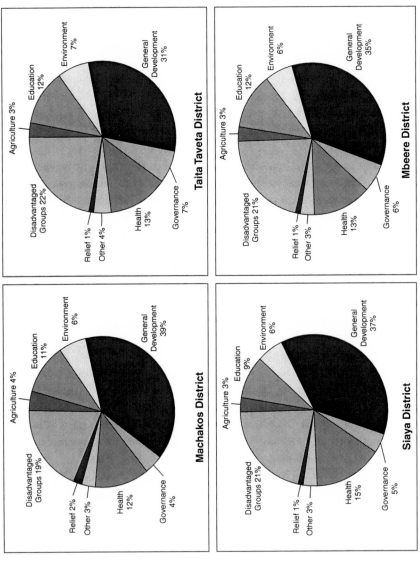

Taita Taveta District

Environment 7%
General Development 31%
Education 12%
Agriculture 3%
Disadvantaged Groups 22%
Relief 1%
Other 4%
Health 13%
Governance 7%

Mbeere District

Environment 6%
General Development 35%
Education 12%
Agriculture 3%
Disadvantaged Groups 21%
Relief 1%
Other 3%
Health 13%
Governance 6%

Machakos District

Environment 6%
General Development 39%
Education 11%
Agriculture 4%
Disadvantaged Groups 19%
Relief 2%
Other 3%
Health 12%
Governance 4%

Siaya District

Environment 6%
General Development 37%
Education 9%
Agriculture 3%
Disadvantaged Groups 21%
Relief 1%
Other 3%
Health 15%
Governance 5%

FIGURE 3.3. Sectoral Distribution of NGOs by District

provinces, are spread across the far western, eastern, and central portions of the country, and include areas with both high and low levels of NGO penetration. They represent areas with long-standing connections to the central government, and those with more limited patronage opportunities. They also represent a wide range of ethnic groups with variation in historical connection to the political center of the country.

Involvement in core state services: education, healthcare, security

At the same time as the broad spectrum of activities was roughly equal in different areas of the country according to the NGO Board data, survey research in case study districts suggests that important variation existed at a more granular level of analysis. For services that are most commonly associated with states – education, healthcare, and security – it was the government, and not NGOs, that provided most services, yet levels varied by setting. A not-insignificant proportion of services were provided by nongovernmental organizations. Many of these services were provided in joint NGO–government arrangements, as shown in Table 3.2 (see Chapter 5 for in-depth descriptions).[17]

Purely government social service provision was notably lower in urban areas than in rural areas in these districts. In the district-wide samples for Machakos and Mbeere, governments provided a similarly high proportion of services: roughly 80 percent of primary schooling and 50 percent of security services. In the two urban area samples, Nairobi and Machakos town, the proportions were closer to 50 percent for all services.[18] Several

---

[17] Respondents were asked about the organizational provenance of each of three types of services they might receive: education, health, and security. Specific questions asked: "At the present time, are there any children in this household attending primary school?" [If yes] "Where do the children currently attend primary school?" "Is [name of primary school] a government school, a nongovernmental (NGO) school, a missionary school, a community or harambee school, or it is a private school?" "In the past one year, what places have you or any member of your household gone for healthcare?" "Is [name of healthcare facility] a government-run facility, a nongovernmental organization (NGO), a Missionary or FBO clinic/hospital, a community or harambee clinic, or is it a private doctor's office?" And "Who are the main providers of security services in the neighborhood where you stay? By this we mean who works to keep crime levels low, prevent theft and violence in your community?" Responses were limited to two different schools and three different healthcare providers per household.

[18] Not surprisingly, the data also show that as urbanization increases, rates of nonstate service provision tend to increase. Private service provision rates were highest in Nairobi, the most urban environment. Urban Machakos, the second most urban area, had higher levels of private health care and security services than the two full districts. These differences make sense when one considers the role of private for-profit actors. These

TABLE 3.2. *Primary social service provision by type of organization*

	Nairobi	Machakos Town	Machakos	Mbeere
Primary school provider[19]				
Government (%)	56	74	81	84
Government and NGO (%)	–	18	6	–
NGO (including religious) (%)	11	3	2	4
Private (%)	31	3	12	12
Healthcare provider[20]				
Government (%)	50	57	75	93
Government and NGO (%)	–	–	<1	–
NGO (including religious) (%)	20	21	7	5
Private	30	22	18	1
Security provider[21]				
Government (police, local administrators) (%)	48	47	50	52
Private guards (%)	23	16	10	–
Community policing (programs with government or community alone) (%)	26	36	40	41
Other (dogs, family, God) (%)	2	–	–	7

NGO representatives explicitly mentioned that government does make a concerted effort to provide basic health, education, and security services: "Government provides the *basics* of life or death, but nothing more" (2008–18). These comments indicated that NGOs see their role as picking up where this service provision lets off, filling the gaps left by a relatively incapacious state.

are much more common in Nairobi than elsewhere in the country, since surplus income is more prevalent in the capital. Thus, while 20 to 30 percent of all services were privately delivered in the capital, only 12 to 22 percent of services in Machakos were private, and in Mbeere, the most rural district, only 12 percent of education services were private, and virtually no health or security services were delivered by for-profit organizations. Thus, the more urban full district of Machakos had consistently higher nonstate provision than the fully rural district, Mbeere. The sole exception to this pattern was private schooling, which is more common in the full districts of Machakos and Mbeere than in urban Machakos town specifically.

[19] Not included in the table are don't know/non-answers. A total of 456 schools were mentioned. Total responses reach over 501 because respondents were asked to name more than one school, medical facility, or security provider, if applicable.

[20] Don't know and NA answers are not reported. Respondents named up to three healthcare providers, for a total of 760 responses.

[21] Respondents were asked for two answers and gave a total of 896 responses.

Looking more carefully at nonprofit provision of services, the data show notable variation in the types of nonprofits that deliver services, as well as distinct regional patterns. For example, NGO services were most common in Machakos town, comprising 21 percent of responses when joint NGO–government services were included.[22] However, whereas education services in Machakos town commonly included joint efforts between governmental and nongovernmental actors, this type of joint service provision was rare for medical services, and non-existent outside of Machakos district.

Across all three districts, most respondents who identified their service provider as nongovernmental also said that these were faith-based organizations, which may or may not be formally registered as NGOs with the government.[23] The urban bias of the results in this case reflects the fact that organizations intentionally locate in towns for access to electricity for their supplies, and so that they are accessible to people from a broad radius of market centers and villages. Many of these missionary facilities have long histories in Kenya, and do not reflect the NGO phenomenon of the past twenty years. Still, it is significant that these faith-based organizations continued to provide services, particularly in the health sector, and that these third-sector organizations provided alternatives to the state and the market at different rates in the four settings.

On the security side, the role of nonstate actors was played primarily by community initiatives, not formalized NGOs – although several formal NGOs did support the development of these programs. "Community policing" in the table, however, includes CBO-type community-initiated and -organized security services, such as neighborhood watch groups, vigilante groups, and formally organized initiatives undertaken in conjunction with the Kenyan Police since such programs began in May 2005.[24]

---

[22] I examine this relationship in more detail in Chapter 6, which shows that NGOs are stronger and more collaborative with their government counterparts in that district.

[23] Because of the survey wording, "faith-based" here may include NGOs connected to local and/or international churches, as well as religious schools and hospitals. Given the history of missionary healthcare and schooling, the latter is more likely than the former. Since the survey questions measure popular perceptions of organizational type rather than their official registration status, it is impossible to know the breakdown among these organizations, a clear limitation in the data.

[24] This information reveals some of the difficulties of conducting survey research across a wide swath of land in Kenya. Workers conducting this survey, although professionally trained by an international survey firm, did not reveal until after the survey concluded that the responses "vigilante group" and "community policing initiative" had more than one meaning and are sometimes used interchangeably. Vigilante groups are considered benign community-sponsored youth groups by some, but hostile and violent

The figure of approximately 50 percent of security services provided solely by the government might give us pause, since a monopoly over violence through government police and security services is a quintessential feature of most states. In Kenya, however, local communities frequently provide this policing service. Kenya in this way recalls Tocqueville's experience in America, where it was not the formal organs of government, but community and voluntary organizations that provided many services. According to the Kenyan Police website,

> Community Policing is an approach to policing that recognizes the independence and shared responsibility of the Police and the Community in ensuring a safe and secure environment for all citizens. It aims at establishing an active and equal partnership between the Police and the public... The Kenya police attach great importance to grassroots community involvement in seeking solutions to crime problems at local and national level through a people driven policing.[25]

These joint government–community efforts are an alternative to vigilante groups, usually self-organized groups of young men charged with keeping crime low in a specific neighborhood or village. According to respondents, vigilantes are quite common, and are not necessarily malignant. A high-ranking police administrator interviewed in Machakos district denied their presence in the district, however – likely due to a nationwide trend of youth security groups employing extortionist and violent practices, as has been frequently documented in local and international news.[26]

NGOs provide many indirect services

Data from in-depth interviews with employees of registered NGOs and government officials from Nairobi, Mbeere, and Machakos reveals that, religious schools and hospitals aside, NGOs tended to provide services that only indirectly facilitate development outcomes. NGOs' education and health programs, for example, rarely directly taught children, built schools, or provided medical services. Instead, education-focused NGOs rehabilitated school facilities; paid for school fees, uniforms, and books

---

extortionists by others. Many of these groups have begun to claim legitimacy through formal community policing projects as well.

[25] http://www.kenyapolice.go.ke/community%20policing.asp (accessed March 25, 2010).

[26] See, for example, "Vigilantes kill Kenyan 'mafia' members in machete attacks," *Guardian UK*, April 21, 2009 (http://www.guardian.co.uk/world/2009/apr/21/kenya-vigilante-kill-mungiki); "Kenya militias turn into criminal gangs, pose threat," *Daily Nation*, February 27, 2010. (http://www.nation.co.ke/News/-/1056/870310/-/vr4bqi/-/index.html) and "The rise of Kenya's vigilantes," *BBC News*, October 9, 2007 (http://news.bbc.co.uk/2/hi/africa/6995577.stm).

for relatively poor students; conducted HIV/AIDS awareness programs at schools; or constructed library or computer labs. Health-focused NGOs were more likely than their education counterparts to build and staff health clinics, provide clean drinking water, or fight a particular disease, but they were equally likely to train community-based health workers and home-based caregivers, or hold rallies or education campaigns aimed at combating the spread of HIV/AIDS. Table 3.3 lists some specific activities mentioned by NGO interviewees in Machakos (roman text) and Mbeere (italicized text), when asked about the work that they do. These descriptions are divided into tangible goods and intangible services, both of which may indirectly affect development outcomes. A complete list of activities undertaken by NGOs interviewed can be found in Appendix A.

The most common form of indirect service provision was "capacity building," which nearly all interviewed NGO representatives included in their programming. Some respondents claimed it was the full extent of their organization's efforts (2008–17, 2008–29). According to the government's NGO Board, 38 percent of NGOs in the country used this approach to meet their goals (NGOs Co-ordination Board 2009). Usually, "capacity building" took the form of group training classes, held at a local school, community center, or hotel. For example, agricultural sector NGOs interviewed in Machakos and Mbeere conducted training on a wide range of topics, including: food security, agricultural productivity, microfranchise development, livestock rearing, horticulture, poultry raising, goat breeding, fruit growing, honey businesses, beekeeping, dairy and confectionary food processing, marketing, drought-resistant crops, and fundraising. Likewise, NGOs targeting the youth[27] provided training on HIV/AIDS prevention, drug abuse, behavioral change, self-reliance and communications, as well as vocational training on tailoring, film, documentary and commercial creation and video editing, conducting research, agriculture, and small-scale business skills.

As will be discussed in Chapter 5, providing services that can only indirectly affect development outcomes makes NGO impacts difficult to measure on a large scale. This measurement challenge lends credence to complaints that NGOs do not accomplish as much as they claim to do, or that their activities do not actually make a difference for those they serve. Incredible numbers of training activities meant to "build capacity" in particular do not appear to have markedly changed standards of living in Kenya.

---

[27] Young people between the ages of 15 and 35, according to the UN.

TABLE 3.3. *Tangible and intangible impacts of NGOs represented in interviews*[28]

Activity	Infrastructure (things produced)	Intangible (people impacted)
Agriculture	• 2 food security training centers/demonstration farms • *3 large fishponds*	• Livelihood program: 5400 people • 312 people in microfranchise program • *1800 cotton farmers*
Education	• 1 small library, with computers • Rehabilitation of and instructional materials for 8 schools • *10 computers, 1 generator brought to 2 schools (5 more schools in progress)* • *Rehabilitation of 7 schools, furniture only in additional 2 schools*	• HIV/AIDS training and awareness programs in 32 schools • *52 adults in literacy program*
Environment	• 2 sand dams • *4 km of water pipeline*	
General Development	• 1 multi-purpose hall • 2 large hostels • *Financial services center built*	• 21 people given microloans • 40 000 beneficiaries of integrated development program • 2000 people in finance program • 3000 members of private sector development program • 312 people for microcredit program • *37 people given small, emergency loans* • *47 people given larger, long-term loans* • *38 training focus groups*

[28] This list is not comprehensive of all activities conducted by all NGOs represented by interviewees. Some NGOs did not provide specific numbers. Nevertheless, this chart gives an impression of the scale of work being undertaken by individual organizations.

TABLE 3.3. *(cont.)*

Activity	Infrastructure (things produced)	Intangible (people impacted)
Health	• 2 maternities/ dispensaries • 10 health clinics (4 more under construction) • 2 VCT centers • 8 boreholes drilled • 9 dams built • 15 service dams • 25 water tanks	• 50 community-based healthcare workers trained • 4 million condoms distributed • Support to 70 HIV/AIDS affected families • *22 home-based HIV caregivers trained* • *Serve 20–40 people per day at health clinic* • *20 groups trained on proper nutrition*
Marginal Groups	• Youth resource center with video equipment, tailoring school • 1 children's home, 2 day care locations	• 9831 sponsored OVCs (orphans and vulnerable children) • 6 youth groups for enterprise training • 5 women trained as tailors • 5 savings associations organized • *50 children helped* • *942 children sponsored* • *14 children sponsored*

Citizen engagement with NGOs

Although NGOs were not providing most core state services, survey research in case study districts confirmed that most Kenyans were familiar with the organizations in the early twenty-first century, and many reported having direct contact with NGOs. Respondents were asked to define the term NGO in an open-ended question, and two-thirds were able to give a proper definition. Of those who could not define "NGO," 88 percent lived in the lowest of seven socio-economic brackets in Kenya, with another 8 percent located in the second-lowest bracket. Only a tiny fraction of well-educated Kenyans could not define the term.

One way to interpret this information is that NGOs are less effective at reaching the poorest of the poor than many NGO taglines proclaim. It's quite possible that the "NGO revolution" appears more prominent in the West than in does in places like Kenya.

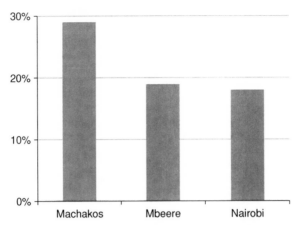

FIGURE 3.4. Percent of respondents having sought out an NGO in the year prior to the survey

Looking from another angle, however, most Kenyans – even the very poorest – do know what NGOs are. In the total pool of respondents 72 percent fell into the two poorest of seven income brackets, yet more than one-third of all respondents identified NGOs that operated in their geographic area.[29] Similarly, more than 25 percent of respondents reported having been approached by an NGO providing goods or services in their area at least once in the previous year. In a separate question, 24.2 percent of respondents reported deliberately approaching an NGO for assistance.[30] The breakdown of these activities by district is show in Figure 3.4.

The level of contact is dependent to some extent on where a person lives. There is a vast difference in the percentage of people seeking services from NGOs in Machakos town – a high of 57 percent – than is observed in either middle-class Nairobi or Mbeere district (see Table 3.4). This observation corresponds to and confirms the conclusion presented in Chapter 4 that NGOs locate not only where they are needed, but also where it is convenient to reach a great number of people. Middle-class Nairobi residents do not particularly need NGOs, and while rural Machakos and Mbeere residents do need them, these communities are

[29] Respondents were asked, "In your opinion, are there many NGOs working in this area, or few?" and chose answers from "Very many," "Some," "Very few," "None," or "Don't know." 53.3 percent said "None." 12.4 percent of respondents said they didn't know.

[30] These groups are not mutually exclusive.

TABLE 3.4. *Respondent opinions on density of NGOs in their area*

	Positive response (%)	Very many (%)	Some (%)	Very few (%)	None	Don't know
Urban Machakos	57.0	1.0	18.0	38.0	39.0	4.0
Machakos district	30.7	1.3	10.0	19.3	64.7	4.7
Urban Nairobi	28.7	1.0	5.9	21.8	43.6	27.7
Mbeere district	26.7	2.7	6.0	18.0	58.0	15.3

less convenient than Machakos town. In particular, there is no large town in Mbeere; its district headquarters at the time of research was not on a paved road, but instead 12 km down a bumpy murram road. These findings confirm data collected by the government NGO Board (2006) and the findings of Chapters 4 and 5 on variation across districts of Kenya.

Delivering intangible symbolic goods

Evidence reveals that NGOs provided Kenyans a symbolic good in the early twenty-first century: the sense that change was possible. During a period in which many service provision levels fell in Kenya, NGOs became a visible emblem to the people of Kenya of someone trying to look after their needs, providing hope for a better life in the future. This optimism effect was reflected in survey responses from 2008. When asked whether they felt more or less confident about the future of Kenya when they thought about NGOs, 50 percent of respondents reported feeling more confident, whereas only 30 percent felt less confident (20 percent didn't know or didn't respond). Nearly 70 percent of Nairobians reported feeling more confident, with a general trend of more urban areas responding more positively – likely reflecting their greater access to and information about NGOs.

NGOs served as a reminder to people that the world outside Kenya had not forgotten about them.[31] This sentiment was reflected in statements made by both NGO and government representatives, as well as those made by Kenyan community members. One NGO leader revealed that he had started his NGO in Mbeere after discovering how hopeless and dejected the rural people around him appeared – a situation he reported having changed in small ways through the NGO's livelihood programs

---

[31] Rachel Stern (2009) finds similar impacts of NGOs among Chinese environmental lawyer communities.

(2008–43). Others said that, "We provide life, education, food...so it gives the people security. They are very appreciative" (2008–13).

The hope brought by NGOs was also reflected in the view that NGOs had the people's interests in mind. In a survey of 500 individuals across the two districts and Nairobi, 70 percent of respondents gave positive answers (i.e. "sometimes" or "usually") to the question; "To what extent do you think that NGOs have the interests of the people in mind?" 30 percent answered "usually," the most positive possible response.[32] In comparison, only 53 responded positively when asked whether civil servants have the interests of the people in mind; only 34 percent responded positively when asked the same question in reference to politicians. Only 20 and 6 percent responded "usually," when asked about civil servants and politicians, respectively. People tended to believe that NGOs were looking after their interests, giving them a sense of hope for the future.

CONCLUSION

This chapter has served three goals. First, it has given an example of the changing political and organizational conditions that create either collaborative or conflictual interactions between NGOs and governments. The conflictual conditions under Moi and their opening during the Kibaki period parallel conditions discussed in theoretic terms in Chapter 2. Second, the chapter has presented a detailed overview of the NGO sector within Kenya in the early twenty-first century. We have learned how NGOs are classified in Kenya, the activities NGOs offered, and their level of engagement with citizens across the urban–rural divide. Finally, for the reader not deeply versed in Kenyan history, this chapter has provided contextual information that is useful for interpreting the chapters that follow.

---

[32] Respondents were given the options "Never," "Rarely," "Sometimes," and "Usually" with respect to whether the people or organizations in question have the interests of the people in mind.

4

Territoriality

NGOs and the broadcasting of state power

"On our side... we cannot feel we're competing [with NGOs]. Actually, they're helping us a lot a lot a lot a lot. Imagine there are four of us [working in the Children's Office]! We cannot be everywhere. There are 6,291 sq. km in this District, and 142 people per square km. We very much rely on these NGOs! We don't even have a vehicle here!"
(Government Children's Office, Machakos district, 2008)

[Speaking about remote North Eastern Province], "You ask yourself, is there a government here? There are no boreholes from government... NGOs alone allow people to survive."
(NGO leader, Eastern Province, 2008)

NGOs have a tremendous ability to expand the scope of the state's reach.
(Sandberg 1994, 13)

Starting from our understanding that "the state, to begin with, is a territorially demarcated entity" (Turner and Young 1985, 12), this first chapter on the four elements of stateness discusses the effects of NGOs on territoriality. Territory is a key element in the Weberian definition of the state, a "human community that (successfully) claims the monopoly of the legitimate use of physical force within a given territory" (Weber 1919). Territory is expressed by states through demarcation, borders, and boundaries reinforced on internationally agreed-upon maps. States need not only claim territory and get others in the international community to recognize their claim, however. They also need to uphold the claim internally by broadcasting their power throughout the geographic space (Herbst 2000, Jackson and Rosberg 1982). States establish territoriality by delineating, occupying, and defending a geographical territory through governing institutions.

In developing countries, the state tends to fade away as one travels outward from the capital. As a result, state territoriality is often poorly articulated in remote areas. In Kenya, the state is "soft" in rural areas, lacking effective government presence (Anangwe 1995). The analysis in this chapter evaluates whether NGOs help or hinder the state in broadcasting power over its territory by evaluating whether ecological factors (Shively 1969) of need, convenience, and politics are associated with NGO placement. Findings reveal that NGOs choose their location based primarily on demonstrable need for services in an area, and not on political patronage, as theories of developing country politics would suggest. Although NGO location also correlates with convenience factors, evidence from interview research reveals that this combination of need and convenience factors is indicative of pragmatic responses to resource constraints on the part of NGOs. This chapter demonstrates how NGOs strengthen state territoriality by providing activities that locals associate with state jurisdiction. In the arid and semi-arid lands (ASALs) of northern Kenya, in particular, NGOs provide a semblance of governing authority, which serves the Kenyan government well.

To assess contrasting theories of NGO placement, this chapter employs regression analysis using an original dataset that combines data from multiple Kenyan government and international development agencies. Qualitative analysis from interview research is used to assess the implications of quantitative results for territoriality.

UNDERSTANDING NGO PLACEMENT

How do NGOs choose to locate within a country? Assuming project locations are not chosen at random, one can imagine several plausible reasons for an NGO to select a place in which to implement its programs. Selection may be based on extreme need – meaning that NGOs choose to work where there is the most poverty, illness, lack of education, or unsafe drinking water. Or perhaps donors decide where NGOs they fund will work (2008–27). NGOs could also choose their locations based on the ease of access or comfort level for the NGO workers themselves. Finally, it is plausible that NGOs are swayed by powerful national politicians, who influence the NGOs to work in their home area either by direct instruction, or because they can offer resources to the NGOs. Each of these reasons would have different repercussions for territoriality.

TABLE 4.1. *Theories and hypotheses on NGO location*

Theory	NGOs are more commonly located . . .	Hypotheses: There are more NGOs in districts with . . .
"Saintly"	Where recipient *need* is great and alternative means of service provision are insufficient	• More poverty • Poor health • Low education levels • Poor social service facilities
"Self-serving"	Where NGO workers or the NGO as an organization have *convenient* access to goods and services	• Greater urbanization • Denser road network • More elite goods
"Political"	In areas that powerful *politicians* help through their patronage networks	• Powerful politicians • Popular politicians

Clustering these explanations of NGO placement into broad categories leads to three very different hypotheses, as shown in Table 4.1. The first hypothesis draws on received wisdom, which regards NGOs as "saintly" charitable organizations: NGOs locate their projects in places where recipient *need* is very great and alternative means of service provision either do not exist or are insufficient. This view corresponds to the mission statements of most development NGOs, which promise such things as: "to promote, encourage and facilitate holistic development that enhances effective and meaningful livelihood changes in the life of the poor and disadvantaged communities"; "to enhance ecology, food security, health, and nutrition in Kenya's arid and semi-arid lands"; or "to help poor . . . needy, desperate, lonely, depressed and disadvantaged orphaned children by providing shelter, education, healthcare, clothing and food" (Republic of Kenya NGO Coordination Bureau 2006).

Need also corresponds to the reason that many highly educated people – both foreign and Kenyan – give for their decision to work for an NGO. NGO workers in general have the skills and abilities to earn considerably higher incomes through employment in the private sector, but choose to work in NGOs for humanitarian or altruistic reasons. As Büthe and his colleagues reason, "[D]ifficult work under often unpleasant conditions for modest salaries leads to self-selection so that those who make a career in transnational aid NGOs have particularly strong normative commitments" (Büthe, Major, and de Mello e Souza 2012, 600). Whether or not their NGOs serve religious purposes, these NGO workers have been referred to as "missionaries," people who put their self-interest, narrowly conceived, behind the pursuit of a greater good (Stirrat 2008, 412).

Studies correlating need and nonprofits, however, are inconclusive. In Bangladesh, Fruttero and Gauri (2005, 784) find little evidence that NGOs base their decisions on levels of poverty or other measures of community well-being, though they are careful to note that some measures of need are difficult to capture. Looking within the USA, Gronbjerg and Paarlberg (2001) likewise find that need does not correlate with density of nonprofits. Others have found that nonprofits tend to locate in relatively affluent urban areas, not the very poor (Bielefeld, Murdoch, and Waddell 1997, Joassart-Marcelli and Wolch 2003, Nemenoff 2008).

Other research finds that nonprofits do locate in areas with great need, although they also locate among the resource rich (Bielefeld and Murdoch 2004). Peck (2008) finds that the number of anti-poverty, human service organizations is a function of neighborhood poverty in Phoenix. Bielefeld et al. (1997) find a correlation between demographic characteristics associated with need and the number of health, education, and social service nonprofits in an area. Joassart-Marcelli and Giordano (2006) see similar correlations when examining career centers. Focusing on international development aid, Büthe et al. find that American private development assistance is dispensed along need-based lines, following idealistic, altruistic, and principled norms of serving places with underdeveloped and neglected populations (Büthe, Major, and de Mello e Souza 2012). Aid is not allocated primarily to prolong the survival of NGOs or the employment of personnel (ibid.).

Should the "saintly" view of NGOs prove true, districts with high poverty and low human development would have more NGOs, all else being equal. Similarly, poor health, education, sanitation, and economic indicators would correspond to higher NGO penetration. High population or population densities would also be associated with NGOs, since this proximity would allow NGOs to do good for the greatest number of people.

Policymakers, NGO workers, donor country representatives, politicians, and academics often present more pessimistic views of NGO placement. These views follow two different logics: the logic of "self-serving" convenience, and that of politics. Both suggest that NGOs select where to provide services not based on need but rather on instrumental considerations.

Convenience theories hold that NGOs choose their location for "self-serving" reasons, either to the benefit of individual NGO workers or to the NGO as an organization. Proponents of these theories often assert that NGO prevalence is correlated with ease of access to a location, to donor resources, and to material quality of life (NGOs Co-ordination Board 2009, 28; Moore et al. 2007, 225). This perspective conforms to the idea that developing country government officials often consider it "punishment" to be sent to remote locations with limited access to elite goods (2005–4; McSherry and Brass 2007). Stirrat (2008) refers to development workers fitting these characteristics as "mercenaries"; Chambers (1983) calls them "development tourists."

Some convenience arguments are less cynical, asserting that NGOs locate where individual members of the organization have connections – both professionally and personally, including family connections. In Africa, this not only helps NGO workers develop their community status as "patrons" (Kaler and Watkins 2001), but also allows them to spend time with people they care about. Research from India offers a variation of this idea, showing that NGOs choose to work where there are already NGOs so as to make use of the existing pool of trained personnel, and because NGOs are more likely to be funded in an area that already receives funding (Jammulamadaka 2012, 40–41).

Organization theorists have long argued that the location of an organization has major ramifications for obtaining resources (Pfeffer 1982). These theories of resource dependence predict that donor-funded organizations like NGOs depend on external funding for their survival. Resource dependence theory is also consistent with the literature on goal displacement, in which the means used to achieve a goal inadvertently become more important than the goal itself, or become goals in their own right.

Empirical evidence on NGO location decisions provides mixed support for these theories. Many scholars have argued or implied that NGOs make decisions based primarily on the survival imperative of the organization itself (de Waal 1997, Hancock 1989, Maren 2002, Doyle and Patel 2008). While Büthe et al. (2012) find no evidence of this self-preservation when looking at the destination of US private development aid, Fruttero and Gauri (2005) find this principle at work in Bangladesh. They assert that NGOs locate largely on their need to secure donor funding, which they achieve by locating in places where their impact can be distinguished from that of other organizations. Liston (2008) also finds an urban bias among NGOs in Kenya.

If it is true that NGOs choose their location based on these "self-serving" convenience factors, then certain correlations should hold. First, NGOs should be more prevalent in places that are accessible and have high population densities. All else being equal, this means that one could expect to find NGOs along major highways, near well-trafficked airports, in areas with well-paved roads, and in larger cities. Second, NGOs should be more common in areas where there is increased access to "elite goods," such as restaurants, entertainment, imported foodstuffs, resorts, and high-quality healthcare and education for workers' families. Third, we should find a correlation between ease of access to donor resources or to stated interests of major donors and NGO location.

There are also *political* theories of NGO location. Arguments in this vein draw on the dominant theory of African political economy, which views African systems as complex networks of patronage relationships. According to these theories, politicians use access to the "national cake" to feed their home areas (Bayart 1993, Ekeh 1975, van de Walle 2001, Jackson and Rosberg 1984b), and areas displaying loyalty to a national government are rewarded by it (Barkan, Geist, and Ng'ethe 2003). The opposite principle also holds. For example, throughout the Moi adminis-tration (1978–2002) in Kenya, the saying "*siasa mbaya, maisha mbaya*" (meaning "bad politics, bad life") was popular – people or areas with "bad" political affiliations did not receive state-based development funds (2008–58). The data from that time confirm the accuracy of the apho-rism (Briggs 2014, Jablonski 2014). Some analysts assert that NGOs have come to play a role in this distribution, as they allow politicians to dis-pense state goods in a sanitized manner (Bratton 1989a, Fowler 1991), although one recent study found that donors deliver aid via NGOs to avoid this type of political capture (Dietrich 2013).

A corollary to this argument is that powerful politicians or administra-tors at the national level directly instruct NGOs on where to locate, often sending the organizations and their resources to the powerful individual's home area. In a patronage-based system, this instruction is particularly important during election periods, when politicians are judged largely on the goods and services they bring to the community, including via NGOs.

These political theories lead to a set of testable hypotheses. If they are true, districts that show strong allegiance to the national government should have more NGOs than those that do not. Home districts of very powerful politicians should also have more NGOs than their less polit-ically connected counterparts, all else being equal. Looking at elections,

NGO placement could follow either of two logics. First, since we expect politicians who can successfully bring NGOs to their district to be more likely to be reelected, we should also see less electoral turnover in districts with more NGOs. At the same time, we would expect the most NGOs in areas where electoral competition is tight, since multiple politicians would likely attempt to garner electoral favor through NGO provision.

Finally, from arguments that assert that NGOs are more accountable to their donors than to their recipient communities (Ebrahim 2003, Mercer 2003), we would infer that donors influence where NGOs locate. While donors might prioritize recipient countries strategically (Koch and Ruben 2008) – for example, the USA currently funds many NGOs in Afghanistan – it is unclear why an out-of-country donor would favor one subnational location over another. At the subnational level, any donor preferences about location would likely overlap with either the need or convenience theories. Moreover, because many NGOs receive funding from a variety of donors, it is unclear how they would prioritize conflicting location instructions. Donors likely defer to their national NGO counterparts to select locations within a country, particularly when they are partnered with well-established NGOs.

Evaluating these hypotheses concerning NGO location helps us understand the implications of NGO location choice for territoriality. If NGOs locate where it is convenient and where politicians are strong, they are less likely to expand the territorial governing presence. If NGOs locate where need for services and for infrastructure is great, however, their presence has the potential to complement that of government officials and offices elsewhere, thereby extending territoriality.

DATA ON NGOS AND TERRITORIALITY

The number of NGOs located in each administrative district of Kenya serves as the dependent variable in most of the linear regression models below. In Model 6, the number of NGOs per 100,000 residents is used as an alternate dependent variable to examine where the density of NGOs is greatest. Data for these variables come from population census databases and the registry of the Kenyan government agency responsible for registering and monitoring NGOs' work in the country, the NGO Board. This registry is used by the Kenyan government to inform its NGO-related policies (Republic of Kenya NGO Coordination Bureau 2011b). Crucial for this chapter, the registry included self-reported locations where each

NGO works, reported at the district level at the time of research.[1] Definitions of this and other variables used in this chapter, as well as descriptive statistics, can be found in Tables 4.2 and 4.3.

Although there are some limitations to using the NGO Board data,[2] results are robust against those using data from the nonprofit organization responsible for coordinating all NGOs in Kenya, the NGO Council (2005), and the variables are highly correlated (Pearson's $r = .95$), suggesting the relative prevalence at the district level is consistent (Model 5). Moreover, there is little reason to believe that errors are systematic.[3] Existing random error should not bias the estimates, but will inflate the standard errors.

---

[1] At the time of research, there were 4,210 NGOs listed in the registry, including all the NGOs registered in Kenya between 1991 (when the NGO Board was created) and late 2006. The registry also includes 58 NGOs registered between 1953 and 1991 that were entered in the database upon its creation. NGOs stricken from the record over the years for various reasons are not included. Because of the nature of the questions posed in this research, these changes should not significantly affect the findings.

[2] There are several limitations to this dataset. One is that financial information was available for only 16 percent of organizations. Data may have been missing for a number of reasons: NGOs may have lacked the administrative resources necessary to calculate financial data or to submit a return; they may not have wanted to share the information with the government; they may not have been aware of the requirement to submit the information; they may not have received any income that year; or they may not have been an active organization. On the last of these possibilities: the NGO Board conducted a national validation survey to understand why such a small percentage of organizations submitted annual returns, and were able to locate only 22 percent of registered organizations (NGOs Co-ordination Board 2009, 25). Additionally, many NGOs have not submitted required annual reports consistently, making it unclear whether the organization no longer existed or whether it had simply relocated its activities. The NGO Board does not have adequate staff to follow up with each registered NGO. Information on organizations that have been officially deregistered was not included in the database. Based on the numbering system of the NGO Board, it appears that 2,164 NGOs were struck from the register between its creation and the time of research – there are organizations numbered to 6,375, but only 4,210 records. This numbering indicates that there have been attempts at maintenance of the database. Board employees recognized their own resource scarcity and did not attempt to hide limitations in their work. They were updating the registry when I spoke with them in late 2006 (2006–8). An equally problematic limitation to the data is that the registry included NGOs' self-reported location – not where the organization could prove that it worked. Because a good number of NGOs register but never get off the ground, or their strategy changes between registration and implementation, we cannot be certain that all organizations actually had a presence in the places listed in the database. Moreover, it is unclear whether the location information an NGO gave at registration was ever updated. For this reason, the count of NGOs used in this analysis is an aggregate value of all organizations listing a district, regardless of time period.

[3] It is possible, though not particularly likely, that the government deregistered organizations based on location, which would systematically bias the findings.

TABLE 4.2. *Variable descriptions and sources of information*

Variable	Definition and source of data
Number of NGOs (*used in principal models*)	Number of NGOs per district Source: Government of Kenya NGO Coordination Board Database, December 2006
Number of NGOs (*used in test of robustness*)	Number of NGOs per district Source: National Council of NGOs (nonprofit NGO coordinating body), *Directory of NGOs in Kenya 2005*
NGOs per capita	Number of NGOs per 100,000 people in a district Source: NGO Board Database; Government of Kenya Central Bureau of Statistics, *Kenya Population Census, 1999*
HIV prevalence	HIV Prevalence rate per district Source: UNDP, *Kenya Human Development Report 2006*
Adult illiteracy	Percentage of Illiterate adults per district (aged over 15) Source: Government of Kenya Central Bureau of Statistics, *Kenya Population Census, 1999*
Percent w/o access to clean water	Percentage of residents in a district lacking access to clean drinking water Source: Government of Kenya Central Bureau of Statistics, *Kenya Population Census, 1999*
Percent w/o access to healthcare	Percentage of residents in a district lacking access to healthcare services Source: Government of Kenya Central Bureau of Statistics, *Kenya Population Census, 1999*
HQ distance from Nairobi	Distance in kilometers of district's headquarters, which is the city or town administrative center for the district Source: Government of Kenya, Kenya Roads Board, 2007
Urbanization percentage	Percentage of district population that resides in an urban area Source: Government of Kenya Central Bureau of Statistics, *Kenya Population Census, 1999*
Population density	Ratio of population levels to land area in square kilometers Source: Government of Kenya Central Bureau of Statistics, *Kenya Population Census, 1999*

(*cont.*)

TABLE 4.2. *(cont.)*

Variable	Definition and source of data
Km of paved roads per 1,000km² of area	Measure of road network density in a district, computed by dividing the total kilometers of paved roads in a district by the total area in the district. *Source:* Government of Kenya, Kenya Roads Board, 2007, and Central Bureau of Statistics
Ave # of MPs per constituency in 1992–2002 elections	Measure of patronage-based turnover. Number of different individuals serving as MP for all constituencies in a district, averaged across the whole district, for the 1992, 1997 and 2002 parliamentary elections (Ranges from 1 to 3) *Source:* Electoral Commission of Kenya
Percentage vote for Moi – 1997	Percentage of voters in the 1997 election who voted for Daniel arap Moi; Computed as the number of votes for Moi in the constituencies that form a particular district divided by the total number of votes cast in the district in the 1997 presidential election *Source:* Electoral Commission of Kenya

TABLE 4.3. *Descriptive statistics of variables in regression analysis*

Variable	District observations	Mean	Standard deviation	Min.	Max.
Number of NGOs (NGO Board)	70	250.0	42.5	204.0	534.0
Number of NGOs (NGO Council)	69	64.0	80.4	4.0	656.0
NGOs per capita	70	93.8	74.0	24.9	441.3
HIV prevalence	70	5.7	4.6	0.0	24.4
Adult illiteracy	70	33.9	15.1	11.1	82.6
Percent w/o access to clean water	70	48.1	17.9	6.1	96.0
Percent w/o access to healthcare	70	65.6	13.8	31.0	94.0
Population density	70	280.3	492.8	0.0	2994.0
Paved road density	70	127.4	389.2	0.0	2867.0
Headquarters distance from Nairobi	70	343.7	190.2	0.0	1039.0
Urbanization percentage	65	13.6	17.6	1.2	100.0
Average number of MPs	70	2.1	0.4	1.0	3.0
Percentage vote for Moi in 1997	70	50.0	31.2	3.3	99.2

Data for the independent variables come from Government of Kenya censuses, UNDP Human Development Reports for Kenya, and seven different Kenyan government agencies or ministries. I divided these independent variables into three categories, relating to the theories detailed earlier: "saintly" need factors, "self-serving" convenience factors, and political factors.

The level of need in a district is measured using the percentage of the *population without access to drinking water* or *healthcare*, as well as *HIV levels* and *adult illiteracy* rates.[4] These variables represent the need for infrastructure, healthcare, assistance fighting HIV, and education, and they largely correspond with the main sectors in which NGOs work in the country, as seen in Chapter 3.[5] None of these variables are highly correlated, nor are they collinear.[6] HIV rate may seem to measure the same thing as lack of access to healthcare, yet the two are correlated at an extremely low level (Pearson's $r = .01$). While both are health-related, HIV infection rates are different from healthcare coverage because HIV cannot be cured and its spread is largely unrelated to treatable medical conditions. If relative need for assistance correlates with NGO placement, regression results will reveal a significant positive coefficient for lack of access to drinking water and healthcare, high HIV prevalence, and illiteracy.

The convenience of a district is measured using several variables, *distance of the administrative headquarters from the capital city, road density, population density*, and *urbanization*.[7] Looking at the district headquarters' distance from Nairobi, we know that, on average, the farther one traveled from the capital at the time of research, the less well

---

[4] I do not use a proxy for "poverty" generally, as many of the poverty indicators, such as that used in the UN Human Development Reports, are composite indices. I choose to tease out the individual factors for greater precision. I do not include GDP per capita, as it is both highly correlated with several other measures included in the models (such as urbanization, population density, and road density) and can be a misleading measure in places with high income disparity.

[5] Many NGOs aim to fight the AIDS epidemic. HIV rates in Kenya at the time of the research were estimated to be between 6 and 14 percent (UNAIDS/WHO 2004).

[6] The mean variance inflation factor (VIF) for all independent variables used in regressions is 1.83.

[7] Greater levels of secondary education in a district would also indicate NGO convenience, as they suggest a pool of educated people from which to draw NGO personnel. Because of the centralized nature of secondary schooling in Kenya, however, students often attended boarding secondary schools outside of their home district, meaning that enrollment rates did not accurately measure education provision. Moreover, high levels of post-university unemployment allowed NGOs to hire university graduates.

maintained the roads were – making travel to remote locations physically uncomfortable and the likelihood of finding elite goods on arrival low. Level of urbanization serves as a measure of physical comfort and quality of life for NGO workers, since urban areas have significantly higher levels of elite goods than their rural counterparts. Donors also tend to locate in urban areas. Places with high levels of road density, likewise, are easier to access and more comfortable to travel in than low road density areas. Since many of the largest districts in Kenya had the least infrastructure at the time of research, road density results magnify the effect of ease of access. Finally, population density levels are a clear "pull" factor for ease of access by NGOs (Liston 2008), using the logic that NGOs motivated by convenience locate where they can access large numbers of people and donors from a single office. If the "self-serving" convenience theory holds, we should see a strongly positive and significant coefficient on the urbanization, population density, and paved roads variables, and a negative coefficient on the district's distance from Nairobi.

Finally, political factors in NGO location decision-making are tested using data on district-level allegiance to the national government from the presidential elections of 1997, in which Daniel arap Moi narrowly retained the presidency after nineteen years in office. Aggregating constituency-level voting data into district-wide average electoral support for Moi determines a particular district's allegiance to the national government in the late 1990s. According to the dominant theories of African political economy, the more a district supported Moi, the more its residents should have been rewarded for loyalty with NGOs. If politics are a major factor in NGO location decisions, *support for Moi in the 1997 elections* should have a significant positive coefficient.[8]

Regressions also report an alternate political variable, the average *electoral turnover of MPs* in a district. This variable measures patronage at the local level, using the logic that MPs who do not provide patronage goods and services tend not to be reelected. Since politics in Kenya is highly personalized, with electoral competition based on the candidate's individual characteristics and not party platforms (Oyugi, Wanyande, and Obdiambo-Mbai 2003), this is a measure not of *party* turnover, but of changes in the individual serving as MP in a constituency. There were three elections in this period, so this variable ranges from 1, meaning

---

[8] Vote share for Moi in 1997 and Kibaki in 2002 are highly (and negatively) correlated with one another. Regression results rely only on the 1997 vote share for Moi as an electoral variable.

a single person served as MP in each constituency in the district during the time period (i.e. there was no turnover in any constituency in the district), to 3, meaning that three different individuals served as MP in each constituency (i.e. turnover in every constituency in every election).[9] If the political hypothesis is accurate, results will reveal a significant and negative coefficient on this variable, all else held constant.[10]

ASSESSING THE CLAIMS ON NGO LOCATION

Results show that the geographic distribution of NGOs in Kenya at the district level is statistically correlated with need and convenience factors, all else being equal. Model 1 in Table 4.4 provides the basic model. Models 2 and 3 show that several need and convenience variables are consistently significantly correlated with NGO placement in Kenya, while political factors have no clear relationship. These results are robust with an alternate count of NGOs (Model 5) and are explained further in this chapter. Model 6 reveals that the results are also robust if we consider the density of NGOs.

Most NGOs claim to locate based on objective need. Analysis of these "saintly" need variables – adult illiteracy, lack of access to clean drinking water, lack of access to healthcare, and HIV rates – reveals that factors pertaining to availability of social services and the HIV epidemic are potential explanatory factors in determining NGO placement. The percentage of people without access to healthcare in a district is significant and positively correlated with NGO presence when we control for alternative measures of infrastructure in Models 2, 3, and 4, all else held constant. The estimated coefficient for HIV prevalence is positive and statistically significant, as hypothesized. Adult illiteracy and lack of access to clean drinking water, which measure both absolute poverty and the need for infrastructure, however, are not significantly correlated with NGO presence. When they are dropped in Model 4, the coefficients and standard errors on the other variables change only slightly. The coefficients

---

[9] At the time of data collection, constituencies (political units) and districts (administrative units) often overlapped, such that multiple constituencies were contained within a single district's boundaries. There were between one and eight constituencies in each district.

[10] Testing the alternative electoral hypothesis that districts with competitive elections have greater numbers of NGOs reveals null results. This test was conducted by calculating both the average margin of victory at the district level for MP elections and close election results at the presidential level. Neither variable was ever significant ($p \geq 0.6$ in all specification for either independent variable) and the coefficient hovered near 0.

TABLE 4.4. *Determinants of the number of NGOs per district*

	Model 1 NGO Board	Model 2 NGO Board	Model 3 NGO Board	Model 4 NGO Board	Model 5 NGO Council	Model 6 NGOs per capita
Need factors						
Adult illiteracy rate	0.365 [0.358]	0.036 [0.275]	0.083 [0.325]		0.41 [0.619]	
Percent w/o access to clean water	−0.318 [0.284]	0.006 [0.195]	−0.118 [0.226]		−0.265 [0.432]	
Percent w/o access to healthcare	0.041 [0.368]	0.479* [0.276]	0.697** [0.337]	0.743** [0.310]	1.403** [0.641]	1.286* [0.69]
HIV prevalence	2.299** [1.040]	1.849** [0.822]	1.906* [0.971]	1.675** [0.803]	1.377 [1.850]	−1.427 [1.79]
Convenience factors						
HQ distance from Nairobi	−0.063** [0.026]	−0.034 [0.021]	−0.057** [0.024]	−0.054** [0.021]	−0.146*** [0.046]	0.109** [0.474]
Urbanization percentage	1.405*** [0.271]					
Paved roads density		0.082*** [0.009]				
Population density			0.056*** [0.009]	0.058*** [0.008]	0.109*** [0.017]	−0.019 [0.018]

Political factors

Ave. # of MPs per constituency in 1992–2002 elections	2.891 [10.124]	-3.252 [7.808]	-3.185 [9.151]		-11.589 [17.412]
Percentage vote for Moi – 1997	-6.664 [20.100]	-0.071 [15.888]	1.633 [18.582]		-1.437 [35.513]
Constant	237.885*** [35.834]	214.641*** [27.514]	205.905*** [33.794]	194.017*** [19.383]	8.16 [64.686]
Observations	65	70	70	70	69
R-squared	0.53	0.67	0.55	0.55	0.26

OLS estimates with standard errors in brackets where * $p < 0.1$; ** $p < 0.05$ and *** $p < 0.01$.

on the statistically significant variables are robust to alternative model specifications.[11]

Because the convenience measures are correlated with one another (except distance from Nairobi), they are alternated throughout Models 1 to 4. District headquarters distance from Nairobi is strongly significant and has consistent substantive meaning in Models 1 to 5; the farther a district's headquarters from the capital, the fewer NGOs present in that district. The other three variables – road density, population density, and urbanization – are statistically significant in the primary models and also confirm the convenience theory of NGO location. Model 6, however, reveals that on a per capita basis, NGOs are more prevalent in places distant from the capital.

Contrary to expectation, the politics-based explanations of NGO presence in Kenyan districts are not statistically significant in any model. Increasing a district's 1997 vote share for Moi, as a proxy for national-level political favor, does not correlate with a higher number of NGOs. According to the hypothesis, support for locally elected politicians (MPs) should have had even greater impact on NGO placement in a district than support for the president, since the patronage relationships between MPs and their constituencies are more direct than those between the districts and the leader of the entire nation. Neither variable has a significant impact on the regression coefficients; when removed from the equation in Model 4, they change neither coefficients, nor significance levels, nor the fit of the model in a meaningful way.[12] Alternate model specifications that included a dummy variable for the various provinces in which districts sat – a loose proxy for ethnicity, which is often said to drive patronage in Kenya – likewise reveals no consistent statistical significance. For example, there is no statistically significant relationship between a district being located in Central province (which is dominated by wealthy and politically powerful Kikuyu) and the number of NGOs in that district, all else being equal. Extrapolating from these data, political pressures do not appear to influence NGO locations in Kenya.

---

[11] An alternate measure of education levels, primary school enrollment rates, is insignificant. This test used the UNDP's *Human Development Report* for Kenya (2006), which estimates the school-age population from the 1999 census relative to the enrollment figures.

[12] Political variables were likewise insignificant when they were included with NGOs per capita as the dependent variable.

TABLE 4.5. *Predicted effects on the number of NGOs per district*

Variable	Table 4, Model 3 coefficient	One standard deviation in the variable	Impact on the number of NGOs in a district (rounded to the nearest whole number; the average number of NGOs is 249)
Adult illiteracy rate	0.083	15.1%	+1
HIV prevalence	1.906*	4.6%	+9***
Percent w/o access to clean water	−0.118	17.9%	−2
Percent w/o access to healthcare	0.697**	13.8%	+10**
HQ distance from Nairobi	−0.057**	190.2 km	−11**
Population density	0.056***	493 people/km	+28***
Ave. # of MPs per constituency in 92–02 elections	−3.185	0.41 MPs	+1

* $p < 0.1$; ** $p < 0.05$ and *** $p < 0.01$.

Robustness tests

The robustness of the results become clear in Model 5, which uses the alternate dependent variable, NGO count data from the National Council of NGOs (2005), which is an umbrella NGO responsible for coordinating NGO activities. Although HIV prevalence is no longer significant, the other key indicator of need, lack of access to healthcare, remains strongly significant. Likewise, both of the measures of convenience that are significant using the first dependent variable remain so using the alternate dependent variable. Most importantly, there is no indication that the political hypothesis needs to be reconsidered when this new data is employed.

MAKING SENSE OF THE RESULTS WITH THE WISDOM OF INFORMED OBSERVERS

In meaningful terms, the quantitative data reveal that both "saintly" need and "self-serving" convenience play a role in determining NGO location. Table 4.5 summarizes the predicted effect of each coefficient in Model 3 of Table 4.4. The second column lists the variable's coefficient in the model; the third, the value of one standard deviation change. The last column on the right shows the predicted impact of this one standard deviation increase on the number of NGOs in a district, all else being equal.

For each standard deviation (13.8 percent) increase in the percentage of people without access to healthcare, we find approximately ten more NGOs in a district. Likewise, for each standard deviation increase in HIV prevalence in a district – or about 4.6 percent increase in prevalence – we find an increase of approximately nine NGOs in a district. Stated another way, as we move from a district with the median HIV prevalence in the country (4.05 percent HIV prevalence) to one at the 75th percentile HIV rate (6.7 percent), we find an increase of approximately five NGOs, all else being equal. This increase is equal to about a quarter of one standard deviation in NGO number.

While less statistically significant than HIV prevalence, the estimated coefficient for the convenience variable, the district headquarters' distance from Nairobi, implies that for each standard deviation increase in the distance of a district's headquarters from Nairobi, we find approximately 11 fewer organizations, all else being equal. This means that being located only 190km (114 miles) away from Nairobi resulted in a district having almost a dozen fewer NGOs than average.

The estimated coefficient on population density implies that a one standard deviation increase in the population density of a district (493 people per square kilometer) leads to an increase in the number of NGOs for that district of twenty-eight additional NGOs. Stated another way, as we moved from a district with the median level of population density (164 people/km^2) to a district at the 75th percentile rate of population density (323 people/km^2), we find an increase of nine NGOs in that district.

Data from interviews with informed observers help to interpret the first-order quantitative results, understand mechanisms of potential causal relationships, and analyze the second-order question regarding territoriality. These data primarily support the "saintly" need hypotheses, but also give a nuanced view of the "self-serving" convenience theories. When asked their motivations for working for an NGO, for example, many informed observers stated explicitly and without prompting that their organizations choose locations based on need (2008–13, 2008–16, 2008–25, 2008–26, 2008–30, 2008–31, 2008–32). Many other organizations hoped to reduce "duplication of efforts" in service provision in order to reach a greater number of people (2008–14, 2008–18, 2008–37), according to respondents.

Although these individual employees were not always directly responsible for the NGOs' location decisions, their expressed motivations for working in an NGO also support the need hypothesis. Respondents frequently reported choosing NGO employment because NGOs offer the opportunity to "do good." For example, one international NGO worker chose to take a 40 percent pay cut to work for a nonprofit, "because I really wanted to give back in some way . . . so [my] main reason is service and mission driven" (2008–3). Another mid-level NGO worker had "a personal interest to work on issues that I had an opinion about and cared for" (2008–7). A third said, "We don't just talk about the bottom line. We get a chance to talk about why we are doing what we are doing, and debate what is the right thing to do" (2008–8). One Kenyan NGO leader reported that before she started her NGO, she earned more money selling meals in a shantytown, but she couldn't stand by and watch so many children remain uneducated (2007–26). Likewise, a young Kenyan left a paying job to start an NGO designed to keep boys in school and out of trouble in a highly turbulent Nairobi slum. He relied on donations to maintain the organization (2007–36). These workers stated their belief that the organizations worked where they did in order to improve the lives of those who truly need assistance.

Qualitative data also provide a more nuanced view of the convenience or "self-serving" theories. From the statistical analysis, we see a decidedly urban bias to NGO placement. Liston (2008) argues that such partiality reflects neglect of the most impoverished, rural areas. My statistical results show that the absolute number of NGOs is correlated with urbanization.

On-the-ground observation confirms that higher levels of urbanization generally parallel NGO capacity. For example, the size and relative strength of individual NGOs in more-rural Mbeere were lower than in more-urban Machakos. Although there were a handful of organizations with significant resources and programs, a greater percentage of NGOs in Mbeere than Machakos were small and local, with few paid staff members and small budgets. Interviews with leaders of Mbeere NGOs tended to offer less sophisticated explanations than in Machakos, and respondent comprehension of the interview questions appeared lower. As a representative example, one NGO leader, located in a remote Mbeere village off a secondary, dirt road, explained how her organization intended to help orphans, encourage employment, and improve food security, but had actually achieved very little. She noted, "People want to do something, but they don't know how" (2008–49). She registered her group as an NGO only because she was encouraged to do so by Peace Corps volunteers.

Nevertheless, on a per capita basis, the data show NGO presence as considerably denser in *sparsely* populated areas – particularly in the

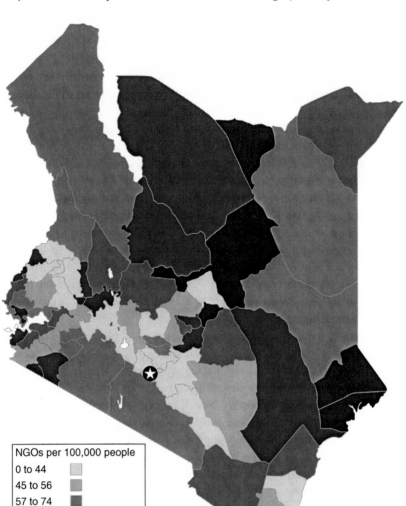

FIGURE 4.1. Map of Kenya illustrating NGOs per capita for each district

ASALs in the north of the country, and in places without government presence (2007–9). This relationship can be seen in Model 6 and in the map in Figure 4.1, which shows the NGO per capita rate for each district. Qualitative evidence confirms that in these areas, NGOs are understood to "be the government," since they more visibly provided goods and services to the populace than did the government (2008–14).

Evidence from informed observers also suggests that location is not based primarily on donor interests or on attracting donors. According to NGO workers in Kenya, most NGOs had multiple donors, often from many countries (2007–26, 2008–10, 2008–11, 2008–14, 2008–21, 2008–22, 2008–26, 2008–29, 2008–30, 2008–31, 2008–33, 2008–44, 2008–53, 2008–54). NGO representatives reported that donors usually supported one or two of several specific programs offered by the NGO, not the NGO as a whole. This means that individual donors affect the *types* of programs that are funded (Cloward 2011), but not the location of implementation. One NGO leader, moreover, reported three different international donors (the United States' PEPFAR, the Global Fund, and the organization's headquarters office in New York), but said that the information "wasn't that important," because "donors aren't so demanding" (2008–33).

Thus, a less cynical explanation of NGO placement in areas of high population density should be considered: NGOs strategically place their projects in areas where they can easily access a great number of disadvantaged people. Since so many people are in need in developing countries, choosing to help the ones that are relatively easy to reach with personnel or supplies is likely to seem reasonable to NGO decision-makers. As one NGO leader in Machakos (70 km from Nairobi) reported, the organization, which registered in 1996, chose to work in Machakos not only because poverty levels, HIV/AIDS incidence, and unemployment rates were high, but also because "Machakos is not too far . . . its easy to coordinate with [our offices in] Nairobi" (2008–32). A Nakuru-based organization (Rift Valley Province) used nearly identical reasoning, though the respondent also said that having a headquarters near its beneficiaries helped to increase local confidence in the organization (2012–6).

In addition, having access to even minimal convenience goods is often hypothesized to draw a higher quality of worker to an NGO field location. Indeed, vastly underqualified interviewees (by their own admission) reported to have gained high-level positions in undesirable locations because more qualified candidates were unwilling to work in that location (2006–9, 2007–22). Just as the World Bank and other elite development organizations argue that they need to pay top-dollar salaries in order to attract the most promising candidates (but still pay less than comparable jobs in the private sector), NGOs need to provide some level of physical comfort in order to entice their workers into the field.

Perhaps need factors are the primary motivation for NGO placement, but pragmatic considerations of how to achieve the greatest impact with the highest-quality workers also play a significant role. This explanation is consistent with interviews with American NGO workers, who reported such things as: "Money was not at all a consideration for me wanting... to work in the NGO domain, but I do value being compensated accordingly for my experience" (2008–5) and "money wasn't critical, but I feel that I *stayed* with [the organization] because despite being a nonprofit, it was a place where I could grow professionally, and feel stable. [It] provides health insurance, 401 K, competitive salaries, and many extra perks" (2008–2).

Finally, interviews with NGO representatives support the finding that patronage politics do not hold sway for NGOs working in Kenya. In no quantitative model do political factors – allegiance to the national government, fidelity to an MP, or high electoral competition – have a statistically and substantively significant impact on NGO placement in the country. We cannot reject the null hypothesis, however, given the large standard errors on the variable and the weak power of the models, but interview evidence does support rejection. According to many respondents, political actors became involved in NGO work *after* a program started by claiming credit for an NGO's positive work (2008–14, 2008–20, 2008–33) – something discussed in detail in Chapter 5. NGO representatives reported avoiding collaboration with politicians for this reason (2008–17). Only one Kenyan informed observer suggested that administrators' home districts might be favored, though not always deliberately (2008–58). He cited an example in which a permanent secretary in the Ministry of Social Services persuaded his home District Development Committee to welcome a child welfare NGO that was having trouble garnering excitement for its work. In a country where patronage and corruption are considered part and parcel of political life, the lack of consistent political interference is a substantial finding.

IMPLICATIONS FOR TERRITORIALITY

There are several ways to view NGO impacts on territoriality, based on these results. In a simplistic count of organizations per district, NGOs do not appear to locate themselves systematically in areas where there is limited government presence. Instead, their prevalence correlates with areas where the state is strongest – such as nearer to the capital city, in high-density areas, and in cities rather than rural areas. One NGO manager reported intentionally locating near government organizations so that the NGO could work in tandem with its government counterparts (2012–1).

Most qualitative evidence as well as regressions estimating correlations with NGO per capita levels, however, reveal that NGOs maintain significant presence in areas of the country where the government is weakest – particularly in the ASALs in the north of the country (see also Oyugi 2004, 48). As the opening quotes of this chapter tell us, NGOs have a more visible presence in remote, poor areas like the North Eastern Province (2008–11). These areas are among the most needy in the country, with the lowest average per capita income and highest poverty rates (Kenya National Bureau of Statistics 2006). As a Ministry of Health employee based in Nairobi said, "Now, NGOs are the only ones in marginal areas of the country" (2007–20).

Since NGOs and governments worked collaboratively in most districts at the time of research (see Chapter 5 for details), we can infer that in the far-flung places where NGOs were relatively strong vis-à-vis government, they still worked to reinforce the state. Even civil servants viewed NGOs as supporting the state; as one said,

"The problem actually is when NGOs are not there. The *wananchi* don't care that government is not there when NGOs are there. As long as one is there [i.e. *either* an NGO or the government], all is okay . . . You rarely find a place where *neither* NGOs nor government is there."

(2008–39)

Likewise, the government workers in the chapter's opening quote noted that NGOs literally helped them to extend their governing presence: the Children's Office relied on NGO vehicles to transport them into rural parts of the district (2008–37). The Ministry of Health officer just quoted pointed out that his ministry had recently started to subsidize NGO-based service provision in distant, marginal regions (2007–20). This support implies a degree of interchangeability between NGOs and government offices – if the government is not strongly broadcasting the signal of the state, NGOs can and do. A manager at a prominent NGO working through Eastern Province said as much, "Where government is not there, NGOs are" (2008–44).

Although not the core focus of this book, a significant proportion of NGOs in Kenya work on issues of humanitarian relief, including refugees. Issues of territorial authority and NGO broadcasting of state power are magnified in these settings, making them worthy of a brief detour.

In areas near the Ethiopian, Somali, and Sudanese borders at the time of data collection, Kenya hosted NGO-managed refugee camps of nearly 450,000 people at Dadaab (making it the largest camp in the world, and Kenya's fourth-largest population center) and nearly 70,000 people at Kakuma. In these administratively far-flung areas, NGOs play a complementary role to the state, helping to reinforce public administration. Dadaab, for example, is run by the NGO CARE, which works with at least seventeen other NGOs in the region. NGOs working in and around refugee camps bring social services and employment not only to foreign refugees, but also to the Kenyan communities near them, strengthening development. In response to persistent drought in the Horn of Africa in the 2000s and 2010s, CARE brought services to over 400,000 refugees living in Kenya, but also to over 300,000 Kenyans (CARE 2011). Education, health, and transportation programs funded by donors and implemented by NGOs created net gains for host populations (Enghoff et al. 2010). Combined with the considerable market opportunities that Kenyan communities gained in responding to refugee camp demands, these NGOs brought approximately $14 million in economic gains in 2010 (Enghoff et al. 2010, 9). Although host communities turned to NGOs for services, their normative associations remained with the Kenyan state (see Chapter 8 and Landau (2002)). The government was able to project a broader face in these areas via NGOs, thereby increasing its territorial scope.

Looking expressly at territorial effects of hosting refugee populations, Jacobsen (2002) argues that the resources from NGOs and other international organizations "represent an important state building contribution to the host state," despite the many challenges associated with large refugee populations (2002, 577). Drawing generalizations from twenty refugee-hosting countries, she observes that since refugees tend to come from contiguous states, refugee populations encourage host states to strengthen their usually weak presence at border regions, extending their bureaucratic reach to these areas. Often via NGOs, refugees also facilitate resource accumulation within states, and draw attention to areas usually out of the public eye (2002, 578).

Turning again to the map in Figure 4.1, we see that the number of NGOs per person at the district level in Kenya confirms these findings. On a per capita basis, NGOs are actually *more* prevalent on the outskirts of the state than they are where the state is strongest. Areas shown in light color have lower NGO per capita ratios than dark areas – as the color deepens, the number of NGOs per capita increases. A clear line of the lightest-possible shading can be seen stretching from the southeast of the country toward the northwest. Remarkably, this lightly shaded strip corresponds to the location of the central highway through the country from the port of Mombasa to the Ugandan border. Along this stretch, population and road density is highest – as is governmental presence – yet NGO per capita ratios are lowest. Each person has access to a greater number of NGOs outside these areas.

These findings concerning NGOs and the broadcasting of power confirm Gibson's analysis (2012) of subnational politics in Latin America and the United States. Although he focuses on subnational authoritarianism in otherwise democratic settings, Gibson demonstrates that subnational units can have a variety of governance structures as part of everyday politics (2012, 4).

CONCLUSIONS

This chapter addresses NGO location in Kenya and its implications for territoriality. Interview data support the findings of regression analysis, and the results largely correlate with a conclusion of Fruttero and Gauri (2005, 761) that NGOs "might be pragmatic and charitable at the same time." To a large extent, this evidence confirms common sense logic about NGOs; yet it counters literature on nonprofits in the US that disputes the claim that NGOs locate their services in places of need. The chapter also provides a preliminary refutation of a very large strand of the literature on Africa that argues that most political economy phenomena on the continent can be attributed to patronage.

From the foregoing analysis, moreover, we can draw conclusions regarding NGOs' complementary role in territoriality and state building. Numerically, NGOs' prevalence in Kenya in 2006 correlates with areas where the state was strongest – nearer to the capital city and in relatively high-density areas. But on a per capita basis, NGOs were more prevalent in places where the state was weak, far from the capital. This finding replicates that of Moore et al. (2007, 230), who find more NGOs per capita in poorer regions of Oaxaca, Mexico, than in wealthier areas near the regional capital, within a general setting of uneven NGO placement across the region. Qualitative interviews show this prevalence worked to the government's benefit by providing a semblance of governing authority. The government was able to project a broader presence via NGOs, thereby "expand[ing] the scope of the state's reach" (Sandberg 1994, 13).

This benefit to state authority is a crucial lesson for those outside of Kenya, as governments in many countries – nearby Ethiopia and Sudan, but also Russia, Nepal, and China – appear threatened by NGOs in their territory. Rather than banning NGOs or their funding from external sources – as these countries have done – they could potentially benefit from NGOs as complements to their own activities.

Understanding NGO placement is important for a variety of additional reasons. Knowing where NGOs locate can help policymakers and donors understand how NGOs work, who they target, and what their priorities are as organizations (Liston 2008, Sandberg 1994). These insights are particularly important as the number of NGOs in developing countries continues to grow, and as nonstate actors increasingly take part in state decision-making and implementation throughout the world.

5

NGOs' role in governance

Changing patterns of policymaking and implementation

"With no NGOs, there's more of government hanging around the office. When there's strong NGOs, more can be done, more impact. Then government gets out there, to the field."
(Ministry of Agriculture employee, Machakos district, 2008)

"To help wananchi *is the work of government. We help* wananchi *to have something in life. So we implement government policies."*
(NGO leader, Mbeere district, 2008)

More than a half-century ago, Robert Dahl (1961) famously asked, "Who governs?" Dahl was interested in the power relations delineating influence among supposed equals in a democracy. Instead of continuing to talk about govern*ing*, today's academics, public servants, and international development administrators employ the term "governance" (Peters and Pierre 1998). As conceptualized in Chapter 2, governance is the process of making allocation decisions for a collectivity and implementing those decisions. Scholars writing on governance recognize that those who govern are not solely found in governments, but also within a range of public, private, and nonprofit organizations. In this chapter, I focus on the way that NGOs have become involved in governance in the provision of services in less-developed countries.

There is some disagreement among theorists regarding how the multiplicity of government and nongovernmental actors ought to work together. As Chapter 2 detailed, some theories emphasize the *privatization* of social service provision, highlighting an important division of labor between government and private actors. For proponents of this view, government actors are meant to "steer" the ship of state by making policy and creating an enabling environment in which private actors can efficiently "row," or implement policy. Other theorists have argued that governments are losing their relevance in an environment of strengthened private actors and globalization.

Evidence from Kenya presented in this chapter, however, confirms that a third set of theories, those focusing on collaborative governance, co-production, and synergies, are most relevant for weakly institutionalized settings. These theories highlight the multiple actors that have become involved in governance, both in policymaking and implementation (Cleveland 1972, Stoker 1998, Peters and Pierre 1998, Rhodes 2000, Rosenau 2000, Frederickson 2004, Bevir 2006, Ostrom 1996). This chapter provides illustrations of this type of collaborative governance shared between NGOs and government actors in Kenya, arguing that the line separating government and NGOs has blurred. The discussion then focuses attention on the many pitfalls that can and have arisen, even in highly collaborative situations, and the fact that this type of collaboration makes the effects of NGOs difficult to measure. The chapter concludes with implications for ongoing state development.

BLURRING BOUNDARIES IN STEERING THE SHIP OF STATE

NGOs help the Kenyan government steer the ship of state by making policy pertaining to service provision. Often at the behest of donors, who prefer for governments to coordinate their activities with private actors, NGOs in Kenya sit on government policymaking boards, development committees, and stakeholder forums. NGOs' strategies and policies are integrated into national planning documents, and their methods of decision-making have, over time, become embedded in government's own. NGOs have become institutionalized in the governing processes of public service provision alongside their government counterparts.

NGOs directly help government to steer

NGOs directly participate in government planning and law-making at the national and local level in Kenya. The following examples from a variety of sectors are representative of this trend. In agriculture in the mid-2000s, one NGO, Cultivating New Frontiers in Agriculture (CNFA), lobbied the Ministry of Agriculture to change the government's policy on farm inputs handouts. Through lengthy collaboration with CNFA, the ministry adopted a new policy: instead of giving free seeds and fertilizer to farmers, the government now subsidizes these items through a voucher system, so as to nurture the development of agro-markets (2008–9, 2008–11). Similarly, the International Livestock Research Institute (ILRI) worked with two government agencies on a Smallholder Dairy Project meant to benefit poor dairy producers and distributers, making access to the lucrative market more democratic. This collaboration led in 2005 to the introduction of the Dairy Development Policy, in which the government agreed to license informal milk producers, whose supply accounted for 85 percent of milk sold in the country, and to legalize their small-scale marketing.

Another NGO worked on youth[1] issues and not only was involved in the development of a National Youth Policy with the Ministry of Youth Affairs, but also represented youth interests for Ministry of Housing annual reports, worked on reforming water policy as part of the national Kenya Water Partnership, contributed to the draft National Lands Policy, and sat on the national steering committee on implementation of the Millennium Development Goals (2008–24). Yet another NGO worked with the government on service provision policies and land reforms, and was a member of the Review Committee of the Local Government Act (2008–10); this NGO also reported working closely on policy and programmatic decisions with the Energy Regulatory Commission, Kenya Power & Lighting Corporation, KenGen, Kenya Water Services Board, Water Service Regulatory Board, Kenya Roads Board, and the Police Service.

At the time I spoke with her, the head of one of Kenya's largest NGOs sat on approximately thirty government policymaking bodies in the Ministry of Health, where her organization helped to create a Code of Ethics for the Kenyan health sector (2006–3). Other NGO representatives reported serving on national bodies such as the National Environmental Management Authority, National Kenya Food Security Steering Committee, and Constitutional Review board.

In addition to influencing policy at the national level, most NGOs are also politically involved at the subnational (local or district) level. Nearly 20 percent of NGO representatives interviewed for this research mentioned, without prompting, that they were members of their respective District Development Committees (DDCs), governing bodies overseeing administrative districts' economic and social development. An NGO

---

[1] In the African development context, "youth" is a broad term, often denoting people aged between fifteen and thirty-five – a large proportion of whom are unemployed urbanites.

representative on the Mbeere DDC said of his role on the committee, "We are part and parcel of government procedures" (2008–52). NGO representatives also sat on their County Council Board, Water Board, Constituency Development Fund Committee, District Peace Committee, District Steering Group, District Environmental Committee, District Stakeholder's Forum, and Locational Development Committees. Analysis conducted by the government's NGO Board suggests that this type of local involvement might be even more prevalent than my interview research indicates. The NGO Board reported that across Kenya 30 percent of NGOs participated in District Development Committees, 20 percent in Constituency AIDS Coordinating Committees, 13 percent in Constituency Development Fund Committees, 10 percent on Area Advisory Councils, and 8 percent on Local Authority Service Delivery Action Plans (NGOs Co-ordination Board 2009, 46).

Small NGOs often contribute to government policy and decision-making through stakeholder forums. At these forums, representatives from different government ministries and politicians congregate with NGOs and other community representatives to gather input on programs or policy. According to a member of one such NGO, "When [government officials] plan, they do not leave us behind" (2008–50). Another NGO representative said that although her organization was not involved in powerful formal meetings, the government wanted input from the organization, and it regularly scheduled local meetings to "share ideas, brainstorm, discuss shared problems... and barriers to work" (2008–12). NGOs reported active participation at the Ministries of Health, Agriculture, Livestock, Local Government, and Children's Department stakeholder meetings, as well as planning the Day of the African Child, the Poverty Reduction Strategy Paper, the Vision 2030 policy (Kenya's long-term national visioning document), the National Policy and Action Plan on human rights, and a variety of other district-level gatherings. Also, during the data collection period, Constituency Development Funds (CDF) given to each MP for development programs in a constituency – collectively constituting 2.5 percent of national government revenue – were distributed via a committee that often included NGO members.[2]

Along with planning committees and policymaking, NGOs have also been recognized as crucial partners in decision-making in District

---

[2] Like other devolved funds, the CDF program, introduced in 2003, has been widely cited as a locus for corruption and patronage. Nonetheless, the participation of NGOs represents a movement toward greater inclusion in the decision-making process.

Development Plans (DDPs), which are the district-level planning documents, akin to Soviet five-year plans, that have been used in Kenya since the 1970s. NGO involvement was clear in the drafting of both the 2002–2008 and 2008–2012 DDPs. In the creation of the 2002 plan – and even more so for the later round of DDPs – government officials wrote DDPs in collaboration with NGOs and other societal groups.[3] Partly in response to donor demands that governments coordinate all development actors and activities in the country, district-level governments began to request NGOs' internal annual plans – and even budgets – which were then integrated into the overall plan for the district. Specifically, when district-level governments listed their revenue and expenditures, they included funds raised by NGOs as well as that of government. NGO inclusion in DDPs went beyond mere tallies to meet donor requirements, however. One civil servant expressed the idea behind the change: "You can't implement a plan you didn't help to make!" (2008–41).[4] The role of these DDPs in bolstering administrative capacity is discussed more in Chapter 6.

Government also influences NGO decisions: not a retreating state

As NGOs melded into the governing process, the Government of Kenya maintained a level of authority over the NGOs, influencing nongovernmental policies and procedures. In addition to the regulations set in the NGO Act and other formal laws, the government continued to influence NGOs informally. When discussing their organization's plans in interviews, NGO representatives referenced government planning documents, such as the Vision 2030 plans, Economic Recovery Strategy, and relevant research reports. "Some objectives are shared by everyone, and are borrowed from government docs," said one NGO worker (2008–17).

NGO leaders also reported meeting regularly with the Provincial Administration officials to make their programmatic decisions in consultation with government officers. Most frequently, they worked with the chief in their location, the government administrator closest to the ground and familiar with the people and their needs (2008–12, 2008–25, 2008–37, 2008–40). Many NGOs also worked with district officers,

---

[3] Some DDPs from the pre-2002 period also mention NGOs, but the countrywide emphasis began in the 2002–2008 DDPs.

[4] NGOs began to be required to submit their plans and budgets to the DDCs in 1986, during the Moi administration. What has changed is the attitude and means of inclusion of NGOs – where this requirement once invoked hostile contestation from NGOs (Ndegwa 1996), it became a largely benign process of coordination.

district commissioners, and Members of Parliament. Just as NGOs sat on government planning bodies, government officials often sat on NGO committees (2008–30). As one NGO worker explained, "Anytime you start working in an area, you have to talk to the local authorities there. Then, you invite them to your meetings . . . so you show solidarity" (2008–12). The leader of a large, influential NGO agreed, "If you can't have good relationships, you can't be an effective organization. We're all targeting the same community, so we work together" (2008–29).

SYNERGIES TO EXTEND THE ARM OF PUBLIC SERVICE PROVISION

On the other side of policy creation is program implementation, where NGOs also work with their government counterparts to extend the reach of state services provision. As one NGO leader said, "we work with almost every ministry because our programs are close to [those of] government" (2008–53). Collaborative efforts can involve merging government and NGO resources together in a single project or NGOs paying for activities that allow the government to fulfill its own mandate. Collaboration can also be seen when government officials embed themselves in NGO programs or vice versa. Furthermore, collaboration is evident when NGOs bring to communities services that the government promises but for which it lacks sufficient resources. Although not universally evident, most data from Kenya confirmed the civil society theory presented in Chapter 2 that NGOs improve government performance by extending the state. Scholars describing this symbiosis elsewhere in Africa have supported this theory, showing that synergy between NGOs and government can facilitate service provision rather than cause conflict (Obiyan 2005, 319; Sandberg 1994, 13).

The first way that NGOs and government line ministries collaborate is by merging resources to provide services. Often, this process entails civil servants providing technical expertise to NGO-funded programs. For example, an NGO and the government collaborated on a blood donor program in Eastern Province in the late 2000s. For this program, funded by the US PEPFAR AIDS program, the government provided social mobilization, sent nurses and technicians to physically collect the blood, and contributed 25 to 40 percent of the total funds needed to run the program. Its partner NGO provided logistical support and the remaining 60 to 75 percent of funding, and coordinated the program from blood collection to cold storage. One NGO employee was based in the government hospital to manage the program (2008–14). This person said that "the technical part is all done by the government workers; I just organize them," and reported that the NGO involvement helped gain support for the program, saying, "We have a human face; people like that" (ibid.).

Around the same time, another NGO worked with the Ministry of Agriculture, the Ministry of Water and Irrigation, the Ministry of Environment and Mineral Resources, the Ministry of Health, and the Ministry of Education on an Orphans and Vulnerable Children (OVC) community-based care program (2008–29). To complete an element of this program that involved training 50 community-based health workers, the Ministry of Health provided the curriculum and educators while the NGO provided the funding.

This NGO also worked with the Ministry of Health on a condom distribution program. The ministry provided condoms and hospital staff to hold demonstrations, and the NGO provided logistical support and transportation. In Mbeere, a similar merger saw an NGO facilitate the government's deworming program in schools; as described in Chapter 1, the government sent an officer and drugs, while the NGO provided transportation and an allowance for the officer (2008–52). NGOs and government sometimes also co-finance funding to CBOs (2008–54). On occasion, multiple organizations simultaneously collaborate with the government: for a water program, one NGO conducted training while another paid for a dam to be built, and the government provided a dam engineering specialist (2008–17).

In addition to merging resources, a second method of collaboration is embedding staff. The Water Department of the Ministry of Water and Irrigation reported that it often embeds its staff in NGO projects. In particular, water engineers and other technical staff were seconded to NGOs to provide the expertise needed to locate the water table and drill boreholes (2008–14, 2008–30, 2008–46). Sometimes these engineers worked on a single well, while others embedded in an NGO for a period of years (2008–14). Likewise, NGOs working with other ministries, such as health, agriculture and livestock, occasionally base their offices within line ministry offices, even paying the government to rent this space (2008–11). This arrangement has mutual benefits: it allows the NGO and government to work very closely, and provides low-cost rent for the NGO and a small amount of revenue to the ministry. NGOs and the government often sign formal memoranda of understanding for these agreements to ensure that the roles and responsibility of each organization is clear (2008–14, 2008–18).

Sometimes, NGOs literally extend the services of government, facilitating existing government services to a greater number of villages or locations. This is the third mechanism of collaboration in implementation. For example, several NGO leaders spoke of government's weakness in addressing needs at the local or village level, which Kenyans often refer to colloquially as "down there." One such NGO working with government line ministries said, "You know government . . . they have structures and guidelines [to get things done], but they don't actually go down there. They can't do everything" (2008–18). Another NGO leader explained that government couldn't undertake the orphan program that his NGO was administering because there were not enough extension officers to do so, explaining "government doesn't have enough machinery in these rural areas," and opining that it was partially due to poor management by government (2008–13). Instead, government projects tended to be concentrated in particular towns or locations, and didn't reach all of a district or constituency (2008–32). As a result, this NGO focused its programs on places overlooked by government.

Government officers, for their part, explained in interviews that their annual budget usually provided adequate funds for activities in a subset of the locations of the district (2008–38, 2008–40).[5] They appreciated when NGOs facilitated the extension of these activities to additional locations. For efforts like installing computers in schools, interviewees reported that it was common for the government to provide some funds for computers, but "then the NGOs bring again more" (2008–51). In other cases, NGOs provided transportation and lunch to the civil servants, who were then able to reach more people (2008–38). In such a case, one division-level civil servant reported that she was only funded annually to work in three of the nine locations in her division, leaving six without the services of her office in any given year. With her government budget, she visited at least one sublocation each week. A local NGO, however, helped her to reach more sublocations (2008–40).

Both NGO and government representatives emphasized the need to reduce duplication of efforts to increase efficiency in meeting needs – they tried to work in different locations from their other-sector counterparts, or, when in the same place, to make sure their efforts were complementary rather than duplicative (2006–1, 2008–23, 2008–11, 2008–18).

---

[5] At the time of research, a location was a formal administrative unit of government; it was smaller than a province, district or division, and larger than a sublocation.

NGO representatives and civil servants agreed that government staff members were, on the whole, pleased with these service extensions. Without them, civil servants often remained idle in their offices for lack of resources to bring services "down there" (2008–30). Frustrated when they ended up "just writing reports in the office," most government interviewees wanted to spend time in the field (2008–39, 2008–30). A civil servant in the Ministry of Agriculture said, "With no NGOs, there's more of government hanging around the office. When there's [*sic*] strong NGOs, more can be done, more impact. Then government gets *out* there, to the field" (2008–38). Likewise, a member of the Children's Office reported that the office relied on NGOs to complete their work (2008–37).

Government subcontracting to NGOs began with occasional projects during the Kibaki administration.[6] For example, in 2008, the Ministry of Planning, Development and Vision 2030 contracted out the activities of a pilot sensitization program called "Localizing Millennium Development Goals" (MDGs) to an NGO in Machakos and other NGOs in at least twenty-one districts (2008–29, 2008–41). After winning the contract by responding to an ad in the newspaper, the NGO worked with the District Development Office to teach *wananchi* about the MDGs and the government's goal to implement them by 2030. The NGO organized workshops at the district, division, and location levels, and arranged for a local *kikamba*-language radio station to play MDG-related public service programming for 15–20 minutes each day for two months. The NGO also worked with several line ministries to conduct trainings about sector-specific MGDs. The ministry performed monitoring and evaluation for the program. The head of this NGO said that they reached many more people working together than either they or the government could have done alone (2008–29). This effort was part of a formal NGO-Government Partnership Program.

Finally, during the Kibaki administration, NGOs collaborated with the Provincial Administration at the local level. NGOs often worked very closely with chiefs and subchiefs, the central government administrators for locations and sublocations respectively. These individuals helped NGOs mobilize participation and support for their work at the community level (2008–17, 2008–35). Relationships between NGOs and subchiefs were generally highly collaborative: "Even particular arms [subchiefs] know where I will be today [because we work so closely]" (2008–17). At the district level, some NGOs also found strong support from the

---

[6] The political implications of this specific activity will be discussed in Chapter 7.

Provincial Administration. NGOs working on Mbeere's cotton-growing initiative, for example, reported that the district commissioner intervened on the cotton growers' behalf when cotton ginners seemed to be taking advantage of the farmers (2008–54). NGO representatives, meanwhile, understood that it was in their interest to show deference to the local authorities that have the power to help or hinder their work: "Let [the government] be informed of what we're doing, so they will add support" (2008–30). However, not all district or provincial-level administrative leaders were helpful (2008–16).

Although most of these examples come from Machakos and Mbeere districts of Eastern Province between 2006 and 2008, interviews in 2012 with service-provision NGOs in Rift Valley and Nyanza province revealed extremely similar stories, suggesting that collaborative relationships were not particular to regions or ethnic groups aligned with the Kibaki administration.[7] One NGO in Nakuru district described how his NGO worked with the government on a waste management project at the municipal level (2012–5). Another NGO in the district collaborated with extension officers from the ministries of agriculture, social services, and the environment to develop programs (2012–4). In Kisii district, likewise, line ministries were supportive of NGOs in achieving their goals (2012–8). A regional manager for an energy access NGO in Rongo district confirmed that NGOs and government work well together, "not like in the past" (2012–9). One NGO representative interviewed went so far as to say that they work as closely as possible with government, in the hopes that their work will eventually be integrated into government entirely (2012–1). On the government side, an energetic official in a line ministry in Kisii explained that she works with NGOs because the workload for her office was simply unmanageable otherwise. In her words, "sometimes you don't know how to divide yourself [to accomplish everything];" she expressed thanks for NGOs because her office "may want to help, but can't help adequately [everywhere]" (2012–7).

Although this collaborative trend therefore appears to be consistent across regions and ethnic groups of the country, some important variation existed across the urban–rural spectrum. Collaboration on service provision between government and NGOs appeared stronger and

---

[7] These NGOs were chosen for interviews because they have at least one program or project involving energy or electricity generation. Interviews were conducted partially to supplement earlier research for this book and partially for a secondary project specific to energy.

more frequent in Machakos, especially Machakos Town, than it did in rural, sparsely populated Mbeere district. Some of the bigger NGOs work-ing in Mbeere noted their joint projects with their government counter-parts, but, overall, the sense of collaboration was less apparent. Because it is difficult and time-consuming to reach Siakago, NGOs were less likely to visit district representatives in Mbeere than in Machakos. As a result, relationships between individuals in NGOs and government seemed to suffer. In the late 2000s, government officials in Mbeere appeared more apprehensive of NGOs than their Machakos peers.

NOT A PURELY COLLABORATIVE RELATIONSHIP

Despite the proliferation of collaborative working relationships during the 2000s, some animosity still exists between NGO and government representatives. This is true not only in Kenya, but also in many develop-ing countries.

Generally speaking, NGO workers I interviewed expressed very posi-tive attitudes toward NGO–government relations. Some, however, con-veyed mild pique through statements like, "[Government officials] take your ideas down, but they don't use them . . . They work with you, but really, not in good faith" (2008–24). Other actors, moreover, did not view relations moving in a positive direction. When the initial euphoria over the democratic change of power in 2002 subsided, some backsliding occurred, notably between the government and Nairobi-based democ-ratization and governance NGOs. Among some of these organizations, relationships with the government declined further after the post-election violence in 2008, during which more than 1,200 people were killed, and again following the harassment and, in some cases, murder of several gov-ernance and human rights NGO leaders (Human Rights Watch 2010).

We could interpret these statements and episodes of conflict as the continuing "true relationship" between NGOs and government – in fact, this was my hypothesis before beginning field research in Kenya. Yet the sentiments expressed in almost all interviews belied this interpretation – acrimonious relationships seemed an afterthought for most NGO repre-sentatives during the Kibaki administration years, possibly because few organizations focused primarily on human rights, anti-corruption and good governance. Although less prevalent than I anticipated, important areas of friction between NGOs and governments did exist, reflecting many of the conflictual conditions described theoretically in Chapter 2. The following discussion examines some of the broad sources of conflict.

Mutual suspicion, lack of trust and insider–outsider resentment

One of the main sources of animus between NGOs and government is a generalized sense of suspicion between the organizations. Jelinek (2006) describes such a relationship of mistrust in Afghanistan, combined with mutual resentment, which I discuss further in this chapter. Researchers have documented similar issues in Bangladesh. In the health sector, government workers are distrustful of NGOs' commitment and capacity, and NGO representatives stated that government officials deliberately create problems and obstruct action (Nurul Alam 2011). The Bangladeshi government has raised concerns that it is losing control over service provision to NGOs (Rose 2011).

In Kenya, some NGO respondents interviewed for this research were frustrated by the long duration of interactions before trust developed. One explained that becoming part of the in-group favored by the district administration is important to NGO success, but difficult to achieve. "They are too suspicious! You have to convince them that you are serious," one NGO leader told me, using the broad Kenyan-English meaning of "serious": well-intentioned, upstanding, judicious, and responsible. He said it took several years and careful grooming to get onto the district government's good side (2008–43). Other NGO interviewees said that distrust can lead to high-level district workers "pulling rank" and explicitly exerting their power over NGOs – particularly small, local NGOs, whose representatives spoke of officials stalling their work (2008–16).

Among NGOs deeply involved in democracy and governance issues, moreover, there remains considerable suspicion of the government. While organizations focused on human rights, corruption, democratization, and transparency represent a small minority of all NGOs, they tend to be quite vocal and visible. Representatives of two organizations that lobby to ban genetically modified organisms (GMOs) and agricultural products from Kenya reported conflicting with government officials (2008–19; 2008–20).

The government did not, however, silence or deregister these organizations. Government officials were often in open conflict with the NGOs: "The government shouts at us as busy bodies," one NGO interviewee said (2008–20). Likewise, in the run-up to the 2013 elections, governance organization were not quieted as CLARION had been in the 1990s (Kidero 2013). Instead, they filed complaints with the court about the government's process; published numerous reports leading up to, during, and after the elections; and monitored the elections at 1,000 polling stations. Members of the government, however – most notably presidential candidate and then-Deputy Prime Minister Uhuru Kenyatta – did attempt to discredit the organizations by associating them with "Western imperialism" and neo-colonialism (Kidero 2013), which he has continued to do as president. Kenyatta is widely believed to have won the election in the first round due to his campaigning against Western meddling in the country's affairs (BBC News Staff 2013, AFP 2013).

Insufficient communication

Much of the mistrust between NGOs and their government counterparts stems from a lack of information flow in both directions. According to interview respondents, sometimes the lack of communication was unintentional – people focus on their work, interacting with the contacts they already have (2008–24). Other times, NGO interviewees reported not knowing what information they should provide to the government. If employees were foreign, moreover, they frequently did not understand the informal protocol of working in Kenya. Likewise, government officers did not realize NGOs like to know what civil servants are working on and how it affects NGO efforts. One NGO leader said that his solution to this information vacuum was to "knock on doors; demand information; demand to know," which led him to cohesive relationships with government (ibid.).

Other NGO representatives reported that they deliberately withheld information from the government (2006–6, 2008–60), either because they didn't want to pay government fees or because they didn't want government to interfere with or skim from their programs. "Briefcase NGOs," those that exist primarily or only on paper for the enrichment of their founders, also withheld information from the government. Such "fly-by-night" NGOs are common, and seen as problematic by both NGOs and government (2008–11).

Government employees can also become frustrated with the NGO sector as a whole, both because they feel they have a right to know what NGOs in their area are doing, and because the NGOs sometimes cause avoidable problems. For example, an agricultural officer complained about NGOs encouraging farmers to grow crops that require access to markets for profitability, yet disappearing after the plants had been grown but before a market could be found (2008–38). She said that her office tried to partner with NGOs so that the farmers were not hurt in the process.

Mutual resentment over resources

Although many NGO representatives in Kenya recognized the government's resource constraints, money issues were a frequent source of conflict. NGO workers resented the "allowances" and per diem that their
organizations paid to their government collaborators (2008–18, 2008–
47, 2008–54). Some NGOs refuse to pay these honorariums, but most
comply, and the fees (around 5,000 Kenya shillings [$70] per day) add
up. At the same time, NGOs reported that the fees were lower than would
be charged by the private sector, so they were willing to pay them (2008–
30). Still, some NGO respondents expressed concern that particular civil
servants would not help them without bribes or other inducements (2008–
14, 2008–16). Others expressed a belief that government was envious of
the money that NGOs receive (2006–3).

On the other side, civil servants said that profligate NGOs caused
problems for government ministries. For example, ministry of agriculture
and livestock officials expressed resentment that NGOs were able to give
material incentives to citizens, when their ministries could not often do
so. The concern that NGOs were spending money carelessly or selfishly
was also expressed from within the NGO sector (2006–2).

These sentiments are not particular to Kenya. In post-conflict countries like Afghanistan, for example, mistrust and resentment are also high
between NGOs and governments (Jelinek 2006). Governments in particular resent the high level of donor funding for reconstruction flowing
through NGOs, as well as the sense that NGOs perceive the government
as lacking capacity. According to one report, "[G]overnment officials
very much want to be a part of the reconstruction effort but through
the gaping lack in resources and access to information, their hands are
tied. A first reaction in all ministry personnel interviewed has been one of
resentment and frustration" (Jelinek 2006, 16).

Promises and policies made, but not implemented

NGO representatives in particular expressed mild frustration that the
government could not always be relied on to hold up its end of bargains.
Sometimes stories of reneging were explicit, as when a government official
promised to bring staff to an NGO-built dispensary or school, but failed
to do so (2008–14, 2008–30, 2008–47). Other times, the lack of "give
and take" was inferred; an NGO regularly assisted the government, but

when the government implemented its own programs, it did not support the NGO in return (2008–54). One NGO leader complained about government contracts, "There's no point to sign a paper if you aren't going to actually [do the] work" (2008–27).

This feeling reflected real disparities between government's strong planning and weak implementation capacity. As one NGO leader said, "Kenya on paper is good! The policy documents are perfect! But they are *very* poor on implementation!...The rules are there. But they are not followed" (2008–14). Another NGO employee had previously worked in Sudan, and felt that collaboration there was more successful than in Kenya, largely because *both* NGOs and government followed through after working together. "The Kenyan context, though, is about meetings, but never what comes out...No one talks about budget. No evaluation is ever done of whether the plans worked" (2008–17). Still, many NGO interviewees that mentioned this lack of follow-through also recognized the limited resources of government. As one NGO leader diplomatically phrased it, "Government acts on these [ideas, suggestions and opinions] at times, but...let's talk of limited resources..." (2008–25).

Taking credit for others' work

One way that governments appear to handle these issues is to claim credit for NGOs' work. For example, one NGO leader in Kenya spoke of a MP announcing to his constituents at a project launch, "You told me to bring someone [to help you], and I have brought [this NGO], and they've done it!" – even though the MP was in no way involved with the NGO's decision to work in that area (2008–54). This observation conforms to Bratton's (1989, 572) analysis of credit taking: "Governments are loath to admit that they have performed poorly because of the implications this has for their right to hold power. They may be unwilling to allow credit to accrue to any organization other than the state."

The strategy, however, often leads to frustration among NGO workers who assert that politicians undermine their work (2008–31). "Don't take the glory if you're not actually my partners!" exclaimed one NGO leader in Kenya when asked about the issue (2008–47). A leader of a lobbying NGO said, "When NGOs do well, politicians come to identify with them. They are not there when you start...but they come in...[and end up] destroying the work!" (2008–19). A third said, "Politicians want people to know that *he* brought these things. But...if it doesn't go well, they turn around and blame you for it!" (2008–17).[8]

A common NGO solution to this credit taking is to implement complementary projects instead of identical ones (2008–14, 2008–17, 2008–18). One respondent, for example, explained that his NGO didn't work on HIV/AIDS information, simple child welfare, or orphanages because so many actors were already involved (2008–14). Another strategy is to focus on work with civil servants rather than politicians (2008–54). As another interviewee said, "When we're opening a project, we'll call [the politicians], okay. But generally we don't work with them. Someone really concerned with helping works without a [political] agenda" (2008–30). One respondent described an alternative strategy, stating that his NGO encouraged former employees and volunteers to become MPs to facilitate better cross-sector relationships (2008–14).

A third method is to insist on public, written acknowledgement for the NGO's contribution (2008–24). NGOs also reported making a point of informing communities of the source of the program by including community members in the delivery of the project and/or using the NGO logo on infrastructure or signboards (2008–14), or putting up their own sign or plaque to mark their work, as shown in Figure 5.1. This strategy prevents politicians from taking over the entire plaque (2008–18).

At the same time, many organizations in Kenya were content with the government taking credit for their work, and some even encouraged it (2008–11). They saw their role as supplementing government in the service of the state and its development. "It happens [that MPs take credit]," says one NGO leader, "But I like it. It means they take ownership and care" (2008–33). Moreover, some politicians worried about inadvertent credit taking, and chose to steer clear of their NGO counterparts. "NGOs don't work with the County Council; they work with communities...We cannot join together with NGOs. Otherwise, who owns the project?" (2008–35).

Some scholars of organizations in Bangladesh, India, and Pakistan draw similar conclusions: NGOs put greater stock in good relationships with their government counterparts than in getting credit for their work, so they allow credit to accrue to government (Batley 2011). However,

---

[8] Politically strategic motivations of politicians frustrate NGOs generally. One NGO worker spoke of an MP drilling a borehole for political reasons 400 meters from the spot where the NGO had just drilled one – even after the organization implored him to put it farther away (2008–14).

FIGURE 5.1. NGO signboard outside an office (this page) and plaque giving credit to an NGO donor who funded the building of a community school's classroom structure (next page)

FIGURE 5.1. (*cont.*)

others have argued that the Bangladeshi government in particular does not view NGOs as giving credit to the government; rather, according to Mayhew's analysis, the government sees numerous NGO program and project signs as taking credit from government or lying about how much NGOs do (Mayhew 2005, 731). Both analyses demonstrate that credit taking is an important issue.

AMID THE COLLABORATION, REASONS FOR SKEPTICISM

Despite these continued areas of discord, the relations between NGOs and the government at the start of the twenty-first century suggest that counter to some claims in the governance literature, the state has not retreated from governance to be *replaced* by nonstate actors. Instead, it has been *joined* by nonstate actors in the governing process, and has been bolstered by the combined efforts. While this collaboration was the dominant story told to me by informed observers and participants in Kenya's development, and is similar to patterns documented elsewhere in Africa,

Latin America, Central and South Asia, and the former Soviet Union[9] (c.f. Rosenberg, Hartwig, and Merson 2008; Brautigam and Segarra 2007; Keese and Argudo 2006; Rose 2006; Zafar Ullah et al. 2006; Taylor 2006; Brinkerhoff 2002), considerable room remains for caution and even skepticism. Four issues related to policymaking and implementation remain problematic: the precarious position that can result for government; the related possibility of government shirking; the potential for co-optation of NGOs rather than interest representation; and the difficulty in measuring the impact of NGO involvement.

A precarious state

Collaboration in decision-making and implementation has the potential downside of leaving the government and public administration, oftentimes already weak, in a precarious position. Although NGOs can add services, training, and goods, reliance on them for implementation makes line ministries vulnerable and leaves them with little recourse if the situation shifts. Should an NGO's funding priorities change, or should the organization decide to leave an area in the middle of a program, the civil service men and women left behind have no means to stop it. Line ministries can benefit if NGOs are there to help them fill their mandate, but they run the risk of poor NGO performance or redirection, since the ministries cannot necessarily hold the NGOs accountable.

For example, NGOs provide a large proportion – as much as 40 percent – of healthcare services in Kenya (Ndegwa 1996), particularly in rural area clinics and in HIV/AIDS prevention and treatment. The organizations provide Kenya with much-needed services, and the government has come to rely on their existence. Should these NGOs decide to close up shop or leave healthcare service provision, however, government capacity would not be sufficient to meet even existing caseloads. A great many Kenyans would be without crucial services, with potentially dire consequences.

The government has little direct authority, moreover, to ensure that NGO programs are conducted in the manner expected, if they happen at all. Ideally, co-production relationships work best if there is a credible commitment among the parties (Ostrom 1996), but this is not always the case. Whereas governments "contract out" to nonprofits in many

[9] This tendency differs from patterns in the West, however (Gazley 2008).

situations (Ferris and Graddy 1986), formalized third-party outsourcing is not the norm in places like Kenya. Instead, privatization of service provision has been largely spontaneous (Cook 2007).

Likewise, although NGOs were formally required to work through the public administration's District Development Committee, many NGO leaders ignored this rule. As a result, even if individuals in the DDC were aware that an NGO was wasting money or implementing a program that clearly would not achieve desired outcomes, the DDC generally could do little to change the situation. Classic examples of badly planned NGO programs are those that were designed to increase livelihoods through the production of a particular crop or good, such as coffee, cocoa, honey, or soap. NGOs trained farmers on growing the crop or producing the good, which the farmers did, only to discover that the area had no market access, that the market was already saturated, or that the cost of access exceeded the proceeds. Had such an NGO consulted with the DDC or a competent civil servant, many such program failures could have been avoided (2008–38).

NGO activities can undermine government efforts in some cases. In Machakos, several civil servant interviewees noted that because NGOs had access to resources that line ministries did not have, it became more difficult for line ministry workers to do their jobs (2008–38, 2008–39). A Ministry of Agriculture worker, for example, pointed out that her ministry ended agricultural handouts in the late 1990s, but that NGOs still gave out agricultural inputs. This caused some community members to assume that civil servants kept goods intended for the community for themselves. She said that because one NGO distributed goods, when the government did not, the NGO "took the community away from government. We can't get quorums for our meetings [anymore]" (2008–38). Researchers elsewhere tell similar stories. In Mozambique, for example, Pfeiffer (2003, 725) found that NGOs not only undermined local control of health programs, but also contributed to the fragmentation of the local health system and to growing social inequality in the country. There, much of the problem stemmed from salary differentials, which drew government health workers away from public service.

Although many NGOs closely engage with government, other NGOs meet only the bare minimum level of cooperation with the DDC or appropriate line ministries, or avoid the government altogether (2008–60). For example, some NGOs only pay lip service to government regulations. One NGO described working with the DDC, but then added, "But really, [we] follow our own mission, [our] strategic plan. [Our] projects then fall from

[our] own planning sessions – not the government" (2008–17; see also 2008–38, 2008–39). Such avoidance of government plans and offices can result in duplication and poor coordination of efforts. Government workers generally do not receive a catalogue of NGOs working in their area; instead they learn of NGO programs through casual observations. As one civil servant remarked, "Oh! There's another [NGO]! They're just working here" (2008–39).

It is important to note that such behavior on the part of NGOs is often a reaction to the weakness of the public administration, creating the potential for a downward spiral of public administration capacity. Particularly for well-funded NGOs with trained and skilled professional staff, working with line ministries and government counterparts can be a frustrating experience. Many NGO workers complained of the slow pace of government implementation (2008–31, 2008–44, 2008–50, 2008–52, 2012–3). One NGO leader described waiting more than nine months for an officer from the Ministry of Trade and Industrialization to provide a promised training, saying "Ah! We are tired [of waiting for government]!" (2008–31). Another explained, "No one is in a hurry to do anything... Like in procurement. The government takes forever because of their procurement process. So we actually provide them a buffer stock of medicines. They have such delays! It's the order of the day" (2008–44; also 2005–07). This person admitted that his organization would prefer not to work with government, but that they couldn't have impact without it (2008–44).

The continued weakness of government service provision extends beyond time delays. Other scholars have outlined the weaknesses of the Kenyan state, which are similar to those of weak states throughout the world. Otiso, for example, points to the following weaknesses in an examination of NGO–government interaction for slum housing improvements in Nairobi: an inflexible, hierarchical administrative structure; corruption, nepotism, and rent-seeking behavior; unattainable regulatory standards; an inability to work with informal groups; and domination by elite groups who enhance their interests at the expense of the poor (Otiso 2003, 223).

NGOs often mitigate some of these issues, but they also recognize that government could make resources go farther if public management were not so poor (2008–13). As in many developing countries, implementation is more challenging than policy creation. As described earlier in the chapter, government offices do not always hold up their end of an agreement to co-produce. For example, in building a health dispensary, the government promised one NGO that it would send health workers, but then reneged (2008–14). Such cases give privatization proponents a legitimate reason to call for reducing government control over service provision.

Government transparency is also low, and corruption remains a serious problem in the country. On the administrative side, one NGO lamented that "[government offices] are never audited – they are four or five years behind, whereas we are audited every quarter" (2008–44, also 2008–14). In some cases, NGOs substitute for the state, making up for government inadequacies that stem more from mismanagement than lack of funding. Although this observation is not surprising, given that Kenya consistently ranks among the world's poorest performers with regard to global corruption and transparency, it is still worthy of discussion.[10] Informed observers directly asserted that "[government officials] have so much money and only think about putting it into their own pockets" (2005–11), and that, "They say they provide services with that tax. I am not sure which ones... they charge double and pocket the rest" (2008–31). One NGO officer who had previously worked for many years as a civil servant remarked, "Government has a lot of money... Heh! I don't know why they're not providing! CDF has 50m [Ksh] when we have 5m [Ksh], but we do more... Something is wrong in the system" (2008–32). Others recognize the corruption, calling government workers "parasitic," while at the same time noting that they help NGOs in the long run (2008–17).

The potential for shirking

Clearly, NGO workers and leaders largely see their work as coping strategies, gap filling, and complementing government (2008–14, 2008–32, 2008–44, 2008–50). Even those critical of government processes see that, as one interviewee opined, "NGOs are *meant* to support government... at least we can do so with supplies" (2008–44). At the same time, they don't want to "let government off the hook" (2008–14, 2008–30). Yet the potential for releasing the government of its duty to provide services to the population is a second cause for concern with NGOs. Indeed, some argue that NGO involvement in service provision facilitates de facto shirking by government (Habib and Taylor 1999, 80), undercutting any benefit NGOs might bring.

---

[10] For example, Transparency International (www.transparency.org) has consistently ranked Kenya among the ten to twenty most corrupt countries.

Although it was not a primary claim made by most informed observers, research in Kenya provided some fodder for the argument that NGOs "let government off the hook." The NGO worker cited earlier regarding his practice of informing the government of his NGOs' work "so they will add support" followed his comment after a long pause by saying, "though...they don't often add support" (2008–30). Often in the same breath, respondents reported being pleased to supplement government activities, yet insisted that government ought to provide the services using taxpayer monies (2008–10, 2008–14, 2008–30, 2008–31). Most NGO workers interviewed were resigned to this fact, saying such things as, "Government *should* do it, but if government is *not* doing it, then an NGO just has to do it, since they are *capable* of helping [the government]" (2008–53).

Some NGO respondents openly expressed concern that NGOs "encourage the government to abdicate its responsibility" (2012–2). For example, one NGO leader, recognizing an unfilled government responsibility, began a "disaster risk reduction program" for road safety.[11] "Someone has to coordinate everyone, so we decided to do it," he said (2008–14). Another NGO representative noted the failure of the parastatal Kenya Farmer's Association, and claimed to have replaced it with NGO programs, which brought more affordable farm inputs to the local level (2008–11). A third mentioned that his NGO revived a cattle dip that the government was meant to maintain, but which had fallen into disrepair. The NGO bought the dip chemicals, repaired the physical infrastructure, and added new pipes, while the government provided advice via the Vet Officer (2008–53). One NGO worker expressed it thus: "In theory, we supplement, but in practice we're there to do what the government fails to do" (2008–17). Another said, "OVCs, for example. Government *should* do it, *but are they able?* They need others to do it for them!...People have given up on government to provide A, B, C, D. So NGOs come to complement government, but sometimes end up the main supplier. Where government is not there, NGOs are. NGOs do *so* much" (2008–44). Indeed, in some cases, respondents opined, "NGOs do more than government" (2008–13).

Government officials admitted that they sometimes shirked, knowing they could rely on NGOs. One civil servant said explicitly, "When the government gets a lot [of money], they might not do the work. So we

---

[11] African roads are notoriously dangerous due to poor road conditions, undermaintained vehicles, and untrained, aggressive drivers.

really require NGO services very much" (2008–35). There was general consensus among respondents that, "Somehow... on the way... things happen..." such that government money does not make it to the people (2008–23). One respondent who was very critical of the government made this comparison: "When NGOs go to the grassroots, the money gets there. When government gets money, it disappears" (2008–19).

As discussed earlier in this chapter, while most respondents spoke of a desire not to duplicate work so as to use limited resources efficiently, some NGO interviewees reported that they avoided parallel programs to prevent the government from taking credit for the NGOs' work, which takes shirking one step farther. As one NGO interviewee said, "When there can be a repetition of duties and actions, then government will take advantage!" (2008–14).

Many NGO informants stated, however, that these problems were common among politicians (2008–23, 2008–30, 2012-8), but not public administrators. For example, one NGO founder reported that his Member of Parliament (MP) unethically wrote the NGOs' programs into his Constituency Development Fund (CDF) reports, even when the NGO received no CDF money or support (2008–10). As discussed elsewhere, several informed observers mentioned MPs publicly taking credit for bringing an NGO to provide services, when they had not done so (2008–54, 2008–19, 2008–17). In contrast to MPs, "Ministries don't do this [credit-taking]" (2008–54). Unlike politicians, NGOs generally had positive things to say about working with civil servants. NGOs most commonly work with technical staff from government line ministries, particularly the ministries and departments of health, water, agriculture, youth, children, and gender, as well as the Provincial Administration.

Interest representation, accountability, and co-optation

A third reason for concern with the state of NGO involvement in governance is that it is not always clear whose interests NGOs represent – those of donors, governments, or *wananchi*. NGOs usually aim to advocate for the interests of the marginalized – in principle, they focus on "downward accountability" to the communities that they serve, and mechanisms exists to maintain such accountability (Edwards and Hulme 1996b, Ebrahim 2003).

Unlike in typical accounts of interest representation, however, the organizations operating in Kenya in the early twenty-first century were often not home-grown, and were usually funded by foreign sources. As described in detail in Chapter 3, more than 90 percent of all funding for NGOs came from outside Kenya. Moreover, rather than arising organically, many NGOs stemmed partially from donor desire to grow civil society since at least the early 1990s (Eikenberry and Kluver 2004). In practice, therefore, even many NGOs that strove for downward accountability in Kenya could be overshadowed by the demands that donors placed on them, leading them to focus instead on "upward accountability" to their source of funds. Donor reporting requirements and short funding cycles, in particular, often draw NGO attention upward (Ebrahim 2005).[12] Such a donor focus was a concern among some informed observers interviewed (2008–14, 2008–15, 2008–27), perhaps because many organizations in Kenya had limited indigenous ties to the community. Short donor cycles are also problematic because they limit the slow and incremental institutional change that is necessary for development.

Accountability to the people is also an issue when NGOs are relied on for service provision associated with the state because mechanisms to ensure it are usually lacking, even where NGOs are locally formed and operated. Democratic governments are held, in principle, to some level of accountability through the electoral system – even if that level is very low in unconsolidated electoral systems. NGOs, on the other hand, are not accountable to societal demands in the same way because they are not elected or appointed through a public system. If they are accountable downward, it is by choice. Where NGOs are accountable, that said, they do not necessarily represent the interests of a specific constituency. Instead, NGOs promote a generally participatory approach. Still, they can set their own agenda without popular participation and in many cases become self-appointed spokespeople for the citizenry.[13] It is therefore exceedingly difficult for citizens to hold NGOs accountable.

Unease that NGOs represent the interests of donors over those of constituents can be exacerbated by concomitant concern that NGOs instead represent the interest of those in power in government. Indeed, NGO–state interactions as described in this chapter conjure Philip Selznick's (1949) discussion of co-optation in *TVA and the Grass Roots*. Selznick defined co-optation as occurring when an organization establishes a formal relationship with a new element or organization, signifying that the new element has a role in decision-making, in order for the original

---

[12] Ebrahim (2005, 52) stresses, however, that as reliant as NGOs are on donors for funding, donors are also reliant on NGOs for information and reputation.
[13] Thank you to an anonymous reviewer for helping me to formulate these ideas.

organization to avert threats to its own stability (1949, 13). This phenomenon occurs either when the legitimacy of the older organization is called into question, such that the new element's legitimacy may be absorbed by the original organization, or when the older organization needs an orderly and reliable mechanism for reaching its public.

Applying this theory to Kenya, we might be concerned that by integrating NGOs into decision-making, the government co-opts NGOs to absorb their legitimacy. Governments may have underhand reasons for integrating plans and activities with NGOs, or even for assigning roles within the government offices responsible for NGOs in a country. In Zambia, for example, White has argued that government departments formed local-level women's groups to participate in department work, but that these groups' involvement was nominal only, used to gain legitimacy and in claims for personnel or financial support (White 1996, 144). She found that seemingly participatory strategies were used as a means of control through co-optation (White 1996). Similarly, Tripp emphasized the crucial role that autonomy from the state played in organizations' ability to press for change in both Uganda and Tanzania (Tripp 2001, 2000). In Kenya, issues of co-optation were mentioned by some interviewees, especially when referring to the large number of NGO leaders who moved into government positions in the early years of the Kibaki administration (2005–4, 2005–7, 2005–11). The threat of co-optation rather than collaboration between NGOs and governments is therefore another cautionary element.

Measuring NGO impacts and use of funds

A final area of concern is the difficulty of measuring or quantifying NGOs' impact on the implementation side of governance, such as on aggregate service provision levels or outputs. The evidence marshaled here shows that NGOs have worked with government counterparts to extend the reach of state services. Clearly, individual NGOs have provided support in education, health, infrastructure, and agriculture. In Kenya specifically, one study has shown that NGOs can be more effective than the government when both implemented the same program (Bold et al. 2012). However, aggregations of these effects proving a significant, quantifiable change beyond the village or town level are rare; it is exceedingly difficult to isolate the effects of NGOs in such calculations.

As described in Appendix A, NGOs interviewed for this research conducted trainings on agro-business, enterprise development, computer use, women's empowerment, vocational skills, hygiene, clean water improvements, child rights, drug abuse, HIV/AIDS awareness and prevention, agricultural techniques and new crops, animal rearing, anti-corruption, food security, peace building, human rights, human resources, community healthcare, management, adding value to agricultural goods, microfinance, and saving. Taken at face value, these programs provided a great number and variety of skills.

Yet it is difficult to know whether NGOs' trainings or civil society and participatory development activities are achieving their goals. On the training side, it is challenging to isolate whether improved conditions or business development are attributable to training. A woman who has completed enterprise development training, for example, does not walk away with a successful business that raises her standards of living. She may never start such an enterprise after training; or she could invest in capital goods for such an enterprise, only to see it fail – which could leave her worse off, at least in the short term, than she was before the NGO training. If she has taken out a microloan, she could also be in debt. NGOs interviewed for this research rarely discussed long-term programming or follow-up meetings with training beneficiaries. They were not incentivized to monitor long-term effects of their programs.

It is not clear, moreover, that the skills NGOs teach relate to outcomes for which there is demand. Although a large number of NGO representatives spoke of beekeeping activities as a source of income generation, it is not clear that there was an untapped desire for honey in the area, or that there was adequate infrastructure to get honey to market elsewhere. If many people in an area are taught skills needed for a single enterprise, moreover, competition among those whose businesses do get off the ground is likely fierce, driving down prices and profits. Microloans, likewise, have been shown to have mixed outcomes; they are not always successful, as recipients' abilities vary greatly (Bauchet et al. 2011).

In Machakos and Mbeere districts alone, tens of thousands of individuals have taken part in capacity-building programs with no clearly discernible effect on development indicators at the district level. Indicators of literacy, for example, have fallen according to census figures during the period of NGO expansion. This decline could be a sign that NGO programs are failing to improve education, but declining literacy rates could also be due to demographic or governmental programming factors.

NGOs working on civil society promotion at the time of research reported positively that, unlike during the Moi administration, they had "sincerely a very cohesive relationship" (2008–11) with the provincial administration, wherein, "We're free to voice issues, say what [we] want" (2008–12). The downside of this collaboration, however, was that it was not always clear that participatory activities like NGO-organized government–citizen forums achieved what they purported to do (2008–24, 2008–27). As one NGO leader explained, "By the time the introductions were over and the presentations [of citizen groups] started, all of the big government people had left... we were bringing complaints to ourselves!" (2008–27). Resources spent in such a way may be having little impact. Programs focusing on peace building, civil education, and governance among citizens on the other hand, could have more of an impact than those between citizens and their government just described, but still be difficult to measure in terms of statistical indicators of development.

One reason why measuring NGO effects at the district level is difficult is that the scale of NGO activities is a drop in the bucket relative to the scope of need. Appendix A, which lists all activities reported by NGOs for this research, illustrates this small scale: while the reported activities do not capture *all* NGO activities in the districts, it is inconceivable that they touch most of the more than one million residents of the two districts in a substantively meaningful manner. Indeed, according to NGO Board figures, there is only one NGO per approximately 800 residents in Mbeere district and one NGO per 3000 residents in Machakos district.[14]

The difficulty of measuring NGO effects on absolute levels of services is also due to the indirect nature of NGO programming, which reflects donor-funding preferences. Most NGO donors prefer to fund one-time expenses; bilateral and multilateral donors fund few recurrent cost items (USAID 1982). Since the 1980s, moreover, there has been an emphasis on long-term financial sustainability at both the NGO and the recipient community level. This imperative means that NGOs and recipient community programs are expected to become financially independent of donors over time, through their own income-generating activities. In the education realm, one-time costs include construction or rehabilitation of classrooms or teacher training. Costs that recur include items like school supplies or teacher and staff salaries – such salaries are among the most difficult to fund. As a result of these conditions on spending, NGOs increasingly turn to one-off trainings and capacity building programs. NGO leaders often recognize that these one-time trainings are not

---

[14] Using data from the nongovernmental coordinating organization in the country, the figure is much closer: one NGO per 5,500 or 7,500 individuals, respectively.

necessarily the most effective use of resources, but must follow donors' specifications. In 1998, for example, less than 14 percent of US-based foundations' funds went to general operating support (Younis 2007).

On the other side, a common critique is that NGOs do not use the funds spent on training or other programs well (2007–1). As one county councillor said, "their capacity building [expenditure] is too high – they come here, spend a lot, waste money. They should spend more in the community, less in town" (2008–35). I observed this firsthand: in Machakos Town I visited a number of hotels to determine where to stay. I was surprised to discover that *all* of them hosted several NGO trainings each week, bringing trainees from around the district and the province. The largest, most expensive hotel in Machakos held one or multiple trainings daily, some of which lasted several days, according to the signboard in the lobby. That hotel charged NGOs the equivalent of $10–15 for vast buffet lunches and dinners – in a town where it was easy to find hearty meals for less than $1 and GDP per capita was less than $300 per year.[15] Clearly, NGO training resources are not always stretched as far as they can go (2006–2).

SUMMARY AND IMPLICATIONS

Let's return to Dahl's (1961) question, "Who governs?" In Kenyan service provision, it became an increasingly joint process in the first decade of the 2000s. Governance was no longer the sole purview of government actors; it was increasingly seen as a shared or networked process among several types of organizations. Governance, therefore, was not the removal of government (Rosenau and Czempiel 1992; Jordan, Wurzel, and Zito 2005), but the addition and acceptance of other actors into the steering process. As a result of government–NGO collaboration on service provision, the total amount of services provided was likely higher than it would have been in NGOs' absence (2008–38).

Indeed, NGOs have had a distinct positive impact on policymaking and service provision capacity. NGOs: (a) contributed to policymaking at the national, subnational, and local levels; (b) provided indirect services that the government was not able to provide; (c) extended the arm of the state to additional places and locations for which government counterparts

---

[15] Other hotels were more reasonable. For example, in the same period, I stayed in a tidy little hotel that also held frequent NGO seminars. The rooms were approximately $15 per night and meals were $1 to $5.

lacked sufficient funds; and (d) worked collaboratively with government on programs neither could do alone.

In providing such services, NGOs and government both saw the role of the organizations as gap filling, complementing, or supplementing the state. As a Nigerian scholar confirmed elsewhere in the continent, "Any expectation that the NGOs will supplant the state in service provision is likely to be utopian" (Obiyan 2005, 302). Instead, NGOs in Kenya expanded the nature of state service provision such that nongovernmental as well as governmental actors began to operate under the aegis of "the state." Working hand in hand on programs and projects, the line between public agency and private NGO blurred. Government civil servants spent months paid by and working for NGO programs. NGOs set up their district or regional offices in government ministry buildings, with public and NGO employees working literally side by side.

As elaborated in the conclusion to this book, this trend is not particular to Kenya. In Brazil, nongovernmental actors help government actors do their jobs, activating both civil society and government actors (Abers and Keck 2009, 291). Also in Brazil (Rich 2013), and in Gambia and Ecuador (Brautigam and Segarra 2007), bureaucrats have come to understand the benefits of working with NGOs. Trust between the sectors built slowly, until government workers realized that it was in their interests to work with NGOs. As a Gambian official said, "If you want NGOs to help with implementation, they have to be part of the policy process" (Brautigam and Segarra 2007, 170). NGOs in India have taken a similar role – they are involved in core policy planning for the government as well as in welfare provision (Jammulamadaka 2012). Batley confirms this observation with respect to India, and argues that similar patterns are evident in Bangladesh and Pakistan as well: NGOs did not lose their autonomy or become co-opted when they attempted to influence policy as advocates (Batley 2011).

On the service implementation side, likewise, in Botswana, Lesotho, Namibia, South Africa, and Swaziland, Rosenberg finds that partnerships between NGOs and governments increased program sustainability of orphan and vulnerable children programs (Rosenberg, Hartwig, and Merson 2008). NGO–government collaboration has been particularly well documented in the health sector (Doyle and Patel 2008; Zafar Ullah et al. 2006; Whaites 1998; Ejaz, Shaikh, and Rizvi 2011). Providing services in Mumbai, India, moreover, is argued to be advocacy in and of itself: advocacy by example, which can also lead to policy change (Batley 2011).

Although these synergistic relations largely strengthened states around the world, Kenya's experience reminds us that they should not be seen as wholly positive. Accountability mechanisms for NGOs have remained weak in Kenya, as has public administration in general. Both of these factors likely have lowered the overall quality of service provision in the country. In addition, government shirking is a constant threat when outside actors step in to "fill gaps," and high levels of corruption in the country have not helped matters. Although Chapter 6 argues that co-optation of NGOs into government was not the dominant trend in the early 2000s in Kenya, co-optation also lingers as a possibility for NGOs in the country. And, finally, although NGOs clearly added services and decision-making capacity to the state, it is difficult to quantify precisely what they accomplish. This challenge is partially due to donor reluctance to fund recurrent costs, partially because of profligate spending by NGOs, and partially because NGO programs often focus on intangible products like training.

It is important, therefore, to continue investigating the long-term consequences of relying on this particular type of private actors – largely foreign-funded NGOs – as key participants in the governing process. Is it realistic to assume that NGOs are in Kenya and other developing countries to stay? Can we be certain that global economic conditions will continue to facilitate their funding?

If Kenya and other developing countries are to avoid a mass exodus of international funds leaving local NGOs, government, and civil society without the capacity to fill the space NGOs now occupy, it is imperative that developing country actors, whether inside the government or outside, also grow their capabilities. I examine this emergent process in detail in the next chapter.

6

NGOs, service provision, and administrative capacity

Isomorphism through learning in the civil service

"It's NGOs that made government open our eyes. We have made a lot of changes."

(Civil servant, Machakos district, 2008)

This chapter focuses on administrative capacity, the ability for officials and civil servants to perform their assigned duties, to manage personnel and resources of the state, and to ensure accountability in service provision (Brautigam 1996, 83). Among scholars of developing countries, administrative capacity has been of interest since at least the onset of Structural Adjustment Programs (SAPs) in the early 1980s. Implemented by the International Monetary Fund (IMF), SAPs were designed to improve economic performance through a series of liberalization and budget cutting measures. Related to capacity, SAPs required governments to downsize the public sector so as to streamline inefficient public agencies. Instead, however, they often resulted in reduced administrative capacity (which had not always been low in all states). Persistent patronage-based hiring and promotion decisions, relatively small budgets, below-market public sector salaries, and the dearth of high-quality education in many countries further eroded capacity.

By the 1990s, development experts called for explicit "capacity-building" efforts in the civil service to raise professionalism, accountability mechanisms, and levels of service delivery. They realized that managing a liberalized economy requires a fairly capable state, able to both enact regulation and administer policy (Chaudhry 1993, Grindle 1996, Levy and Kpundeh 2004). The World Bank provided nearly $9 billion in loans and $900 million in grants to support public sector capacity building between 1995 and 2004 (World Bank 2005, vii).

Some donor support for increasing administrative capacity has been channeled through NGOs. NGOs have likewise instigated their own capacity-building programs at the local level. This chapter addresses how NGOs influenced government practice *within* the civil service in the early years of the twenty-first century in Kenya. As NGOs were integrated into both decision-making and service implementation, the administrative capacity of the state also strengthened in novel ways. NGOs affected the ways in which line ministries and district administrators planned and implemented programs, and how public servants did their jobs. As a result, there was a nascent turn toward more democratic processes in public service administration. Service provision, not only by NGOs but also by government offices, became more participatory and accountable. As seen elsewhere in the world (Evans 1996, Lam 1996, Abers and Keck 2009), cross-sectoral synergies created conditions in which civic engagement was more likely to develop and thrive, and where bureaucratic organizations became stronger.

As outlined in Chapter 2, theories of social learning (Brautigam and Segarra 2007), institutional isomorphism (DiMaggio and Powell 1983), and civil society help explain how administrative capacity within the Kenyan government increased as a result of interactions with NGOs. Government agencies learned from successful NGO strategies, and in working alongside NGOs adopted some of their institutional characteristics – namely participatory methods and a focus on documenting results. This trend accords with collaborative governance theories that focus on synergies. Where synergies exist, civic engagement and accountability grow, while bureaucratic organizations become stronger (Evans 1996). This chapter tests the relationship between growing civil society and improved government performance (Putnam 1993). Similar to Ndegwa (1996, 4), it demonstrates that NGOs' "mundane activities" can empower individuals.

This chapter outlines three capacity-building means used by NGOs in Kenya, and discusses their implications for accountability and participation. It demonstrates that the modifications within government represent a movement toward democratic values and participatory approaches. The analysis also emphasizes that this move is tentative, small, and new, and there are a number of ways in which it could be more illusory than real. The chapter concludes by noting recent national changes that will affect this trend in the years to come.

MECHANISMS FOR INCREASING STATE CAPACITY

During the early years of the twenty-first century, NGOs affected state capacity via three mechanisms. First, NGOs implemented training activities and capacity-building programs designed to influence the way civil servants carry out their jobs. Second, government officials worked to integrate NGOs into their internal processes, seeking to extend the formal, coordinated administration of the state to these organizations. Both of these mechanisms are straightforward, deliberate strategies that merged NGO and governmental activities. The third, however, is where social learning comes most prominently into play: government actors adopted strategies and approaches they had seen to be successful when employed by NGOs – sometimes knowingly mimicking NGO strategies and other times doing so unintentionally. Through all three mechanisms, government began to isomorph toward NGO traits.

Deliberate NGO attempts to build or facilitate capacity

Spurred by donor interest and funding, as well as by a growing recognition among development practitioners of the need for a functioning, capable state, NGOs have undertaken programs to address state capacity. This attempt has manifested in training programs held by NGOs around the world, many of whose primary activity is to educate civil servants. For example, more than half of NGOs in Cambodia provide training to government employees, according to a survey by Suarez and Marshall (2014). NGOs also address state capacity by filling gaps and/or joining forces with government where it is weak (Oyugi 2004), or by relieving some of the managerial and financial burden placed on a government agency (Bratton 1989a). Through training efforts, both direct and indirect, NGOs reorient the priorities of civil servants so that they are more accountable to the poor, and respond more directly to their needs, while also removing some of the isolation for remote civil servants (Clark 1992, 152). Information provision, in particular, often allows civil servants to do jobs that would be impossible without the data provided.

Through both direct training of civil servants and government program managers and also the provision of information, NGOs work to change government officials' conduct using the institutional strategies of coercive isomorphism identified by DiMaggio and Powell (1983, 150). Kenya's experience in the early twenty-first century exemplifies these relationships. Indeed, some NGOs in Kenya designed programs with the explicit goal of enabling ministries to enact their formal mandates. The Ministry of Education, for example, lacked sufficient funding to train public school management committees and hold in-service trainings for government teachers. Knowing this, an NGO in Machakos facilitated these trainings, providing transportation, fuel, meals, supplies, and an honorarium for trainers (2008–32). As a result, the capacity of these government school management committees improved. This NGO had similar training programs with three other ministries and the Horticultural Crops Development Authority. A governance NGO, likewise, implemented training programs that instructed new police officers on protecting public safety while respecting human rights (2005–9). These programs and others like them explicitly aimed to train the government to better achieve its goals.

Several other NGO representatives interviewed for this research stressed the importance of information sharing with the government, which also strengthened the government's ability to meet its objectives. One NGO, for example, supported the Ministry of Agriculture mandate by sharing famine and relief distribution data with the ministry, and helping it with logistical support in these sectors (2008–25). Likewise, program officers in another NGO continuously updated their government counterparts in the ministries of health, education, water, and agriculture, as well as in the Children's Department and the Provincial Administration (2008–18). Even more directly, the Ministry of Livestock offices in Machakos were provided Internet access through one of the NGOs working in the area at the time (2008–38). Without this technology, ministry workers would have difficulty gaining information on weather patterns, fluctuations in livestock and meat prices, animal diseases, and other issues pertinent to their jobs.

During the post-election violence of early 2008, moreover, the Government of Kenya relied heavily on NGOs for information. The government made use of one large NGO to assess levels of movement to internally displaced people (IDP) camps around the country (2008–14). Instead of spending limited resources to count IDPs in each location, the government informally outsourced this data gathering to NGOs, allowing government resources to be used for other ends. The government not only trusted the NGO to be better able to collect this data, it also wanted to avoid duplication of efforts (2008–14). In situations like this, NGO programs became government programs; the government achieved its public administration goals through the NGO.

In these examples, NGOs extended the reach of the state by providing government with information necessary to achieve its missions, particularly information that might otherwise have been difficult to obtain. As one NGO program manager explained, the NGOs had more access to information than the government, but the government had access to the NGOs, "So the government mechanism *is* the NGO. The way government achieves its aim is through the [NGO]" (2008–14).

Intentional moves by government to integrate NGOs into their internal processes

The use of NGO information by government workers ties to the second mechanism by which public administration capacity increased in the early 2000s through the involvement of NGOs. Here, I refer to deliberate strategies of government to increase their ability to set and achieve objectives by integrating NGO programs into their work – in some sense adding capacity by co-opting nongovernmental agencies or offices into a broader, polycentric state. As discussed in the previous chapters, many government officials think of NGOs as their "collaborators in extension" (2008–39), and applaud their increasingly integrated methods of service provision (2008–38). Indeed, most districts and ministries explicitly relied on NGOs to achieve some of their goals in the early twenty-first century. For example, a civil servant in the Children's Office of the Ministry of Gender and Children's Services reported that his office incorporated NGO activities into its annual budget. Because the NGOs provided the government with an annual financial return, the Children's Office started factoring NGO budgets into their own financial planning (2008–37).

Most districts also integrated the work of NGOs into their District Development Plans (DDPs) as a means of bolstering capacity. As discussed in Chapter 5, a new feature of the 2002–2008 DDPs was the across-the-board inclusion and elaboration of the role that NGOs would play during the plan period. While some districts' plans included references to NGOs more than others, the sense of reliance on NGOs for service provision was present throughout. The local administration clearly integrated NGO activities in an attempt to increase state capacity to achieve goals, merging the activities of nongovernmental actors under the aegis of "the state" writ large.

Although my interview evidence for this research comes primarily from Eastern, Central, and Nairobi Provinces, content analysis on the DDPs from all parts of the country confirms this integration of NGOs for increased capacity throughout Kenya. In Butere-Mumias District of Western Province, for example, the language of the DPP specified that NGOs were "expected" to provide "credit, grants, and material support" to cooperatives, to manage and promote good governance, and to undertake agricultural extension services jointly with government (Republic of Kenya Ministry of Planning and National Development 2002a, 27–29). They were "required" to provide financial support and capacity building in Nyando in Nyanza Province (Republic of Kenya Ministry of Planning and National Development 2002g, 43); they "would provide" "credit facilities, physical infrastructure, educational and health services" in Kakamega (Western Province) (Republic of Kenya Ministry of Planning and National Development 2002b, 50); and were "expected to continue complementing the Water Department's efforts" in Rachuonyo (Nyanza Province) (Republic of Kenya Ministry of Planning and National Development 2002h, 34).

Moreover, at the end of each 2002–2008 DDP was an extended table detailing all projects proposed for the plan period, and how each would be carried out. Very frequently, this round of plans stated that NGOs would do such things as "Supplement extension services; Carry out training and awareness campaigns" (Republic of Kenya Ministry of Planning and National Development 2002c, 36), or "provision of textbooks, bursaries and physical facilities" (Republic of Kenya Ministry of Planning and National Development 2002d, 48). In its 2002–2008 DDP, Makueni District proposed 149 projects to be undertaken; of these, 44 (just under 30 percent) explicitly mentioned involvement of implementation and/or funding by NGOs (Republic of Kenya Ministry of Planning and National Development 2002e, 71–86). The specific NGO responsible for such programs in these districts was mentioned only occasionally, suggesting that some of these documents resembled "wish lists" more than true plans, but the District Development Committees that wrote the DDPs clearly recognized the importance of NGOs for effective service delivery.

Here, as in the previous chapter, the overarching trends suggest that the Kenyan government considered NGO activities to be part of the work of the Kenyan state. The government counted on NGOs to help provide basic services. As a powerful example, the DDP section concerning "public administration, safety, law and order" from Nyandarua District stated that "development partners, NGOs, and the government work hand in hand providing finances, technical, and logistical support and training services in carrying out various research and development activities" (Republic of Kenya Ministry of Planning and National Development 2002f, 54). Even some civil servants who did not yet see NGOs as fully integrated with government hoped that this integration would occur one day: "NGOs and the Ministry will be streamlined, so they are working in the same same[1] direction" (2008–38). In their district plans, Kenyan officials aimed to "seek closer working relationship with the community, CBOs, NGOs, religious organizations, and other private providers to increase the range and quality of provision" (Republic of Kenya Ministry of Planning and National Development 2002b, 49).

This integration of NGOs into government plans has taken place in many other developing countries as well. In Ecuador (Keese and Argudo 2006), NGOs have helped local government develop administrative capacity by working together to develop development plans. As in Kenya, NGOs in Ecuador trained civil servants through explicit capacity-building programs and helped to equip government facilities (ibid.). Likewise, in Brazil cooperation between NGOs and the government led to learning processes by both parties, making both sectors more effective (Kasa and Naess 2005).

As the expectation that NGOs will undertake the administration and funding of many public services has solidified, the boundary between the end of government and the beginning of civil society has blurred. In practice, the implementation of these activities blends government and NGO resources. This melding occurred in Kenya as NGOs and government contributed partial resources to create full joint projects and as government personnel seconded NGO offices, and vice versa. The Rift Valley Province district of West Pokot endorsed these integrated efforts explicitly in its 2002–2008 DDP: "Lessons Learnt: Projects that were implemented with assistance from NGOs and other development agencies performed better than those that were implemented by the government alone. There is thus need to collaborate with all stakeholders during the preparation of the current plans" (Republic of Kenya 2002, 17). Government actors in this district wanted to improve the quality of services they provided, and they recognized that they could learn from NGOs in this regard. Working together became one solution: "Extension [services in agriculture] will be undertaken jointly between the government, the NGO, and the farmers themselves through Farmers Field Schools, agricultural demonstrations and exchange visits" (Republic of Kenya Ministry of Planning and National Development 2002a, 27).

Integrating NGO programs and budgets into government plans is simultaneously both reasonable and dubious. The strategy is in many

---

[1] Kenyans often repeat words intentionally for emphasis. Thus, "same same" is used the way "very same" or "exact same" would be used in the US.

ways reasonable, considering that NGO and government employees both confirmed that NGOs provided services traditionally associated with the state. NGOs also sponsored governmental special events including ministry stakeholders' meetings and the "Day of the African Child" celebrations (2008–11, 2008–39). In some sectors, including the HIV/AIDS health subsector, the government lacked the resources to implement programs on its own and relied on NGO resources (2008–19). Working with NGOs, government officers could identify problems, but rely on NGOs to help the people solve them (2008–37). Given this ongoing service provision and collaboration, why not incorporate these vital players into planning?

At the same time, it is also unrealistic for a government to "expect" and "require" NGOs to undertake activities. At the start of the twenty-first century, NGOs received few funds from Kenyan government agencies. Thus, relying on NGO activities left government offices in a precarious position – without purse strings to pull, the government had few enforcement mechanisms to ensure NGOs continued their work. This dynamic is significantly different from nonprofit–government relationships in wealthy countries, where governments tend to "contract out" to NGOs, providing governments with contractual enforcement mechanisms. Moreover, in cases where NGOs push for democratic change explicitly, a tension remains between NGO integration into state processes and the need for the NGOs to be functionally autonomous (Tripp 2000, Dicklitch 1998).

Participatory approaches: mimetic isomorphism through social learning

In addition to deliberate strategies to improve administrative capacity through NGO trainings and NGO integration into a polycentric administrative state, government officials in Kenya also changed internal public service processes to imitate NGO approaches. In the early years of the twenty-first century, throughout the Kenyan public administration, government offices mimicked NGOs' focus on participatory development and accountability. Specifically, government ministries directly copied successful NGO programs and enacted new NGO-like measures, such as line ministry "report cards," service charters and performance contracts – mechanisms of accountability that will be discussed in detail in this chapter. As explained in Chapter 2, many of these changes reflected the influence of donors, who had been exhorting these approaches for some time (Brautigam and Segarra 2007). Yet these changes also represented social learning, considering that NGOs have been a major force advocating for accountable governance in Kenya since at least the early 1990s.

This story is not particular to Kenya. In Gambia, for example, donors required the government to partner with NGOs as a condition of funding in the early 1990s (ibid.). When donors withdrew most of their presence following the 1994 military coup, however, the government continued to work with NGOs, recognizing that it could maintain or expand its capacity in the social sector by doing so (ibid.). A government official there explained, "ten years ago...NGOs were seen as interfering, but we have now seen that they have strategic advantages" (Brautigam and Segarra 2007, 160).

In Kenya, a similar process of government partnering with NGOs occurred in the 1990s, as discussed in Chapter 2. Unhappy with the Moi administration, donors largely withdrew direct funding from the Kenyan government, though they continued to fund many NGOs in Kenya (Chege 1999). When Kibaki came to power, a significant number of NGO leaders and employees were brought into government, some even serving in senior positions. Once inside government agencies, former NGO leaders implemented strategies and programs familiar to NGOs, thereby making the government organization resemble its nongovernmental counterpart. As a result of these moves to professionalize by mimicking NGOs, one senior NGO worker declared, "Government is more of an NGO than NGOs are!" (2008–33).

Acknowledging that some scholars are skeptical of NGOs' true commitment to participation and accountability (White 1996, Mercer 2003), NGOs do champion these values loudly and consistently (Carr 2011, Cleaver 2002). They may not always succeed at "practicing what they preach," yet NGOs seek to serve the public good and to use participatory methods (Barr, Marcel, and Trudy 2005). As evidence of NGOs' participatory intent, a survey of NGOs in Uganda found that 90 percent of organizations reported involving host communities in the delivery of services, and nearly 60 percent of beneficiaries of these NGOs agreed that the NGOs seek community participation (Barr, Marcel, and Trudy 2005). Although NGOs claimed more participatory involvement than the respective communities experienced, it is significant that a clear majority of community members reported that NGOs sought their involvement. The authors of the study also report that NGOs are well regarded in the country, especially when they are accessible to beneficiaries (ibid.). Relative to the Kenyan government and its public administration during the past forty years, NGOs have unquestionably led the way in making public service provision more participatory and accountable.

At the time of data collection, Kenyan citizens agreed that NGOs looked after the interests of the common man. When asked, "To what extent do you think NGOs have the interests of the people in mind?" in a survey on service provision and service providers, 70 percent of respondents answered positively, and only 20 percent responded negatively.[2]

Government workers in Kenya were not blind to these popular perceptions of NGOs and their strategies. I discuss government attitudes toward NGO reputations in greater detail in Chapter 8. Here, I argue that civil servants have learned from NGOs' positive reception in the community, and have responded by adopting NGO tactics to improve their own administrative capacity.

Mimicking NGO approaches

Some development strategies of government ministries at the time of research were exact copies of NGO programs, reflecting true mimetic isomorphism. For example, to measure the success of some of their programs, more than thirty government ministries introduced a public "scorecard" system, in which they publicly posted citizens' reactions to and perceptions of service provision by the agency. These scorecards were nearly identical to an NGO's "report cards" of various government agencies started several years earlier (2008–10). The head of this NGO noted that, upon seeing popular support for the NGO report cards, the government began to produce its own scorecards as part of their "Citizen Service Delivery Charters." The charters explained the mission, range of service, clients, commitments to delivery, and complaint mechanisms of the agencies that use them[3] and were prominently displayed throughout

---

[2] The remaining 10 percent of respondents either had no answer or didn't know. Respondents were asked the same question with respect to Kenyan politicians and civil servants; only 34 percent and 53 percent of respondents respectively felt that these government actors had the interests of the people in mind. Interviewees report that government actors are frequently perceived as corrupt, but NGOs are not (2008–11, 2008–14, 2008–16).

[3] According to a brochure for the Kenya Public Service Week (2008a), the following ministries and departments were involved: Office of the President (Provincial Admin, Internal Security, Defense, Special Programs); Office of the VP (Home Affairs, Heritage and Culture, Immigration and Registration of Persons); Office of the Prime Minister (Public Service Minister, planning/national development, ASALs, Trade, Agriculture, Local Government, Cooperative Development and Marketing, EAC, Education, Energy, Environment and Mineral Resources, Finances, Fisheries, Foreign Affairs, Forestry and Wildlife, Gender/Children, Higher Education/Science/Tech, Housing, Industrialization, Info/Communications, Justice/National Cohesion/Constitutional Affairs and Labor.)

government offices. The Ministry of Livestock service charter, for example, labeled itself "a tool to enhance awareness on the range of services offered by the Ministry . . . and to express our commitments to offer satisfactory services to all our clients. [It] represents a paradigm shift in the manner in which public services will be delivered, now and in future" (Republic of Kenya 2008b).

On the programmatic level as well, the government started perfect copies of NGO activities, reflecting mimetic isomorphism. For example, the government began piloting an Orphans and Vulnerable Children (OVC) Cash Transfer program in Machakos that was based on a successful NGO program in the district at the time of research. In the program, the government gave 1,500 Kenya shillings (about $25) per month, plus regular medical checkups and medicine, to households fostering OVCs (2008–37). This mimicry highlights the ability for NGOs to act as arenas for experimentation in development strategies at the local level (Rose 2011, Carrard et al. 2009). Rather than rolling out a large-scale cash transfer program with an unknown chance of success, civil servants were able to monitor the NGOs' in-family orphan program. Upon seeing the program achieve its goals in the community, the government assumed the NGO approach.

In addition to adoption of NGO programs and accountability measures, in the early 2000s, the civil service and some political offices introduced annual performance assessments and service contracts for the first time, which resemble those used in NGOs to rate individual and office performance (2008–35). In some offices, very specific outputs and outcomes were targeted, reflecting a move toward greater capacity, as determined by concrete measurement of activities (2012–7). While these reviews are not particular to NGOs – many organizations use annual assessments – government officials credited NGOs for these and other changes, saying, "It's NGOs that made government open our eyes. We have made a lot of changes" (2008–37). Another interviewee pointed out that "service contracts are new in government, but are old at NGOs" (2008–52).

For similar reasons, many government offices installed suggestion boxes and even highly visible, staffed customer care desks. One such customer care desk in Machakos district entailed a table placed under an awning outside of a central administrative office. Two women staffed the desk, labeled "customer service," although "customers" were rare.

It must be emphasized here that these changes do not indicate a complete institutional shift in norms. They were first steps. In Kenya, almost *any* type of accountability mechanisms among line ministries at the local level remains relatively new. According to civil servant interviewees, until recently, there were few accountability mechanisms to be found among government offices. Although the Kenyan civil service was highly professionalized during and after colonialism (Leonard 1991), years of economic crisis and political decline had left those professional norms all but forgotten. To reinforce what a significant change these steps toward accountability represented, a civil servant explained, "In the 1990s, government ministries had no money, and employees of government could do what they wanted with the money that was there. But now . . . things are changing. No you have to work. You have to go down there, to the Divisions" (2008–39). Another civil servant reinforced this point, saying, "you have to report to duty now" (2008–41). The fact that merely *showing up at work* was considered a novel requirement might be read as a discouraging sign for Kenya's prospects. Yet as DiMaggio and Powell assert, even when changes begin as ceremonial or nominal, they can become institutionalized over time (1983, 150).

Borrowing other NGO tools of accountability

Another element of the changes in the internal dynamics of government service provision was a push toward "demand-driven development," which added participatory elements that NGOs popularized to programs.[4] These approaches encouraged *wananchi* to be proactive in making their voices heard and to demand services from government. For example, the Ministries of Agriculture and of Livestock successfully revitalized demand-driven extension services, teaching people that if they wanted services, they needed to approach the ministry for them. One agricultural officer reported success in this program, "It's taking root! 60 percent of people come and demand" (2008–41). Crucially, the extension services also became more participatory: civil servants working in both the agriculture and livestock ministries explained that instead of handing out ministry-chosen agricultural inputs, they began to develop community action plans with input from the community. First, they investigated the conditions in the area, and they then floated several possible strategies to the farmers, who were allowed to decide on

---

4 Scholars writing on Kenya during the first decades of independence note that demand-driven development is not new (Leonard 1977). The participatory element on the part of government, however, is. Moreover, it is interesting that young civil servants and NGO workers *believe* demand-driven development to be new. It is likely that these programs declined during the Moi administration and have been reinvigorated in the 2000s.

the course of action. The ministries then provided training on the chosen agricultural techniques (2008–38, 2008–39). These ministries also sponsored food security, agro-forestry, water development, and livestock improvement programs, which self-help groups and private businesses could implement. Potential projects were discussed and chosen publically in an effort to ensure that government was "now being held accountable" (2008–41).

A representative from an NGO that has worked throughout Kenya since the 1980s provided insight into one way that these changes in government were based on social learning from NGOs (2008–18). He described the organization's decision-making process, which was based on a "Participatory Learning and Action" (PLA) assessment that the NGO completed every three years. Each time the assessment was conducted, this participatory approach brought together community forums, focus groups, surveys of residents, and other techniques to identify and discuss issues of importance to the community. Following these NGO-led processes, the community met to prioritize the various areas discussed in the PLA. The NGO representative made a point of describing how the government was invited to take part in the participatory process each time it occurred, and he reported that all of the government ministries sent someone, including the Ministry of Health, Ministry of Water, the Children's Department, Ministry of Agriculture, and the Provincial Administration. These civil servants, then, witnessed the participatory PLA process and the concomitant project design session.

Since 2007, the government has also held a "Kenya Public Service Week" (KPSW) set of events at the conference center in Nairobi and in every provincial and district headquarters. This program, begun by the UN in 2006 as a Public Service Day, was nationalized the following year. According to the KPSW brochure from 2007, "domestication into the KPSW in 2007 is a significant development. It represents a shift towards 'openness' in service delivery to the public besides encouraging citizens to demand better services from the Government . . . It is also to build recognition of the role public officers play towards achievement of efficient and effective service delivery to citizens" (Republic of Kenya 2008a). As one politician said, the KPSW allowed the community to see the things they spend money on; it was an accountability measure designed to let citizens "know that their taxes are getting plowed back" (2008–35). These and other stakeholder forums that provide a means for citizens to voice their concerns became important conduits for greater administrative capacity in Kenya.

MOVEMENT TOWARD DEMOCRATIC VALUES
THROUGH ISOMORPHISM

In borrowing these new internal strategies of service provision, government agencies and actors in Kenya slowly began to adopt more democratic governing styles than those usually associated with African public administration. These new strategies began to increase public administrative capacity during the early years of the twenty-first century. According to one authority on international development, this ability to change attitudes and practices of local officials is one of the greatest attributes of NGOs (Clark 1995). Looking at local governance in Ecuador, moreover, Keese and Argudo argue that such NGOs not only complemented local government, but were necessary for its democratization (Keese and Argudo 2006). Taylor (2006) likewise demonstrates that NGOs working collaboratively with the government in Russia strengthened democracy. He asserts that direct NGO collaboration with law enforcement agencies in performing core organizational tasks moved Russia in a more liberal direction (Taylor 2006). Combined with NGO involvement in policymaking and implementation, public organizations' modeling of programs and actions on those seen within NGOs has begun to increase transparency, accountability, and responsiveness within civil services, cracking open the door to the development of a vibrant interest-group democracy.

NGOs are not always successful at being participatory (Mercer 1999), nor are they usually internally democratic (1996b, Bebbington 1997, Edwards 2000). This inconsistency can be attributed largely to perverse incentives created in the competition for foreign donor funding (Fowler 1991, Cooley and Ron 2002, Martin 2004). NGOs do preach democratic values, however, and have been lauded for teaching populations about their rights as citizens, lobbying governments to administer transparently, acting as information conduits between local communities and public officials, providing a voice for the disempowered, and explicitly pressing for democratization (Clark 1991).[5] NGOs have also been cited for reducing corruption (Deininger and Mpuga 2005, 183), spreading power to more people and groups (Matthews 1997), diffusing liberal ideals around the world (Keck and Sikkink 1998), and encouraging activism in authoritarian regimes (Stern 2013).

---

[5] See also Hyden (1983), World Development (1987), Bratton (1990), Sanyal (1994), Ndegwa (1994), ICNL (1995), Meyer (1997), Salamon et al. (1999), Besley and Ghatak (1999), Garrison (2000), Cannon (2000), Mercer (2002, 8–10), Martin (2004, 25), Doyle and Patel (2008).

In addition to the civil service's increasingly participatory approach, three other signs pointed to increasing democracy within the public administration in early twenty-first-century Kenya: adoption of the language of democratic governance, willingness to work with organizations that are openly critical of the government, and devolution of funding. Not only did these changes stem from NGOs, but they also reflected the influence of NGOs in new patterns of collaborative governance, as well as the integration of NGOs themselves into decision-making and programming.

At the level of service provision, the Kibaki administration unquestionably adopted the *language* of open, collaborative governance. Its ambitious plan to implement the Millennium Development Goals by the year 2030, for example, "[a]dvocated a consultative approach ... involving as many ordinary Kenyans and stakeholders as possible. Consequently, this was done through workshops with stakeholders from all levels of the public service, the private sector, civil society, the media and nongovernmental organizations (NGOs)" (Government of Kenya 2007, 3).

Most key informants I spoke with – even *after* the violent election period in early 2008 – were convinced that these changes were more than window-dressing and fancy language. Instead, NGO–government collaboration was seen as part of a slow-moving long-term turn toward increasing accountability and participation in the governance of service provision. A district officer told me that government workers appreciate the transformations, and gave credit for them to the integration of NGOs into the Kibaki administration. Despite the aberrant post-electoral violence, he said, "2002 catalyzed people – they want to move forward. Once change comes, it's hard to stop" (2008–36). An NGO worker agreed, saying that civil servants "are now more proactive. They really try to do their jobs since 2002" (2008–14).

Another senior district administrator talked animatedly of things "changing dramatically: *everyone* is being brought on board!" (2008–41). Working with NGOs became part of an overall new strategy of the Kibaki government, expressed in the government's "2030" plan, which stated that a "participatory approach is one of our new 'core values'" (Government of Kenya 2007). At the time, these were innovative ways of thinking for Kenya's government. One high-level civil servant reported that Kenya changed to an environment of, "Focus and work as a team ... we're talking about a 24-hour economy, not business-as-usual. We need to work together now" (2008–41). Other civil servants agreed (2008–35, 2012–7).

Even leaders of NGOs that had been key players in the struggle for democracy during the 1990s described a relative opening in governance in the first decade of the twenty-first century. For example, a representative of a nationwide, Kenyan-based NGO that battled the Moi administration as the self-proclaimed "voice of the voiceless" described how her organization successfully engaged with the Kibaki administration when it began to bring NGOs into the governing process: "Government has not asked us to compromise ourselves" (2008–26). In fact, the Kibaki government contracted the organization to run human rights, civic education, and other trainings and programs on political topics. This organization was not politically affiliated with Kibaki or his Kikuyu ethnic group – it was truly a national organization. This informed observer reported that during the Moi administration, Provincial Administrators sent her on "wild goose chases," and forced her to conduct service provision secretly to avoid harassment. This ended, she said. "Now . . . I'm able to work" (ibid.).

The capacity of public administration increased as a result of the integration of NGO efforts. Beginning in 2008, the organization just mentioned was also asked to coordinate the National Policy and Action Plan (NAP), a program to reform human rights policy in Kenya. The NAP was a government program implemented through NGOs that had a highly participatory, locally oriented approach. According to the government's Kenyan National Human Rights Commission website at the time, the government's approach to creating this policy was to conduct "regional hearings . . . in all provinces, whereby they will receive submissions and discuss with the residents their human rights concerns, challenges and priorities towards informing the human rights policy and action plan."[6] Organizers of this process in Eastern Province revealed that hundreds of NGOs and community groups presented planning documents, group opinions and memoranda at a public engagement stakeholder forum. These documents were collected by the government agency with the goal of integrating them into the national plan.

Another governance NGO representative involved in the NAP program told a similar story. Even though his NGO acts as a critical, outspoken watchdog of the government, it was another governance organization that was contracted by the government to conduct NAP activities in Eastern Province. He spoke of successfully demanding the government to hold

---

[6] Kenya National Human Rights Commission website http://www.knchr.org/index.php?option=com_content&task=view&id=46&Itemid=89 (accessed June 2009).

open-to-the-public meetings. One of his strategies involved "gate crash-ing" meetings that appeared to be only nominally open, reporting on these meetings to *wananchi*, and providing detailed information to *wananchi* on how the government's devolved funds were meant to operate (2008–27). This NGO representative's goal was to mobilize people to, in his words, "Raise concerns! Be lively! Demand to know!" at local and district-wide government meetings (ibid.). Such rabble-rousers would never have been welcomed as partners with the government during the Moi administration. Working with critical organizations rather than sti-fling them represented a significant opening in governance patterns during the Kibaki administration.

Aside from the NAP, the government also invited NGOs to disseminate information on its behalf during the country's annual "Kenya Public Service Week" (KPSW). The KPSW, inaugurated in 2006, was designed to improve service provision by informing citizens of their rights and government obligations regarding services (2008–26). Into the 2010s, the KPSWs provided a public forum, held in accessible locations throughout the country, for government offices to bring information to citizens, and for citizens to engage with public service providers. The expectation was that with better knowledge of their rights, citizens would be more able to hold the government accountable.

Such NGO–government collaboration also extended to civic education campaigns in the run-up to the 2013 general elections. Although the government administered some of these efforts, it also allowed a large range of NGOs to do so – something that would have been unimaginable just a decade or two earlier. As a representative example, the Institute for Education in Democracy (IED) designed and disseminated educational election-related information on seven radio stations that focused on thirteen of the country's counties. The organization aimed to reach more than 3,000 people.[7] Likewise, a range of civil society NGOs, mostly based in Nairobi, aggressively produced and disseminated reports and monitoring publications that were critical of the government leading up to the elections (for example, see Kenyans for Peace with Truth & Justice 2012, Kenya Human Rights Commission 2013, International Crisis Group 2013).

Although most of these reports cited a lack of voter education and cau-tioned that this dearth of civic education could have spilled into a second violent election, the message of civil engagement appears to have worked.

---

[7] IED website http://www.iedafrica.org/news.asp?ID=113 (accessed March 2013).

The 2013 elections witnessed very little violence, 86 percent voter turnout, and an incredible amount of election monitoring. Not only did international observers monitor the election, but a Kenyan NGO, the Elections Observer Group (ELOG), also sent approximately 7,000 observers to polling stations around the country for the March 2013 election.[8] Social media groups like Uchaguzi and Twitter provided means for citizens to monitor and report in real time as well. Uchaguzi, a monitoring platform created by civil society groups during the post-election violence of 2008, was used in both the 2010 constitutional referendum and the 2013 elections.[9] Whereas the government would likely have clamped down on these groups ahead of elections in the past, it now engages them, largely through a strengthened judiciary system (Kenyans for Peace with Truth & Justice 2012).

Finally, the Kibaki government devolved funds from central to more localized levels of government to increase accountability and concomitant administrative performance. These programs, including seven funds for local authorities and constituencies, bursaries for secondary and university school students, road maintenance, AIDS efforts, and youth enterprise development, were meant to increase accountability by bringing the distribution of funds to a lower, more local level. Much of the devolution represented a push from donors toward decentralization, yet NGOs were often involved as well. In many cases, committees containing both government and NGO representatives determined the distribution of these funds. Individual ministries also developed devolution efforts, giving funds to CBOs as part of community initiative programs. Examples include the Ministries of Agriculture and Livestock, both of which funded small self-help groups and larger private businesses for programs in areas like food security, agro-forestry, water development, and livestock improvement (2008–38, 2008–39). These projects were discussed publicly using a participatory approach. Although this devolution of funds has been rife with allegations of corruption, the government invited NGOs to conduct monitoring and evaluation for some of these efforts (2008–24). Considerable improvements are still needed, but external evaluations represent a step in the right direction. According to one interviewee, the funds were "so appreciated by the community" and signified that government was "now being held accountable" (2008–41).

---

[8]   From their website, http://www.elog.or.ke/ (accessed March 12, 2013).
[9]   Their website is: https://uchaguzi.co.ke/ (accessed March 12, 2013).

The government under Kibaki also became less centralized, with public administrators given a freer hand in deciding how to use ministry funds. At the same time, donors, pleased with the transfer of power in the 2002 presidential elections, began to fund the government to a greater extent, including a major shift to general budgetary support instead of support for specific line items. As one civil servant stated, "Government has more funding now, and it's managed better. With the change of government, there is now more control of funds" (2008–39). Direct budget support has not been a consistent donor policy, however.

TWO STEPS FORWARD, ONE STEP BACK

Although movement toward a more capable and democratic state occurred during the early years of the twenty-first century in Kenya, this observation does not imply that the administration of public services became efficient, accountable, and participatory. The argument of this chapter is modest, stating simply that public administration at the local level *moved in this direction*. It remains the case that getting civil servants to appear in the offices where they are paid to work is considered a step forward. Movement has been very slow; service provision levels remain low, and corruption is still common. The degree to which public administration changes – or whether it backslides – is yet to be determined, and will be a very long-term process.

For example, some periods of backsliding occurred during the Kibaki administration. As mentioned in Chapter 3, governance NGOs experienced a period of discord with the government in 2005, both as anti-corruption "tsar" John Githongo left the country in fear for his life (2005–4, 2005–5, 2005–7) and in the lead-up to a failed referendum on a new constitution in the same year (2006–6). Based on information from informed observers, such tensions were acute among governance NGOs, while many service providers were unaffected (2006–2). In general, NGOs, whether they focused primarily on governance issues or not, said that improvements occurred much more in service provision than in political areas. One NGO respondent who talked about collaborative policymaking with eight different ministries or agencies of the government said, "The only problem with government is governance. They don't respect human rights, right to education, etcetera. Especially politicians. But water, health, sanitation . . . it's all okay" (2008–24). Representatives of two highly political organizations, however, said that their organizations had figured out how to collaborate with the government successfully (2008–26, 2008–27).

It is possible that these changes were more illusory than real. Aid recipients can manipulate their donors, and it may be that both NGOs and government offices simply played the "politics of the mirror" (Chabal and Daloz 1999), in which governments reflect back to donors what the donors want to see or hear, while following their own preferences behind the looking glass.[10] Some officials in the Kibaki administration certainly appeared open to working with NGOs for such instrumental reasons. Since donors wanted NGO involvement in governance, it was in the interest of the Kenyan government to include them. It is also possible that NGOs and government colluded so as to achieve greater success at mutually beneficial resource extraction from donors. Some government workers even sanitized their corrupt practices through briefcase NGOs they created for the purpose of diverting government monies (2008–11).

Governments can also use "participation" as a tool to avoid real institutional change, and to shirk their responsibilities (Botchway 2001). For example, one NGO working with the Ministry of Justice and the governmental Kenya National Human Rights Commission on the National Action Plan (NAP) worked to coordinate Community-Based Organizations and other interested civic groups to participate in the day-long event in their home district. A representative of the NGO complained that while the government officials came to the introduction of the day's events, the high-level officials from the Ministry of Justice, along with the District Commission, many of the Chiefs, and the local politicians left before the CBO presentations began (2008–27). He was left asking, "Will the memos even be read?" (ibid.). In this case, the follow-through needed for CBO engagement to be true participatory development did not take place.

Questioning the "participatory" in NGOs

NGOs, of course, are not a "magic bullet" miraculously instilling civil society and consolidated democratic governance in all walks of public management in developing countries (Edwards and Hulme 1996a). The

---

[10] Ebrahim (2003) agrees. While he discusses five methods of NGO accountability, he also cites Najam's (1996) description of NGOs' claims of participation as "sham rituals," in which "the sham of participation translates into the sham of accountability" (Ebrahim 2003, 818).

example above is a reminder that participatory development strategies may be little more than "performances" of participation and partnership, creating an illusion of good governance (Mercer 2003). NGOs can also promise participation, but not deliver among their beneficiaries (Brunt and McCourt 2012). In some cases, NGO activities may even reduce the level of participation in an area. Igoe (2003), for example, documented a diversion in programs from advocacy and engagement among pastoralist NGOs in Tanzania toward less participatory activities whose effects were easier to measure and report to donors. The result was lower accountability toward constituent communities and less pressure on the state to improve its performance (Igoe 2003). Other accounts of donor–NGO interactions have told a similar story in Uganda (Tripp 2000, Dicklitch 1998, Katusiimeh 2004).

There is considerable debate about whether NGOs as a set of organizations can be associated with democratic values (Fowler 1995, Cammett and MacLean 2011, Kasfir 1998, Dicklitch 1998). Variation in NGOs exists, and the internal organization of organizations – their structure, decision-making processes, and the composition of their personnel – can make a difference for democratic outcomes (MacLean 2004, Baggetta 2009). Few NGOs, however, are formed through democratic processes in the way that representative governments are.

Efficient use of capacity-building resources?

Along similar lines, and echoing Chapter 5, we should refrain from unquestioning optimism about the success of NGO capacity-building programs. Profligate spending by NGOs was a common complaint articulated by informed observers in Kenya: "NGOs use a lot of funds. They pour them out, but when you quantify the amount of benefit, it seems not to be equivalent with the amount poured. They employ a lot of staff, but the remuneration of staff! It is so enormous! It takes almost half of what has been allocated!" (2008–37, also 2008–31).

In particular, spending copious amounts on "capacity building" – especially trainings that take place at local hotels and include large meals and tea breaks – was a frequent critique of NGOs, both from within NGOs and from government. One local politician said, "Most of the NGOs are good. But their capacity building [expenditure] is too high – they come here, spend a lot, waste money. They should spend more in the community, less in town" (2008–35). Some observers went so far as to suggest that trainings were all NGOs did: "I've not seen [NGOs' impact]. But I'm not sure what they do. They do so many seminars, but the output isn't visible. I can't say this NGO did X, Y, Z. Mostly they have seminars in the big hotels" (2008–36).[11] Some NGO leaders agreed with this critique, saying that the community has been "so trained" that they are "becoming fatigued" (2008–33). "Capacity building" is not without noble aspirations. Many NGO workers and their participants truly believe the way to development is to "teach a man to fish" – an oft-cited phrase among development practitioners, but one whose "talk"-based efficacy has been questioned (Swidler and Watkins 2009; Watkins, Swidler, and Hannan 2012; Barr, Marcel, and Trudy 2005).[12]

CONCLUSION

The integration of NGOs into governance reflected a clear move toward synergistic, collaborative governance in Kenya during the early twenty-first century. This chapter has demonstrated how this collaboration also led to some improvements in the internal administrative capacity of the state. In particular, drawing on theories of social learning, the chapter showed how many government agencies noticed the successes achieved by NGOs and, whether intentionally or not, mimicked their actions, recalling DiMaggio and Powell's (1983) mimetic isomorphism. As a result, government offices began adopting more transparent, participatory, and accountable approaches to their work. This was most obvious in their attempts at participatory engagement, in which citizen opinions from the village to the city were solicited (if not always addressed), but also in performance reviews, service charters, and a demand-driven approach. In addition, government learned to integrate NGO plans into its own district plans, and NGOs provided training and information to further grow administrative capacity (if not always by the most efficient means possible). The result of these changes was that governance within the public administration in Kenya slowly began to become more democratic, moving away from its hierarchical, authoritarian past.

---

[11] Not all government officials felt this way. One civil servant appreciated the trainings she had received from one of the larger NGOs in Machakos – in fact, she had attended six such trainings between January and October 2008 (2008–37).

[12] Of course, NGOs provide "capacity building" partially because of donor rules regarding funding. Donors, both governmental and nongovernmental, often refuse to pay the "recurrent costs" of programs, under the assumptions that NGOS' work should become self-sustaining and that repeatedly paying for things encourages dependency. As a result, donor-raised funds must be used for one-off expenses, making training programs a natural outlet.

The findings presented here, however, are based on recent and tenuous changes in the public administration of services. It is far from clear that they will persist. On the one hand, political and administrative devolution required in the 2010 constitution has begun to come online and has the potential to reinforce these changes. Yet countervailing forces could easily sway trends away. Even now, it can be difficult to tell whether respondents in my study described true changes in administrative capacity and political will within the bureaucracy, or whether the government was merely "performing" participation (Mercer 2003, White 1996), reflecting what officials know donors want to see in a continued "politics of the mirror" (Chabal and Daloz 1999).

Today, administrative capacity in Kenya remains very low. Services are not provided in a democratic manner. Upheaval in Kenya following the 2007 presidential elections, moreover, reminds us that democracy in Kenya is still young and unconsolidated. Although NGOs may help to move public service administration and decision-making in a more democratic direction, these efforts exist in a broader and fragile political context. Success in public management improvements will depend largely on the trajectory of the political system as a whole.

7

Have NGOs decreased perceptions of state legitimacy over time?

"If I don't give services, I won't be elected."
(County Council member, Masaku County, 2008)

"You don't see NGOs reflecting poorly on government. You see government being helped by NGOs!"
(NGO leader, Mbeere district, 2008)

Whether a state broadcasts physical presence throughout its territory, exerts capacity to provide services, or governs with finesse all have implications for how citizens perceive their state. Such perceptions, specifically of the state's right to rule – its legitimacy – are the subject of the next two chapters. These examinations take a close look at what happens to the social contract between state and society when NGOs step between a government and its people to provide services.

What is legitimacy? *Legitimacy* is an expression of consent by the people to be governed, without reliance on coercion or bribes, and is therefore the lowest-cost method of gaining compliance (Etzioni 1965). It is also a means to evaluate authority, as people judge how fairly and morally authority is exercised (Sunshine and Taylor 2003). Legitimacy derives from acceptance by those in the organization's environment, who are informed by the rules, belief systems, values, and relational networks of the broader social context (Selznick 1949, Lister 2003).

The idea that NGOs could affect state legitimacy stems from the concept of the social contract between states and their populace, in which citizens willingly exchange freedoms for security and services. Post-colonial states, in particular, reacted against colonial governments' reliance on coercion to exploit subject populations and lands. Newly established states instead worked to govern legitimately by providing services and promising economic development (Jackson and Rosberg 1984a). Governments in Africa developed a paternal role, acting as caregiver, provider, and source of security to the citizen-children of the nation (Schatzberg 2001, 1).

As such, patron–client relationships became the norm. In the early twenty-first century, Africans continued to consider politicians legitimate when they were able to deliver services. In a 2011 nationwide survey in Kenya, for example, 95 percent of respondents said that an MP's "development record" affected their support, and 75 percent said that the MP's ability to "assist them with their needs" influenced their attitude toward that politician (National Democratic Institute and Institute for Development Studies 2011). In the same survey, 89 percent and 82 percent of respondents who believed their MP had "very badly" or "badly" addressed constituents' concerns said they would not vote for her/him in the 2012 elections. On the flip side, 57 percent and 86 percent of those rating MP performance as "good" or "very good" at responding to constituent needs said they would cast another vote for the MP (ibid.). The question therefore arises as to whether a government itself has to provide services for legitimacy to accrue to it, or whether other, nongovernmental actors can contribute to positive perceptions of the state.

This question is not particular to Kenya, nor indeed to Africa. Examining citizen–state interactions throughout the world, scholars have investigated the relationship between service provision and state legitimacy generally (McLoughlin 2015), and between NGO services and state legitimacy specifically, in numerous settings. The common understanding – not only in Kenya (Otiso 2003), but also in Afghanistan (Jelinek 2006), Uganda (Parkhurst 2005), Pakistan (Batley 2011), China, Taiwan, Vietnam (Heurlin 2010), and weak states throughout Africa (Bratton 1989b, 410; Waal 1997) and the world (Batley and McLoughlin 2010) – is that NGOs delivering public services deflect or threaten state legitimacy (McLoughlin 2011).

This chapter tests whether the legitimacy of the Kenyan state decreased in the face of NGO growth, comparing survey data from 1966, before the proliferation of NGOs, to replicated results in 2008, after NGO numbers surged. Both popular and scholarly opinion supports the idea that legitimacy in Kenya decreased during Moi's presidency. Only 34 percent of eligible voters participated in the 1997 presidential elections, a clear indicator of citizen disengagement. The Moi period, however, was a time when researchers were restricted in the types of questions they could ask about politics (Schatzberg 1986), and political survey research was not allowed. Surveys were reintroduced in the early 2000s after Moi volunteered to step down from the presidency and the country experienced an electoral change of party in office. Scholars noted high levels of support for government, but considered it a post-election "euphoria" (Wolf, Logan, and Owiti 2004; see also Branch and Cheeseman 2005). The elation had passed by 2008, when Kenya experienced violence that left more than 1,000 people killed and half a million displaced in the aftermath of the flawed 2007 elections.

Despite the violence, this chapter demonstrates that once changes in demographics are included in the analysis, legitimacy levels in the late 2000s were nearly identical to, if not higher than, those in the immediate post-independence era. The analysis then reveals that even in cases where state legitimacy decreased, NGOs were not a major factor affecting this decline. Endemic corruption and heightened insecurity, among other state-specific factors, had a stronger negative impact on citizens' perceptions of the government than did NGOs.

DATA ON NGOS AND CHANGING LEGITIMACY

Data presented in this chapter come from a 1966–1967 survey of secondary school students in Eastern Province (Prewitt 1971, 2010) and my own replication of that survey in late 2008.[1] In addition to an exact replication sample, I asked approximately half of the 2008 respondents

---

[1] Time series data would have been ideal for this project, but do not exist. The search for such data did yield some enlightening email exchanges with many scholars of Moi-era Kenya. The original survey was conducted as part of a larger project directed by political scientist and former US Census director Kenneth Prewitt (Prewitt 1971). Prewitt's original survey queried students throughout East Africa on issues of nationalism, state building, and socialization via schools. I replicated portions of the survey most closely related to issues of state legitimacy. Because of significantly altered demographic conditions in the past half-century, and because the original survey authors removed school names for confidentiality reasons, the schools visited in the late 1960s could not be replicated exactly. Instead, after consultation with Prewitt, now a Columbia University professor, I selected schools that matched the *type* of school selected in the 1960s. These schools were long-standing, well-established schools of good reputation – important because all secondary schools in Kenya in the early post-independence era would have had these characteristics. While Prewitt's full sample came from multiple grade levels across all of Kenya's provinces, I compare only his results from Eastern Province that correspond to today's Form Three students in that area. To meet requirements regarding the protection of human subjects, all respondents in my survey were aged 16 or older and were in their second-to-last year of secondary school.

questions that included new answer choices about NGOs. These modified questions allowed for a comparison over time that includes information about NGOs in the present time period. The 1966 data contained 144 responses from four schools; the 2008 data, 500 respondents from six schools.

Table 7.1 provides a description of each variable used in this chapter, and Table 7.2 provides descriptive statistics. Two dependent variables are used to measure different types of legitimacy: moral and procedural legitimacy. Moral legitimacy indicates a congruence between societal values, morals, and ethics, and approval of the state (Suchman 1995). Procedural legitimacy, on the other hand, relates to citizen willingness to voluntarily comply with the rules and laws of the state (Levi, Sacks, and Tyler 2009). Surveys measured the state's *moral legitimacy* using a question asking whether the respondent believed that the Government of Kenya usually knows what is best for most Kenyans. The measure of *procedural legitimacy* asked whether a person has the right to disobey laws they believe are immoral or wrong. These variables have become common measures of legitimacy in survey research, used in the World Values Survey (www.worldvaluessurvey.org), and Afrobarometer surveys (www.afrobarometer.org), among others (Gilley 2006a, 2006b). Both variables are used dichotomously such that a positive relationship corresponds to greater legitimacy.

The independent variable of interest in the first set of analyses in this chapter is change over time, which is measured using a dichotomous variable for the *year* of the survey. If legitimacy has decreased over time, results will reveal a significant negative correlation on this variable.

In the later analyses, several variables measure respondents' perceptions of or contact with NGOs. One variable queries whether respondents believe that *NGOs are needed* to improve the country, a measure of faith in NGOs. A similar variable for *faith in NGOs* examines whether respondents think that NGOs know what is best for most people. A priori, this variable best measures a respondent's view of NGOs, since it is identical to the question asked about the government as an indicator of moral legitimacy. A third variable measures an individual's reported *contact with NGOs*, and a fourth provides a straightforward measure of *trust in NGOs*. If positive views and interactions of citizens with NGOs undermine state legitimacy, coefficients will be significant and negative, all else constant.

Other factors are likely to affect a respondent's perception of the legitimacy of government. Whether or not a person trusts government leaders,

TABLE 7.1. *Variable description and measurement*

Variable	Survey prompt and measurement
Moral legitimacy	*The government usually knows what is best for most people.* 0 = disagree or strongly disagree; 1 = agree or strongly agree
Procedural legitimacy	*If someone believes a law is wrong or immoral, he has a right to disobey it.* 0 = agree or strongly agree. 1 = disagree or strongly disagree.
Year	Measure of change over time. 0 = 1966; 1 = 2008.
Corruption	*How much would you say you trust government leaders?* Measure of faith in government leaders and politicians. 1 = never; 2 = not always; 3 = sometimes; 4 = usually.
Insecurity	*How much would you say you trust the police?* Measure of faith in the police. 1 = never; 2 = not always; 3 = sometimes; 4 = usually.
Democracy	*Which sentence is more true about voting?* Measure of faith in democratic processes. 0 = Voting has very little effect on what government does; 1 = Voting is a good way to control government.
NGOs needed (in new replication)	*The people of Kenya cannot improve their country unless NGOs lead them and help them.* Measure of faith in NGOs. 1 = strongly disagree; 2 = disagree; 3 = agree; 4 = strongly agree.
Faith in NGOs (in new replication)	*NGOs usually know what is best for most people.* Measure of faith in NGOs. 1 = strongly disagree; 2 = disagree; 3 = agree; 4 = strongly agree.
Contact with NGOs (in new replication)	*Which statement best describes how much NGOs do for you and your family?* Measure of contact with NGOs. 1 = NGOs do not do much for my family; 2 = NGOs do some things for my family; 3 = NGOs do many things for my family.
Trust NGOs (in new replication)	*How much would you say you trust NGOs?* Measure of trust in NGOs. 1 = never; 2 = not always; 3 = sometimes; 4 = usually.

(*cont.*)

TABLE 7.1. *(cont.)*

Variable	Survey prompt and measurement
Gender	*Are you male or female?* 0 = Male 1 = Female
Age	*What is your age?* Ranges from "16" to "20 or older"
Urban/rural	*Where do your parents live now? (In a location; In a town or city)* Measure of urban vs. rural respondent; In 2008 data, it can also be a measure of insecurity, which is considerably higher in urban areas. 0 = rural; 1 = urban.
Father's education	*Did your father attend school? If so, what is the highest standard he attended?* Measure of family class, using father's education level. Ranges from 0 = primary education or less; 1 = secondary education and more.

TABLE 7.2. *Descriptive statistics of variables in regression analysis*

Variable	Observations	Mean	Standard deviation	Min.	Max.
Moral legitimacy (all)	643	0.48	0.50	0	1
Procedural legitimacy (all)	638	0.53	0.50	0	1
Moral legitimacy 2008	500	0.47	0.50	0	1
Procedural legitimacy 2008	495	0.48	0.50	0	1
Insecurity	642	2.02	0.77	1	4
Corruption	636	2.03	0.75	1	4
NGOs needed	265	2.39	1.09	1	4
Faith in NGOs	266	2.67	1.08	1	4
Contact with NGOs	263	1.81	0.67	1	3
Trust NGOs	264	2.29	0.76	1	4
Gender	644	0.47	0.50	0	1
Age	641	17.45	1.08	16	20
Urban/rural	637	0.39	0.49	0	1
Father's education	595	4.22	1.65	1	6
Democracy	632	0.82	0.38	0	1

a proxy measure for government *corruption*, should correlate with perceptions of legitimacy. Perceived *insecurity*, likewise, is measured using trust in the police, as the presence of trustworthy police heightens a sense of security. Since insecurity was higher in cities than in rural places in Kenya at the time of research, a variable for whether the student comes from an *urban or rural home* is also included. I expect insecurity to be negatively associated with state legitimacy.

Finally, the variable *democracy* measures whether the respondent believes in procedural democracy as a way to control government. This variable was important in 2008 because of the flawed – arguably stolen – general election of 2007. We would expect that respondents who believe that voting is a good way to control government would have more negative views of the legitimacy of the state shortly after a stolen election.

Because of changes in Kenyan demographics between the 1960s and the 2000s, the 2008 students tended to be younger and to have better-educated parents than their 1966 counterparts, and there were a greater proportion of females in the sample. Analyses therefore control for *gender*, *age*, and level of a respondent's *father's education* in all regression analyses.

A TWO-STEP PROCESS TO ASSESS NGOS AND LEGITIMACY

Because data on perceptions of NGOs in the 1960s do not exist, a two-step approach is needed to analyze the relationship between NGOs and changing perceptions of government legitimacy in Kenya. First, I compare legitimacy levels in 1960 to those in 2008. Here, the period before NGO proliferation serves as a baseline, and the 2008 data serve as a post-treatment measure, where NGOs are the treatment. Second, I examine whether reported perceptions of or contact with NGOs were associated with state legitimacy in 2008.

Legitimacy and change over time

Counter to the general perception, respondents' views of state legitimacy were not statistically different in 2008 than in 1966, according to t-tests of both moral and procedural legitimacy, and controlling for a variety of demographic factors. Logistic regression model results in Table 7.3 reveal that the passing of time (*year*) is not significantly correlated with measures of legitimacy when gender, age, and upbringing are taken into account. This finding holds for both measures of legitimacy, moral and procedural.

TABLE 7.3. *Impact of time on legitimacy in Kenya*

Variable	Model 1 Moral legitimacy	Model 2 Moral legitimacy	Model 3 Procedural legitimacy	Model 4 Procedural legitimacy
Year	0.0732	0.0468	−0.294	−0.252
	(0.281)	(0.279)	(0.288)	(0.281)
Gender	−0.0968	−0.0753	−0.446***	−0.502***
	(0.166)	(0.164)	(0.167)	(0.165)
Age	0.0965	0.0953	−0.0709	−0.0709
	(0.0944)	(0.0931)	(0.0964)	(0.0952)
Urban/rural	−0.304*	−0.381**	−0.00740	0.0111
	(0.183)	(0.180)	(0.183)	(0.181)
Father's education	−0.0352	−0.0107	−0.0939	−0.0993
	(0.243)	(0.240)	(0.242)	(0.236)
Democracy	0.660***		−0.339	
	(0.219)		(0.220)	
Constant	−2.149	−1.574	2.129	1.865
	(1.782)	(1.761)	(1.839)	(1.808)
Observations	621	633	616	628

Robust standard errors in parentheses where *p < 0.1; **p < 0.05; and ***p < 0.01.

Models 1 and 3 in Table 7.3 include a measure of a respondent's belief in procedural democracy as a way to restrain government.[2]

Predicted probabilities provide a substantive interpretation. In 1966, an average-aged female urban respondent who believed in the effectiveness of electoral democracy, and whose father had attended at least some secondary school, had a slightly lower than 1 in 2 chance of regarding the government as morally legitimate (predicted probability = 0.44). In 2008, a person with similar characteristics had a nearly identical predicted probability of granting the government legitimacy (0.46).

An examination of other variables of interest reveals that when all else is held constant, a 2008 urbanite's predicted probability of a positive view of government was 8 percent lower than that of her rural counterpart. Having a positive view of democratic procedures, however, increases the likelihood of a view of government moral legitimacy by 15 percent. The 1966 data reveals similar comparisons in predicted probability

---

[2] Changes to demographics over time were also tested by interacting these variables with the variable of interest, change in time. These interaction effects did not reveal significant information.

with respect to urban status and attitudes toward voting efficacy, where the respective changes in location and beliefs about electoral democracy were −0.07 and 0.15. These results support the commonly held notion that urban residents are more skeptical of government than are their rural counterparts.

As a test of robustness, Models 3 and 4 in Table 7.3 examine procedural legitimacy. Again, the results do not provide statistically significant indicators that legitimacy fell over time. The only significant independent variable in these models is *gender*. It appears, interestingly, that women are more likely to follow their own moral compass, rather than that set out by the laws of the government.

NGOs and legitimacy

Although the common perception that state legitimacy fell in Kenya following the growth of NGOs is not statistically evident in regression analysis, there is still the possibility that people with varying experiences and perceptions of NGOs likewise varied in their perception of state legitimacy. Data from the 2008 subsample of students who responded to survey prompts about NGOs allow us to address this question. Tables 7.4 and 7.5 show the results of logistic regression with robust standard errors using the same moral and procedural legitimacy measures and the same controls as above. In these models, I am also interested in the impacts of corruption and high insecurity, which are hypothesized to negatively affect perceptions of state legitimacy.

Table 7.4 reveals inconsistent and inconclusive results about perceptions of or experiences with NGOs and opinions about the government's moral legitimacy. Model 1 shows that respondents who agreed or strongly agreed with the statement that NGOs are needed to improve Kenya appear less likely to find the government legitimate, although this result is not statistically significant. Likewise, the more strongly respondents reported trusting NGOs, the less likely they were to find the government morally legitimate (Model 4). When asked a parallel question about NGOs, however, the opposite result emerges. People who agreed that NGOs know what is best for the country were more likely to also perceive the government as morally legitimate (Model 2). Receiving help from NGOs, a measure of contact with the organizations, appears to be associated with greater likelihood of finding the government to be legitimate, but, again, was not statistically significant (Model 3).

TABLE 7.4. *Relationship between NGOs and moral legitimacy in Kenya*

Variables	Model 1 Moral legitimacy	Model 2 Moral legitimacy	Model 3 Moral legitimacy	Model 4 Moral legitimacy
Corruption	0.735***	0.838***	0.767***	0.824***
	(0.244)	(0.278)	(0.248)	(0.249)
Insecurity	0.192	0.102	0.163	0.348
	(0.232)	(0.242)	(0.236)	(0.245)
Gender	−0.161	−0.0867	−0.141	−0.303
	(0.269)	(0.273)	(0.270)	(0.276)
Age	0.00717	−0.0166	0.0238	−0.0564
	(0.160)	(0.165)	(0.160)	(0.161)
Urban/rural	−0.476*	−0.441	−0.457	−0.446
	(0.279)	(0.287)	(0.281)	(0.281)
Father's education	0.280	0.275	0.241	0.168
	(0.412)	(0.435)	(0.408)	(0.392)
Democracy	0.0368	−0.192	−0.0579	0.00284
	(0.351)	(0.369)	(0.348)	(0.342)
NGOs needed	−0.0351			
	(0.119)			
Faith in NGOs		0.528***		
		(0.136)		
Contact with NGOs			0.170	
			(0.208)	
Trust NGOs				−0.547***
				(0.197)
Constant	−1.751	−2.718	−2.344	0.246
	(2.875)	(3.027)	(2.889)	(2.931)
Observations	255	256	253	256

Robust standard errors in parentheses where * $p < 0.1$; ** $p < 0.05$; and *** $p < 0.01$.

Assessing procedural legitimacy in Table 7.5 shows a clear lack of a statistically significant relationship between beliefs related to the government's procedural legitimacy and respondents' views of, or contact with, NGOs. Regardless of the measure used, the NGO variables are never significant. The signs on the variables again suggest an inconsistent relationship. Combined with the models in Table 7.4, these results suggest that NGOs do not affect government legitimacy.

Using predicted probabilities to interpret the coefficients in Table 7.4 reveals that the average female respondent had about a 2 in 5 probability

TABLE 7.5. *Relationship between NGOs and procedural legitimacy in Kenya*

Variables	Model 5 Procedural legitimacy	Model 6 Procedural legitimacy	Model 7 Procedural legitimacy	Model 8 Procedural legitimacy
Corruption	−0.0692	−0.0546	−0.0357	−0.0486
	(0.214)	(0.210)	(0.211)	(0.211)
Insecurity	0.114	0.120	0.0768	0.109
	(0.224)	(0.224)	(0.224)	(0.227)
Gender	−0.451*	−0.486*	−0.458*	−0.480*
	(0.270)	(0.270)	(0.270)	(0.274)
Age	−0.240	−0.246	−0.227	−0.251
	(0.167)	(0.165)	(0.164)	(0.165)
Urban/rural	0.293	0.272	0.309	0.288
	(0.265)	(0.265)	(0.266)	(0.265)
Father's education	−0.676*	−0.706*	−0.683*	−0.699*
	(0.392)	(0.392)	(0.391)	(0.390)
Democracy	−0.807**	−0.812**	−0.864**	−0.838**
	(0.374)	(0.369)	(0.364)	(0.364)
NGOs needed	−0.190			
	(0.121)			
Faith in NGOs		−0.0921		
		(0.125)		
Contact with NGOs			0.0981	
			(0.196)	
Trust NGOs				−0.0251
				(0.185)
Constant	5.914*	5.849**	5.122*	5.759*
	(3.021)	(2.984)	(2.971)	(3.008)
Observations	254	255	252	255

Robust standard errors in parentheses where * $p < 0.1$; ** $p < 0.05$; and *** $p < 0.01$.

of perceiving the government to be morally legitimate (pp = 0.42). Table 7.6 shows that if an equally average person responded that NGOs always know what is best for Kenya (Model 2), the predicted probability rose to 0.59, or about a 3 in 5 chance. If she responded that NGOs never know what is best for Kenya, however, the same type of respondent would have only a 1 in 4 likelihood of a positive perception of government legitimacy.

TABLE 7.6. *Changes in predicted probabilities for variables in Table 7.4*

Model number	Variable	Range of change	Predicted probability of finding the government legitimate at bottom of range	Predicted probability of finding the government legitimate at top of range	Change in the predicted probability of finding the government legitimate
2	"NGOs know best" for Kenya	From 1 = strong disagree to 4 = strongly agree	0.24	0.59	0.35***
2	Corruption	From 1 = never to 4 = usually	0.27	0.80	0.53***
4	Trust in NGOs	From 1 = never to 4 = usually	0.87	0.59	−0.28***
4	Corruption	From 1 = never to 4 = usually	0.25	0.88	0.63***

* $p < 0.1$; ** $p < 0.05$; and *** $p < 0.01$.

Model 4 in Table 7.4 reveals that a respondent who reported trusting NGOs is likely to have a lower perception of the government's procedural legitimacy that someone who does not trust NGOs.

It is important to note, however, that the effect of trusting NGOs is smaller than the effect of believing the government to be corrupt. Across the models on moral legitimacy, corruption is the main driver lowering legitimacy. Examining predicted probabilities for Model 2 in Table 7.4 reveals that the otherwise average female respondent who reported never trusting government leaders (likely due to perceptions of corruption) had only about a 1 in 4 probability of finding the government legitimate in general. The otherwise average female respondent who always trusts government leaders, on the other hand, had a 4 in 5 likelihood of finding the government legitimate in 2008. These results accord with a priori expectations that trust in government leaders reflects a respondent's belief in government legitimacy generally. Similarly, belief that a government is corrupt is a strong driver of generally negative views of government legitimacy. Interpreting results in Model 4 of Table 7.4 using predicted probability reveals a similar finding about the effects of corruption. Even where NGOs decrease respondents' views of legitimacy, it is views on government leaders and their levels of corruption that are the main drivers of legitimacy in Kenya.

Other factors have a more consistently significant relationship with a respondent's attitude toward abiding by the law, or procedural legitimacy, as shown in Table 7.5. In general, all else held constant, female respondents were more likely to support disobeying laws on moral grounds than male respondents, as were those whose fathers completed at least some secondary school, and those who believe that voting is a good way to control government.

Interpreting the log-odds of Model 6 in Table 7.5 using predicted probabilities reveals that, again, setting age, views on NGOs, government leaders, and the police at their mean, with each other independent variable set at 1 (positive response), then the predicted probability that a person thinks the government is legitimate is 0.44, or again about a 1 in 2 likelihood. Being female in this instance lowers the predicted probability of a positive view of procedural legitimacy by 0.12; having more highly educated parents lowers the probability by 0.17; believing in electoral democracy drops the probability by 0.19. These variables not only have a greater impact on views of procedural legitimacy, they are also consistently significant statistically.

IMPLICATIONS OF THE RESULTS FOR STATE LEGITIMACY

What wisdom do these results impart? They provide key additions to the literature on state legitimacy in developing countries, especially post-colonial states. First, comparing data from the immediate post-independence period and from 2008 reveals that reported legitimacy has not statistically decreased over time in Kenya, even when controlling for a number of demographic factors. Unexpectedly, young people in this sample in 2008 were either as or more optimistic than had been the case among students in the late 1960s. While it is possible, and even probable, that legitimacy decreased during the Moi administration (1978–2002), in 2008 students' views were similar to those expressed forty years earlier.

One way to interpret these findings is to dismiss the respondents in both time periods as secondary school students, who tend to be relatively optimistic about the future. Yet only about half of the students responded favorably to questions about the government's moral or procedural legitimacy in either time period, suggesting a healthy level of critical thinking. Results from a second original survey conducted in 2008 among Kenyan adults, moreover, reveals similar findings. As is detailed in Chapter 8, contact with or appreciation for NGOs does not induce a person to find the government illegitimate; if anything, the opposite is true.

Recall also the electoral violence that occurred approximately ten months before the surveys were conducted in 2008. One would expect perceived state legitimacy to fall after a crisis in which many people died or were displaced, meaning that in more normal times, survey responses would likely have been even more positive. Apparently, hope springs eternal.

Second, looking at the relationship between respondents' views on NGOs and those on government legitimacy shows that it was likely not NGOs, but a variety of other factors that drove 2008 levels of voluntary compliance with government. Contrary to concerns, ordinary people were *not* "ceasing to regard the state as their own . . . and refusing to comply with official injunctions" under the influence of NGOs (Bratton 1989b).

Instead, the data in this chapter clearly suggest that the main drivers of low legitimacy perceptions, where they existed, were corruption and socio-economic background as expressed in higher parental education levels, urban upbringing, and female gender. It should not come as a surprise that people who distrusted their leaders were not likely to find the government and its procedures to be legitimate. And where people were more urban, the same holds true, as the insecurity Kenyans felt in urban settings reflected poorly on the government. In this way, the data from Kenya tell a modernization story – people who were more urban and better educated tended to be more critical of government. This critique could be indicative of greater awareness of and responsiveness toward the government and its actions.

CONCLUSIONS

This chapter is the first of two chapters that use original survey data to assess the relationship between NGOs and state legitimacy. The analysis reveals that, counter to popular perception, state legitimacy in Kenya was not lower in the late 2000s than it was in the late 1960s, at least not among secondary students. Moreover, secondary students in 2008 with exposure to or positive impressions of NGOs were no more likely to find the government illegitimate than those without such exposure. These findings are confirmed by data from a second original survey of adults conducted in Kenya, the subject of Chapter 8. The final sections of that chapter provide lessons from both analyses pertinent to state development.

8

NGOs

Increase state legitimacy or undermine popular support?

"The problem actually is when NGOs are not there. The wananchi don't care that government is not there when NGOs are there. As long as one is there, all is okay. But if none are there, then they get angry at government."

(Civil servant, Machakos district, 2008)

"The common people end up thankful to government for allowing the NGOs to operate there."

(NGO Leader, Machakos district, 2008)

"People are just happy that something is done that wasn't there before."

(NGO leader, Mbeere district, 2008)

In this chapter I conclude the question of legitimacy begun in Chapter 7. At least since Tocqueville (1835) examined the role of civil society in the US, governments and scholars have been concerned that nongovernmental provision of services can threaten government authority. Many scholars have made the argument that organizations that become very independent from government can compete with it for loyalty when they perform otherwise public functions (Whittington 1998, Jelinek 2006, Heurlin 2010). When NGOs take away "what the state does best" – service provision (Whaites 1998, 346) – NGOs can erode the social contract (Schuller 2009). According to some scholars, NGOs can even use donor resources deliberately to compete with government for legitimacy (Obiyan 2005, 82). They intentionally sway legitimacy by publically opposing politicians and their credentials, or drawing attention to their mistakes (Sandberg 1994, 11).

Even when unintended, NGOs' participatory approach mobilizes people, encourages increased information sharing, fosters alternative political ideas, and empowers the disadvantaged, all of which can threaten extant political authority, power and order (Bratton 1989a, Fowler 1991, Boulding and Gibson 2009 citing Putnam 1993 and Putnam 2000, Martin 2004). In all, as Fowler writes, "Of the five imperatives that are a constant source of political concern to African governments, legitimacy is potentially the one most susceptible to NGO expansion" (1991, 78).

Developing country governments often feel their authority threatened by NGOs, given their relative newness as states, the artificiality of many of their borders, and their history of fighting colonial powers through civil society organizations (Fowler 1991, 58). Even where high-performing NGOs provide a net benefit vis-à-vis service provision, politicians sometimes see NGOs' greater capacity as "embarrassing" for the state (Guber 2002, 141) or as a visible criticism of state shortcomings (Farrington, Bebbington, et al. 1993, 50). This tension is especially evident where governments are weak, lack confidence in their control of the country, and are nondemocratic or not accountable (Bratton 1989a, 576). Post-conflict settings can exacerbate governmental perceptions of competition from NGOs: donors often favor NGOs for service provision, which can lead to low levels of capacity within local governments, unsustainable facilities, and insufficient upward and downward accountability among service providers (Batley and McLoughlin 2010, 132). These trends are reinforced by NGO workers often forming a large part of their country's educated middle class, meaning they have access to the resources with which to challenge state authority (Obiyan 2005, 81).

The implied assumption here is that citizens in developing countries make comparisons between NGOs and the government, such that NGOs' work reflects poorly on the government. Using an original survey of Kenyan adults, this chapter reveals that this assumption does not always hold. The analysis first demonstrates that, in Kenya at the beginning of the twenty-first century, NGOs were generally regarded favorably – often more so than their government counterparts. However, the analysis also reveals that contact with and appreciation for NGOs did not translate into more negative perceptions of government. In Kenya, there was little evidence of NGOs replacing the government as the new legitimate authority. Indeed, NGO presence either bolstered the way people saw their state, or appeared to have little effect.[1] Nevertheless, although NGOs appear not to have had a major impact on legitimacy *in general*, there was evidence

---

[1] Blattman (2009) also finds that NGOs do not affect political participation levels among ex-combatants in northern Uganda.

of a significant difference in responses from urban versus rural dwellers, and from more- versus less-educated individuals. These findings indicate that those sounding the alarm that NGOs are overwhelming weak state legitimacy may not only be crying wolf, but may actually be undercutting a potential ally in state development.

This finding runs counter to most expectations, highlighting the importance of investigating the mechanisms at work. This chapter reveals that the primary reason government legitimacy did not decrease in the face of NGO service provision is that the people of Kenya had exceedingly low expectations of their government. Most Kenyans failed to make the link between NGO provision and the government not fulfilling its end of the social contract because they understood and even accepted the limitations of their government. In some cases, Kenyans were even more likely to expect goods and services from NGOs than from the government. Analysis of interview data suggests several less prominent mechanisms as well: government actors successfully took credit for NGO work or for facilitating its occurrence, Kenyans sometimes mistook NGOs for government organizations, and some scholars made incorrect assumptions about the sources of state legitimacy in Africa. These trends are also discussed in this chapter.

THE DATA: SURVEY INSTRUMENT AND INTERVIEWS

This chapter draws on data from an original survey of 501 individuals taken at the household level in Machakos, Mbeere, and Nairobi districts in August and September of 2008.[2] Random representative samples of 150 respondents were taken in two full districts, Mbeere and Machakos, and samples of about 100 individuals were conducted in two urban settings, Nairobi and Machakos Town.[3] Survey responses are supplemented

---

[2] The Steadman Group (later Ipsos) translated the survey into three local languages (Swahili, Kamba, and Kimbeere), administered it and converted the data to digital format using high-speed scanners (15 percent of which were rescanned and 10 percent of which were checked manually for quality control purposes). Respondents were told that the survey was conducted for a researcher at the University of California, and trained enumerators were adult Kenyans who spoke in the preferred language of the respondent.

[3] Sampling was done in clusters of ten or fewer individuals in proportion to the population of each location or sublocation according to the most recent government census. In Mbeere, sampling took place in twenty-three locations representing the entire district. In Machakos, sampling was done in twenty-five locations. Neighborhoods were carefully selected for being long-standing communities inhabited largely by educated and formal-sector employed – but not wealthy or "elite" – Kenyans. For the most part, they

by data from in-depth one-on-one interviews with Kenyans, NGO workers, civil servants, and politicians. Respondents explained the mechanisms by which NGOs and legitimacy are related.

Because the survey was conducted in late 2008, less than a year after post-election violence in the country, I selected whole-district case studies where there had been little or no violence, deliberately controlling for ethnic conflict. The sample used is therefore not ethnically representative of the country as a whole, a clear limitation of the data. Nevertheless, although the responses are numerically biased toward ethnicities living in Eastern Province, many responses did not vary significantly by ethnicity. Descriptively, for example, a smaller percentage of ethnic Luo selected to describe Kenya as "not a democracy" (4 percent) or "a democracy with major problems" (37 percent) than the whole-sample averages, a question on which we would expect there to be a difference in the opposite direction. Statistically, when ethnicity variables are included in regression models, they are never significant. Follow-up interviews conducted in Western, Rift, and Nyanza provinces in 2012 suggest that the role of NGOs does not vary among different ethnic groups. This evidence conforms to the findings of Dietrich (2013): donors deliver aid via NGOs in order to avoid political capture. In Kenya, such capture generally occurs along ethnic lines to maintain patronage relationships (Briggs 2014, Jablonski 2014). That said, one NGO leader interviewed said that government ministers sometimes also deliver services via NGOs in order to ignore party politics (2006–2).

Table 8.1 provides a definition of each variable used in this chapter and Table 8.2 provides descriptive statistics. Moral and procedural legitimacy are each operationalized in several ways. As defined in Chapter 7, moral legitimacy indicates congruence between an individual's societal values, morals, and ethics, and approval of the state. Procedural legitimacy, on the other hand, relates to citizen willingness to voluntarily comply with the rules and laws of the state. On the former, individuals reported the extent to which they *agreed with government* values, responding to the prompts, "What the Government believes is good for Kenya is what I think is good for Kenya" and "The Government of Kenya *shares my values* and does the right thing." This language allowed respondents to

were neighborhoods where one would expect civil servants and their families to live and included Umoja I, Mbotela, Buru Buru, Bahati, Maringo, Ofafa Jericho, Uhuru, Kayole, Makadara, and Donholm. In Machakos Town (population 150,000), sampling was done in Bondeni, Katoloni, Kariobangi, Kenya Israel, College, Mjini, Miwani, Muthini, Eastleigh, and Majengo II.

TABLE 8.1. *Variable descriptions and measurement*

Variable	Survey prompt and measurement
Moral legitimacy: government shares my values	*The Government of Kenya, in general, shares my values and does the right thing.* 1 = disagree; 2 = neutral; 3 = agree.
Moral legitimacy: agreement with government	*What the Government believes is good for Kenya is the same as what I think is good for Kenya.* 1 = disagree; 2 = neutral; 3 = agree.
Procedural legitimacy: laws	*The laws of Kenya express the values and morals of people in this country.* 1 = disagree; 2 = neutral; 3 = agree.
Procedural legitimacy: police	*The police always have the right to make people obey the law.* 1 = disagree; 2 = neutral; 3 = agree.
Legitimacy: organizations have interest of people in mind	*To what extent do these organizations have the interests of the people in mind?* 1 = never; 2 = not always; 3 = sometimes; 4 = usually.
Legitimacy: trust institutions	*How much confidence do you have in the following organizations or institutions?* 1 = none at all; 2 = not much; 3 = quite a lot; 4 = a great deal.
Contact with an NGO	*In the past year, how many times have you gone to an NGO seeking training, information, a service or for a physical good?* 0 = Never; 1 = Once or more.
Education	*What is the highest level of formal schooling that you finished?* Ranges from 1 = No formal education to 8 = Finished university.
Class	Index measuring living standards based on respondent's answers to 22 prompts. This index is based on the Living Standards Measurement Survey (LSMS) developed in the early 1980s in the World Bank, which has been used in more than 70 countries (http://go.worldbank.org/WKOXNZV3X0). Ranges from 1 (extremely low) to 17 (extremely high).
Gender	*Respondent Gender?* 0 = Male 1 = Female.
Age	*What is your age?* Ranges from "16" to "20 or older."

(cont.)

TABLE 8.1. (cont.)

Variable	Survey prompt and measurement
Urban/rural	*Setting* 0 = Rural; 1 = Urban.
Protest	*In the past one year, have you attended a demonstration or protest march?* 0 = No; 1 = Yes.
Raised issue with government	*In the past one year, have you ever gotten together with others to raise an issue with a local politician or administrator?* 0 = No; 1 = Yes.
Views on the economy	*In general, how would you describe the present economic conditions of this country?* Scale from 1 = Very Bad to 5 = Very Good, with 3 being neutral.

comment on the state broadly, rather than on a particular regime, individual, or office. Respondents also assessed the extent to which they believed that different types of organizations have the *interests of the people in mind*, and the amount of *confidence* they had in various institutions. Indicators of procedural legitimacy ask whether the *laws* of Kenya express the values and moral of the people of the country, and whether or not the *police* always have the right to make people obey the law.

The key independent variable of interest in the analyses is *contact with NGOs*. Respondents reported whether or not they actively sought out or visited an NGO for training, information, goods, or services in the past year. Proactive NGO seekers are, in principle, more likely than others both to transfer legitimacy to NGOs and also to already be irritated by the government's underprovision of services.[4] Respondents who reported having visited an NGO would therefore be expected to find the government less legitimate than those who have not done so.

A wide variety of control variables are included in the analyses, some of which might be expected to be associated with higher or lower levels of perceived government legitimacy. Controls include continuous variables measuring *age*, *education* level, socio-economic *class*, and *views on the*

---

[4] Other possible survey questions asked respondents whether they thought there were many or few NGOs working in their area, and whether they had been approached by an NGO for services or goods in the past year. The nonresponse rates on these questions were much higher (12 percent and 6 percent respectively versus less than one percent) than the question about visiting an NGO, with similar results.

TABLE 8.2. *Descriptive statistics for variables in regression analysis*

Variable	Obs.	Mean	Std. Dev.	Min.	Max.
Urban areas					
Moral legitimacy: government shares my values	200	2.44	0.82	1	3
Moral legitimacy: agreement with government	200	2.30	0.89	1	3
Procedural legitimacy: laws	196	2.51	0.80	1	3
Procedural legitimacy: police	197	2.64	0.70	1	3
Contact with an NGO	200	0.25	0.43	0	1
Age	200	31.46	11.67	18	78
Education	198	5.27	1.41	2	8
Gender	201	0.45	0.50	0	1
Class	201	6.18	4.34	1	16
Protest	199	0.09	0.29	0	1
Raised issues with government	199	0.16	0.36	0	1
Views on the economy	193	1.98	1.13	1	5
Rural districts					
Moral legitimacy: government shares my values	299	2.44	0.82	1	3
Moral legitimacy: agreement with government	298	2.28	0.85	1	3
Procedural legitimacy: laws	298	2.56	0.75	1	3
Procedural legitimacy: police	297	2.77	0.58	1	3
Contact with an NGO	298	0.24	0.43	0	1
Age	300	35.28	13.79	18	85
Education	300	3.81	1.60	1	8
Gender	300	0.62	0.49	0	1
Class	300	1.88	1.97	1	12
Protest	300	0.14	0.34	0	1
Raised issues with government	300	0.30	0.46	0	1
Views on the economy	297	1.88	1.09	1	4

economy of Kenya at the time of the survey, as well as dummy variables for *gender* and *urban or rural* setting (in the full district sample only).[5] The variables regarding *protest* and *raising an issue with a government* official gauge the respondents' civic activity level, using their history of

---

[5] In analyses not presented in the tables in this chapter for the sake of parsimony, a number of ethnicity variables are also used as controls. Specifically, these were dummy variables for each ethnic group with ten or more respondents: Luo, Luhya, Kisii, Kikuyu, Kamba, Mbeere, and Embu. One might expect responses to vary among these ethnicities. In no model were they significant, nor did they significantly change the coefficients on other variables included.

TABLE 8.3. *Survey responses to organizational legitimacy questions*

	Government of Kenya	NGOs
Organization "shares my values and does the right thing"		
Strongly agree (%)	7.4	5.2
Agree (%)	57.3	52.7
Neither agree nor disagree (%)	13.8	17.6
Disagree (%)	18.4	10.4
Strongly disagree (%)	2.8	2.2
DK (%)	0.4	12.0
What organization "believes is good for Kenya is what I think is good for Kenya"		
Strongly agree (%)	8.0	5.6
Agree (%)	47.9	50.3
Neither agree nor disagree (%)	16.4	14.8
Disagree (%)	22.6	11.8
Strongly disagree (%)	4.6	4.2
DK (%)	0.6	13.4

attendance at protests or demonstrations and whether they are generally the type of individual who raises issues with government administrators or politicians.

NGOS VERSUS GOVERNMENT LEGITIMACY

Survey results reveal that at the start of the twenty-first century, Kenyans tended to think very highly of NGOs – often more positively than they thought of the government. NGOs in Kenya were considered legitimate organizations and were accorded respect and appreciation by most respondents. As one said, "People are just happy with NGOs" (2008–32). For example, when respondents were asked questions regarding the moral legitimacy of NGOs, nearly 60 percent responded affirmatively, while only about 15 percent responded negatively (the rest were neutral or didn't know; see Table 8.3). Specifically, respondents were asked to what extent they agreed or disagreed with the statements, "NGOs in general share my values and do the right thing," and, "What NGOs believe is good for Kenya is the same as what I think is good for Kenya."

Afrobarometer survey data from the same year confirm this result. The survey, which collected data from a representative sample of the entire country, asked respondents how much international NGOs and donors help the country. Fewer than 4 percent of Kenyan responded negatively, while just under 75 percent said they help a little bit, somewhat, or a lot

(Bratton, Gyimah-Boadi, and Mattes 2008).[6] Similar to results presented in this chapter, Afrobarometer found little variation in the level of negative views of international NGOs and donors, comparing across ethnic groups.[7]

Such responses are not particular to Kenya. In a survey of individuals in the Kyrgyz Republic, researchers found that more than half of the population felt positively about NGOs (Pugachev nd). Likewise, in Afghanistan, Jelinek found considerable support for NGOs – one of his respondents reported, "we have a very good perception of NGOs, and why not? Most of the work done in our village has been done by NGOs" (Jelinek 2006, 15). Not all parts of the world have such positive feelings about NGOs, however. In a study of the Balkan states of Serbia, Bosnia and Herzegovina, and Macedonia, for example, views were mixed. Skepticism of NGOs (particularly in Serbia) sat alongside recognition of their contribution to society, as well as a general desire to join local NGOs (Grodeland 2006).

In Kenya, thoughts on NGOs were either more favorable or broadly comparable to those held about the government (Table 8.3). When asked questions about government, 65 percent of respondents agreed that the Government of Kenya shares their values, while 56 percent felt that what the Government of Kenya believes is good for Kenya is the same as what they believe is good for Kenya. More people had negative views of government than they did of NGOs, however; 21 and 27 percent of respondents disagreed or strongly disagreed with the statements respectively.

Respondents were also asked, "To what extent do you think that Kenya-based or internationally-based NGOs have the interests of the people in mind?" As shown in Figure 8.1, just less than 65 percent of total respondents thought that Kenya-based NGOs "sometimes or usually" have the interests of the people in mind, while a full 75 percent of people felt this way about international NGOs.[8] As one informed observer said, "The common man likes NGOs ten times government! Go ask anyone on the street" (2006–6). When asked whether Kenyan politicians or civil servants have the interests of the people in mind, only 33 and 53 percent of Kenyans respectively responded "sometimes" or "usually." Considerably

---

[6] The remaining 23 percent responded that they did not know. Unfortunately, the question does not allow respondents to distinguish between NGOs and donors.

[7] Looking at groups with over 35 respondents, only the Somali have more than 3 percent of respondents answering negatively, with 12.5 percent negative responses.

[8] Respondents were given the options "Never," "Rarely," "Sometimes," and "Usually" have the interests of the people in mind.

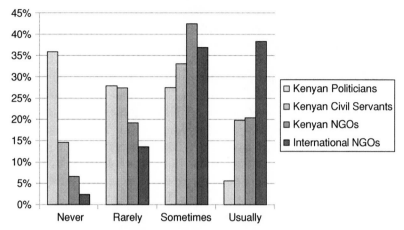

FIGURE 8.1. To what extent do various organizations have the interests of the people in mind?

fewer Kenyans thought that government officials had their interests in mind than thought NGOs did.

Figure 8.1 reveals that Kenyans were most likely to say that Kenyan politicians never – and international NGOs always – have the interests of the people in mind. Kenyans tended to have less strong opinions about civil servants and Kenyan-based NGOs.

Finally, respondents were asked how much confidence they had in various governmental and nongovernmental organizations and institutions, ranging from individuals like the president to organizations like the police to Kenyan-based NGOs. "Government of Kenya" rated very highly as an aggregated category; nearly 74 percent of respondents gave it a positive assessment. NGOs, particularly internationally based organizations, held the confidence of 69 percent of respondents. Arguably, the aggregate government category rated so highly because Kenya – and Africa generally – has highly personalistic political systems, leading to a tendency among citizens to associate the state with the person of the president. Nearly 81 percent of respondents said they had a great deal or quite a lot of confidence in president Kibaki.[9] Confidence levels in organizations like

---

[9] This is a remarkably high percentage, given that Kibaki was widely thought to have stolen the presidential election that took place less than a year before the survey was conducted. Some of this incongruence can be explained by the fact that there was little electoral violence in the areas where the survey was conducted, and most Kamba and Mbeere, the largest ethnic group living in Machakos and Mbeere respectively, tended to support Kikuyu politicians like Kibaki. Moreover, Kibaki's vice president at the time came from the Kamba group.

TABLE 8.4. *Respondent confidence in various organizations*

	Generally positive* (%)	A great deal (%)	Quite a lot (%)	Not very much (%)	None at all (%)	N/A
How much confidence do you have in the following organizations or institutions?						
President	80.8	37.1	43.7	16.8	2.2	0.2
Government of Kenya	73.7	30.1	43.5	22.0	4.0	0.4
International NGOs	68.5	25.0	43.5	19.4	6.2	6.0
Prime Minister	62.1	23.6	38.5	27.2	10.6	0.2
Parliament	61.3	19.4	41.9	31.4	5.8	1.6
Kenyan NGOs	58.7	21.4	37.3	26.4	8.4	6.6
Civil Service	58.1	16.4	41.7	37.1	4.2	0.6
Police	53.7	13.4	40.3	33.5	12.0	0.8

* "Generally positive" figures sum the responses of "A great deal" and "Quite a lot."

Parliament, the civil service and the police were lower, at 61, 58, and 54 percent confidence respectively.

It is worth noting that nearly all of the survey responses presented here were much more positive than were expected a priori for a survey of Kenyans. Afrobarometer researchers in 2003 and again in 2008 (Wolf, Logan, and Owiti 2004; Bratton, Gyimah-Boadi, and Mattes 2008) report very similar "euphoria" among their respondents. For example, my original survey data results indicate that 71 percent agreed or strongly agreed with the procedural legitimacy statement about laws. In a representative sample of the whole country done in the same year by Afrobarometer, respondents reported whether they agreed or disagreed with the statement, "The courts have the right to make decisions that people always have to abide by." In the survey 65 percent of respondents agreed or strongly agreed (Bratton, Gyimah-Boadi, and Mattes 2008). This tendency toward very positive answers accords with the findings on government legitimacy reported in the previous chapter, which were gathered in a separate survey.

NGOS DO NOT NEGATIVELY IMPACT STATE LEGITIMACY

Moral legitimacy

The evidence presented above indicates that Kenyans thought highly of NGOs in the early twenty-first century. Ordered logistic regression results displayed in Table 8.5, however, reveal no statistically significant relationship between perceptions of government and contact with NGOs. These results are valid to a wide variety of model specifications. There does

TABLE 8.5. *Effect of NGOs on moral legitimacy of government*

Variables	Full rural districts	Urban areas
	The govt shares my values and does the right thing	The govt shares my values and does the right thing
Contact with an NGO	0.03	0.13
	(0.30)	(0.37)
Education	−0.05	0.38***
	(0.10)	(0.14)
Class	−0.17**	−0.03
	(0.07)	(0.04)
Gender	0.38	0.54*
	(0.28)	(0.33)
Age	0.01	0.00
	(0.01)	(0.01)
Urban/rural	2.08*	
	(1.11)	
Protest	0.74	−0.97*
	(0.47)	(0.59)
Raised issue with govt	0.02	1.84***
	(0.32)	(0.61)
Views on economy	0.24**	0.19
	(0.12)	(0.15)
Cut Point 1	−0.74	1.27
	(0.66)	(0.92)
Cut Point 2	0.01	2.00**
	(0.66)	(0.93)
Observations	294	188

Coefficients are log-odds. *** $p < 0.01$, ** $p < 0.05$, * $p < 0.1$.

not appear to be a "transfer" of legitimacy from government agencies to NGOs; Kenyans who held NGOs in high esteem did not view government less favorably. If anything, having visited an NGO in the year prior to the survey raised a respondent's view of the government very slightly. This result holds whether one examines rural or urban Kenyan populations, and for both moral and procedural legitimacy.

To validate the robustness of the results above, the models of Table 8.5 were run with an alternate measure of government legitimacy. Respondents were asked whether they believed that their government held the same values as they did. Results revealed the same variables were significant with the signs pointing the same direction, in both urban and rural areas. Having sought services or resources from an NGO in the year prior to the survey remained insignificant, and was positive with respect to views of government legitimacy, in all models.

Using the results of Table 8.5, predicted probability analysis (which helps to interpret the results of logistic regression) reveals, moreover, that a politically active, rural man of average age, education, class, and views on the economy who sought assistance from an NGO was no more likely to view the government as legitimate than one who had not sought out an NGO. His probability increases a mere 0.005 in the full rural districts subsample, and 0.01 among residents of Nairobi and Machakos Town.

Table 8.6 displays predicted probabilities for an average Kenyan male in the two subsamples, noting the important statistically significant variables in the results of Table 8.5.[10] These results clearly indicate that the average Kenyan felt the government to be legitimate, a finding that corresponds to the results in Chapter 7.

Within the full rural district subsamples, a respondent's social class and his views on the economy correlated with his perceptions of government legitimacy. Specifically, the wealthiest respondents had only about a 1 in 5 probability of finding the government legitimate, while the poorest – the vast majority of people in these districts – had a 3 in 4 likelihood.[11] The wealthier a rural individual was, the more likely he was to view the government negatively. The same is true for those who had negative views about the economy. The relationship between social class and legitimacy in the full-district rural subsample can be seen clearly in Figure 8.2. The dark gray area represents the predicted probability of finding the government legitimate over the range of economic classes.

Turning to the urban subsample results of Table 8.5, different variables are correlated with government legitimacy than in rural districts, but the NGO variable of interest remains insignificant. In urban areas, education, gender, and prior political involvement had a significant relationship with perceived government legitimacy.[12] Table 8.6 thus reveals that holding all other variables at the average, an urbanite with the lowest possible level of education was far less likely to find the government legitimate

---

[10] Note, however, that in this sample of 300, only 10 respondents or 3.3 per cent are coded as living in urban areas.

[11] Results were consistent using different measures of economic status, such as the type of housing and the respondents' access to television.

[12] Analysis revealed similar findings using different measures of political participation and inclinations, including being registered to vote, level of disappointment with the 2007 elections, and having voted in the 2002 and 2007 elections.

TABLE 8.6. *Predicted effects of variables on moral legitimacy of government*

Variable	Range of change	Predicted probability of finding the government legitimate at bottom of range	Predicted probability of finding the government legitimate at top of range	Change in the predicted probability of finding the government legitimate
Full rural districts subsample				
Social class	Full range (from 0 to 17)	0.76	0.22	−0.54**
Views on economy	From negative to positive view of the economy (1 to 5)	0.69	0.84	0.15**
Urban areas subsample				
Education	Full range (from 1 to 7)	0.38	0.83	0.45**
Gender	From male to female (0 to 1)	0.81	0.89	0.08*
Raising an Issue with politician or administrator	From no to yes (0 to 1)	0.48	0.88	0.40***
Raising an issue with politician or administrator	From no to yes (0 to 1)	0.48	0.88	0.40***
Protesting	From have never protested to have protested (0 to 1)	0.93	0.79	−0.14*

*** $p < 0.01$, ** $p < 0.05$, * $p < 0.1$.

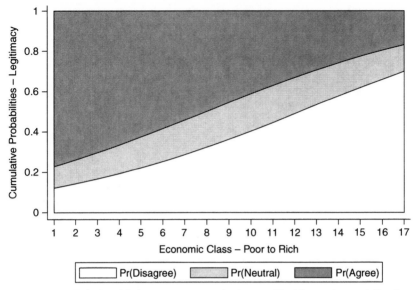

FIGURE 8.2. Relationship between economic class and legitimacy in rural districts

than one with the highest level of education. The predicted probability changes from 0.38 to 0.83 across the range of education.

In urban areas, a propensity toward political activity was also significantly correlated with views on government legitimacy. If a person had ever raised an issue with a local administrator or politician, they were much more likely to feel positive about the government than if they had not – going from a close to 50 percent chance of a positive view of government to a 90 percent probability of giving the government legitimacy. If they had protested or demonstrated, however, they were less likely to view the government as legitimate.

Procedural legitimacy

As for moral legitimacy, contact with NGOs is not statistically significantly related to procedural legitimacy, using either of two measures. Ordered logistic regression output is shown in Table 8.7 for both questions included in the 2008 survey. The results are largely consistent within the rural and urban samples. While contact with NGOs did not appear to drive citizens toward lower regard for government, economic variables among rural respondents and political participation in urban areas were correlated with views on the state's right to govern.

TABLE 8.7. *Effect of NGOs on procedural legitimacy of government*

Variables	Full rural districts		Urban areas	
	The laws of Kenya express the values and morals of people in this country	The police always have the right to make people obey the law	The laws of Kenya express the values and morals of people in this country	The police always have the right to make people obey the law
Contact with an NGO	0.357	−0.328	0.353	0.431
	(0.342)	(0.398)	(0.390)	(0.459)
Education	0.0460	−0.0995	0.156	0.201
	(0.106)	(0.133)	(0.145)	(0.163)
Class	−0.306***	−0.211**	−0.0212	−0.0496
	(0.0779)	(0.0897)	(0.0463)	(0.0498)
Gender	0.240	0.161	0.325	−0.0613
	(0.313)	(0.399)	(0.340)	(0.370)
Age	−0.00881	−0.0197	0.0173	0.0100
	(0.0103)	(0.0128)	(0.0154)	(0.0161)
Has protested	0.695	0.0913	−1.461**	−1.541***
	(0.501)	(0.629)	(0.580)	(0.541)
Has raised issues	−0.113	0.573	0.651	0.115
	(0.338)	(0.468)	(0.517)	(0.524)
Views on economy	0.143	0.0380	0.506***	−0.0245
	(0.135)	(0.164)	(0.173)	(0.162)
Cut Point 1	−1.889**	−3.712***	0.873	−0.974
	(0.740)	(0.954)	(0.969)	(1.069)
Cut Point 2	−1.137	−3.040***	1.549	−0.341
	(0.733)	(0.941)	(0.973)	(1.062)
Observations	283	282	185	185

Coefficients are log-odds. *** p < 0.01, ** p < 0.05, * p < 0.1.

MECHANISMS LINKING NGOS AND STATE LEGITIMACY

The statistics featured in this chapter corroborate those of Chapter 7 in demonstrating that NGOs do not undermine state legitimacy. If anything, the opposite appears true: contact with NGOs improved support for the state. This finding suggests that loyalty accrues to the state regardless of who provides services.

This counter-intuitive finding raises questions about the mechanism linking NGO activity with state legitimacy. I therefore use inductive analysis to elucidate the mechanisms giving rise to correlations found in the statistical analysis. Specifically, qualitative knowledge from informed observers in Kenya facilitates analysis of three possible mechanisms, outlined in Table 8.8.

TABLE 8.8. *Causal mechanisms underlying NGOs' relationship to government legitimacy*

Cause	Explanation	Assessment
Political	• Government successfully takes credit for NGOs' work.	Sometimes.
	• People expect services of government, and they view the government to have delivered if the government creates an environment in which NGOs provide services.	Occasionally.
Cognitive	• Africans do not understand the difference between NGOs and the government – they are all government in the eyes of Kenyans.	Rarely.
	• Scholarly error in assumptions on the sources of African state legitimacy.	Sometimes.
Expectations	• African citizen expectations of their government are extremely low, particularly among the rural poor.	Frequently.

Political explanations

One explanation for the neutral or positive association between NGOs and government legitimacy is that politicians – from local county councillors to Members of Parliament – successfully claimed credit for the services that NGOs provide. As discussed in Chapter 5, governments do not want to lose the credit for socio-economic progress to nongovernmental organizations (Bratton 1989a, 572). As patrons in a clientelist system, it is important for government officials to be seen as having brought resources and services to the people of Kenya (Berman 1998; Oyugi 1995). Politicians can not only gain legitimacy indirectly from NGOs providing services in their constituencies, but under certain conditions they can also claim credit for bringing NGOs to the area and for the work that they do (Cannon 1996, 263; Boulding and Gibson 2009).[13] Indeed, evidence from the 1990s indicates that Kenyan politicians did bring overseas development assistance to their constituents (Briggs 2014; Jablonski 2014). When NGOs facilitate or allow this type of credit taking to occur, NGO service provision legitimates political authority (Sandberg 1994).

Credit taking by government officials assumed many forms in Kenya in the early twenty-first century, ranging from relatively subtle removal of NGOs' names in the authorship of jointly created documents (2008–24) to public and unambiguous declarations of personally arranging for – or even funding – an NGO to work in the area. Such political sleight of hand was at work, for example, in Constituency Development reports (2008–10), project openings and launches (2008–17), and dedication plaques on infrastructure (2008–18, 2008–14). A local politician in Machakos District explained the rationale: "The community might not like to know where their services come from, but for politicians, when it comes to election time, it really matters! So they really make sure to specify to the people" (2008–35). A human rights NGO respondent had a different explanation, however, saying that after an NGO dug a borehole with its own funds, an MP might take credit for it, budget it as a CDF-funded project, and then take the CDF-listed monies for it for his own pocket (2005–9). Thus, as was identified in Chapter 5, credit taking is a potential source of friction between NGOs and governments. On occasion, politicians also attempted to garner political legitimacy by acting the hero, publically denouncing NGOs for unrest or problems in the area (2008–54). Most commonly, however, the attitude of people depended on their local-level public administrator – the chief or subchief of the location or sublocation. "For local people, the government *is* the Assistant Chief," explained one respondent (2008–30).

Some informed observers also said that governments can gain legitimacy by creating an environment in which NGOs choose to be present and conduct their work – work that often could just as easily be

---

[13] Boulding and Gibson (2009) call this the "status quo argument," in which NGOs – whether explicitly or inadvertently – support existing political authority (measured in electoral support for incumbent politicians) by creating opportunities for politicians to claim credit for their work. Sometimes this happens through state capture, as when NGOs depend on state contracts or funding.

undertaken elsewhere, such as in other countries with needy populations (MacLean et al. 2015). Indeed, many of the NGOs in some parts of Kenya served neighboring countries, especially war-torn Sudan and Somalia, from within Kenya, due to Kenya's more open political climate and lower levels of violence. One leader of a small NGO, when asked how NGOs affect government legitimacy, said, "[T]he common people end up thankful to government for allowing the NGOs to operate there," since, "Most people know that government has to allow the NGO to participate before they start in an area . . . " (2008–13).

To reiterate a point made in Chapter 5, some NGOs encouraged the government to gain legitimacy from the organization's work – they saw their role as improving the state as a whole, not undermining it. As such, they were happy to share accrued service provision-based legitimacy with local civil servants and politicians. On the whole, however, NGO representatives interviewed only wanted credit to go to government when government actors actually contributed in some way. While NGOs did not work to *undermine* the state,[14] many would have liked to see government being more responsive to its citizenry.

Cognitive explanations

A second explanation relies on a rather pessimistic view of the cognitive abilities of people in developing countries. This line of reasoning holds that they are not smart enough (or not well educated enough) to understand the difference between NGOs and government. Thus, when they see services coming from an organization external to the village or town, they assume that the services come from some branch of government. Interview data, however, suggests that this was not the case in Kenya – though confusion does happen sometimes as the line between NGOs and government blurs.

For individuals in poor or remote areas of Kenya, the start of a new service provision program was big news – everyone in the village knew about it and how it came into existence. Projects were discussed seriously throughout the village. Communities had management committees who worked with NGOs to complete projects – so, "they know who brought what!" (2008–33). People also knew that it was uncommon for the government to fund certain localized programs: "So if something comes,

---

[14] Cannon (1996, 263) similarly found that NGOs in Uganda are there to meet needs, not worry about whether or not they are undermining government by providing services.

they know it's not from government" (2008–18). Even if individuals did not know particulars about the NGO bringing goods, informed observers insisted that they understood that the resources were not coming from the government (2008–34, 2008–50, 2008–52).

In addition, nearly all NGOs made a point of informing the local community of their work – by including locals in the project, holding meetings in the village, and/or leaving their logo on infrastructure or signboards (2008–18, 2008–25, 2008–30, 2008–32). These practices made it difficult for a government official to successfully claim credit for something she or he had no part in. For example, when a district officer in one area tried to take over a community borehole provided by a large NGO, he was unable to convince the community that he drilled it because they had been actively involved with the NGO on the project (2008–14). In many cases, one interviewee said, "*wananchi* are mobilized before the project and throughout, so they know that when a politician takes credit, it's usually not true" (2008–54).

Still, confusion of this type did happen sometimes, allowing NGO activities to reflect positively on state legitimacy. Most informed observers thought that such misunderstandings were very context-specific – they were more likely in extremely poor or remote areas (2008–31), or in situations of great uncertainty, as in refugee or internally displaced persons camps (2008–14). Confusion started to arise around government funding decentralization initiatives that were fairly new at the time of research. Efforts like the Local Area Transfer Fund, government bursary funds, and local HIV/AIDS funds increasingly looked like NGO programs, but were run by the government. A local research company, Research International, found confusion between these programs and those of NGOs when it conducted research on nonstate provision of services (2008–59). As NGOs and government have worked together more and more, the line between them has blurred for most Kenyans as well: "People don't know what's government funded, what's NGO, especially now that they are working so much together," according to a mid-level civil servant (2008–37). An NGO representative similarly reported that the government was doing many "wonderful things," with gaps filled by NGOs, and as a result, "government has started being more respected" (2006–2).

Expectations-based explanations

A third way to understand the relationship between NGOs and legitimacy requires reassessing our prior assumptions about the relationship between African states, service provision, and legitimacy. In particular, evidence from Kenya suggests that previous theories have been mistaken at the level of understanding citizen expectations. Political scientist and development expert Norman Uphoff writes that legitimacy derives from "having satisfied people's needs and for having met their normative expectations over time" (Uphoff 1993, 614). Rarely, however, have scholars considered the role of these citizen expectations in the social contract (McLoughlin 2015 is an exception).

Data from informed observer interviews in Kenya suggest that NGOs did not lower government legitimacy because Kenyans' expectations of the government in these areas were *already extremely low* (2008–32). Most informed observers felt that Kenyans don't make the link between NGO provision and government not fulfilling its end of the social contract (2008–30, 2008–34, 2008–51) because, as one said, "People tend to understand that government can't do it all. They see the government representative living in their same conditions, etcetera." (ibid.) Another reasoned, "A lot of people don't think that they pay tax, so they don't think government needs to give anything" (2008–27) – explaining that some people didn't realize they pay VAT when they make purchases. These Kenyans didn't become frustrated because, to a large extent, they were not holding expectations that were not being met. The scholarship on public expectation disconfirmation theory has found similar results in the US, where people rate government performance higher when they have very low expectations of it (Van Ryzin 2004). Such a process was likely at work in Kenya.

Indeed, Kenyans seemed to accept the limitations of their own and the government's situation (2008–18). There was a sense of understanding – even empathy – for the government on the part of many Kenyans, particularly in rural areas. One said, "People understand government has an obligation, but no capacity to reach down so far. They know." (2008–25). Even when they thought it was the government's responsibility to take care of them, they understood that NGOs were simply trying to fill in where the government could not provide (2008–23, 2008–24). This psychological strategy reflects a high level of pragmatism on the part of Kenyans.

On some level, Kenyans simultaneously understood that the government was unlikely to provide for them, and still vaguely hoped that it would somehow do so. An NGO representative who brought financial services to a market town in Mbeere district, for example, said, "People expect government to do things, like bring a bank here. But people also understand the government is slow, so they are happy that the [NGO] is here for now, even if it's not a full bank . . . In the long-term, though, they expect a lot more from government, because NGOs will leave one day" (2008–45).

Other survey results conformed to this interpretation for rural populations. Citizens were asked the following: "Which statement do you agree with more: A) It is the responsibility of the Government of Kenya to provide my family with services, and I expect that the Government itself will provide them, or B) It doesn't matter who provides my family services as long as they are provided." In rural districts, approximately 60 percent of respondents said that it was the government's responsibility to provide services, and they expected services from it. Even though they didn't receive many such services, most rural dwellers still found the government legitimate nonetheless. Urbanites tended to care less about the source of services than did their rural counterparts. Seventy percent of respondents in Nairobi said that it did not matter who provided services as long as they were provided. As one Nairobi resident said: "Nairobians are now realizing that the Government is incapable of solving all of the city's problems. Their solution lies in the will of Nairobians themselves" (Onyango 1998).

Interviewee responses recall Schatzberg's (2001) extended analogy in *Political Legitimacy in Middle Africa: Father, Family, Food* of the African state as a family. Comparing the state to a mother and NGOs to a caring neighborhood woman, one senior Kenyan NGO worker said,

"Imagine that you have a mother, who is supposed to provide you with care. But what if some lady from the neighborhood is the one who always takes care of you. How do you feel? You don't know her interests! You'd rather still have your mother's love. So . . . You understand that you are being taken care of, but you really want your mother to come and do it. There is just something special about a mother's care, and that other woman, you don't know why she's doing it, what other motivations she has . . . "

(2008–10)

Several NGO managers independently expressed concern that NGOs inadvertently lower people's expectations of public officials and agencies (2008–18). One noted that Kenyans pestered the government for services less frequently when NGOs were in the area, because people knew they could get the services from the NGO (2008–44). This meant to him that government could be less accountable, but it also suggests that NGOs lulled Kenyans into making fewer demands on their public administrators and officials. Along these lines, a government official said that people expect things only from NGOs, taking pressure off government: "People have come to associate NGOs with getting stuff. They don't expect as much from government" (2008–39). A generalized sentiment of, "People know government *should* provide, but is not able to, so they count on NGOs," prevailed in many interviews (2008–54). Looking at NGOs in Nigeria, however, Smith (2010) found that even when NGO leaders are corrupt, the values that they espouse lead to rising expectations for political and economic development.

Many informed observers linked the role of expectations to extreme poverty. They stated that NGO service provision benefited state legitimacy because people living in dire, precarious situations didn't have the luxury of caring where services and goods came from – they were just relieved to have some of their needs met (2008–12, 2008–26, 2008–33, 2008–34, 2008–45, 2008–47, 2008–49, 2008–50, 2008–51, 2008–53). This relief resulted in diffuse support for governing institutions. As a woman working in rural Machakos explained it, "Desperate people don't think about *where* things come from – because of their poverty. They just want more, so as to get out of the place they're in. So they generally feel better about the government, because someone is helping them at least!" (2008–12). In a display of gallows humor, one respondent said that for the uneducated, "so long as there is food on the table . . . Actually, if there even *is* a table . . . well, they don't care where [help] comes from" (2008–26). Another gushed, "People are just very happy. It's wonderful, the [NGO], for bringing these things," and then said that the NGO's work made the government look good (2008–45). Explaining the link explicitly, a respondent observed, "You don't see NGOs reflecting poorly on government. You see government being *helped* by NGOs," increasing overall satisfaction levels (2008–50).

In conditions of extreme poverty, the mere fact of an outsider bringing poverty relief may offer people hope that their lives could become less precarious over time. They may gain the sense that people "out there" – or "up there," as they say in Kenya – care about their small village and its problems. Such lifting of aspirations is also not particular to Kenya. Researchers in Ethiopia have shown that citizen aspirations and mental models of their future opportunities can increase due to small interventions (Bernard et al. 2014). Specifically, they find that merely watching a one-hour documentary about agriculture or business successes in similar communities raises aspirations among treated individuals (ibid.). Whether intentionally or not (and I believe it is not), Kenyans transferred this positive fellow-feeling to the state, excusing its limited performance.

THE REAL DRIVERS OF LEGITIMACY

Evidence from Kenya clearly demonstrates that NGOs do not necessarily threaten government legitimacy, and it provides clues as to what does, holding all else constant. First, correlates with legitimacy differ between rural and urban settings. In rural areas, economic factors were strongly associated with individual perceptions of state legitimacy. As rural wealth increased, individuals became more likely to be skeptical of government. Likewise, if they believed the economy was doing poorly, they tended to feel less positive about government.

For town and city respondents, civic participation and education appears to be relevant. Urbanites who engaged with government in a positive, individual manner by raising an issue with their local administrator or politician tended to find the government more legitimate, while those who protested in urban areas found it less so.[15] This finding could mean that people who raised an issue with an individual government official generally had good experiences in doing so, while those who protested remained disenchanted, ceteris paribus. It could also mean that those with high expectations of government thought it worth their time to talk with their representatives, while those who had low opinion of government protested.

Among urbanites, education levels also corresponded with perceptions of legitimacy, but not in expected ways. In Nairobi and Machakos Town, the least educated were the most likely to have negative perceptions of the government. This finding about education in urban areas runs counter to the theory that as people become better educated, wealthier and more urban, they began to expect more from government, citing their "rights" as citizens (Moore 1966). Low-education urban dwellers in Kenya, however, likely had low employment opportunities, and lacked the land and community available to their rural counterparts, which could influence them to deny government legitimacy. The most educated citizens in urban areas were much more likely to have employment and steady income, particularly in the middle-class neighborhoods of Nairobi.

Qualitative data from informed observer interviews presented some mixed findings, however. Responses aligned more closely with expectations than with survey results. Many NGO and government officials interviewed reported that more educated, wealthier individuals realize

---

[15] Of course, the direction of causation here is unclear; it is possible that low legitimacy leads to protest.

TABLE 8.9. *Respondent views on responsibility to provide public services*

Which statement do you agree with more:
A) It is the responsibility of the Government of Kenya to provide services and I
    expect the government to provide them;
B) It doesn't matter who provides services as long as they are provided.

	Rural districts	Urban areas	Total
Responsibility of government	172	70	242
Doesn't matter	128	131	259
Total	300	201	501

they should have services that the government is not providing (2008–25). They expressed the opinion that educated people would hold the government responsible for service provision, and expect services directly from the government (2008–10, 2008–14, 2008–26, 2008–27, 2008–33, 2008–36, 2008–37, 2008–47), when asked the question about service provision responsibility presented in Table 8.9.

Often, interviewees made the distinction between those who understand they pay taxes and those who don't, believing people who know they pay taxes will expect more from the government. One senior NGO leader said, "But we pay taxes! So the government has to provide from those taxes. It's unfair otherwise, and it's unsustainable. Should we pay taxes to NGOs?" (2008–10). One government official felt the same way: he initially laughed when asked the question about responsibility and expectations. He then said,

"Let's say both are true. They carry the same weight, but statement B is slightly heavier than A. People have been enlightened, like about taxes. Before, they just thought government is there to misuse funds. Now, they even query their MP in Parliament: Why are there no lights? Why the road isn't tarmacked? But it depends on literacy levels. In places without literacy, they will say A. They don't care who gives what."

(2008–37)

Finally, counter to expectations regarding ethnic politics in Kenya, views on the moral and procedural legitimacy of the government did not vary by ethnicity in this sample, ceteris paribus. When dummy variables for key ethnic groups are included in each analysis presented above, none is ever near statistically significant, nor does their inclusion change other regression results meaningfully. Nonetheless, these results are not conclusive about the relationship between ethnicity and legitimacy. Responses may reflect the fact that the survey was conducted primarily in Eastern Province among the Kamba, Mbeere, Embu, and Kikuyu, who tended to support the Kibaki presidency. Similar questions related to moral legitimacy for a representative sample of Kenyans using the 2008 Afrobarometer data reveal somewhat lower positive response rates, although they were still positive responses. Fifty-seven percent of respondents in that survey affirmed that they trusted the president (Bratton, Gyimah-Boadi, and Mattes 2008). Luo and Luhya Afrobarometer respondents, who tended not to have voted for Kibaki, were significantly less trusting of the president, with only 35 percent positive responses. At the same time, one might expect the Kalenjin, who also voted against Kibaki, to accord with the Luo and Luhya, yet 53 percent gave positive responses in the survey.

CONCLUSION

This chapter demonstrated that although scholars and politicians have claimed that NGOs threaten to undermine state legitimacy, in Kenya there was little evidence of this pattern in the early twenty-first century. Indeed, while NGOs were regarded quite favorably – often even more favorably than their government counterparts – they did not take away legitimacy from the government. Rather than a zero-sum game where a positive view of NGOs brought about a negative view of the civil service or politicians, NGOs appear to either have had no impact on popular perceptions of the state, or to have improved them. These results confirm those presented in Chapter 7.

The limited scholarship on this topic examining other parts of the world reaches similar conclusions. Jelinek (2006) examines the question in Afghanistan, asking about the effect of NGO assistance on communities' perceptions of government, for example. While he reports some bitterness toward the government on the part of citizens, as well as government concern that NGOs, which would only be in the country temporarily, had stronger service structures than the state, he also notes that where citizens felt physically secure, they had faith in the government (ibid.). They came to expect security from the state, but other services from NGOs.

With respect to Uganda, Parkhurst (2005) comes to a parallel conclusion, arguing that NGOs helped the government to increase its legitimacy – not only within the country, but among the international community as well. Specifically, he argues that in response to the

HIV/AIDS crisis, the Ugandan government strategically and proactively collaborated with NGOs. It was able to, in essence, contract out the technical response to nonstate actors, recognizing the crucial role played by NGOs, while at the same time maintaining leadership in the area (ibid.). This strategy allowed the state to build both legitimacy and capacity.

Sacks (2012) confirms these results cross-nationally. She finds clear evidence using Afrobarometer data from 2008 that the provision of services by donors and NGOs strengthened the relationship between citizens and the state. Specifically, nonstate social service provision strengthened the fiscal contract – people were more likely to pay taxes to the state when they believed nonstate actors were delivering services (ibid.).

Finally, Dietrich and Winters (2015) find that external funding of service provision in India has no relationship with government legitimacy. Emphatic NGO and donor branding of projects for their own credit claiming does not "interrupt the virtuous circle in which government performance leads to legitimation of the government among citizens and to citizen compliance with the government," they report (ibid., 2).

****

The findings of this chapter have practical implications for developing countries. In the recent past, NGOs have been decried by politicians in many parts of the world as undermining their legitimate authority. Governments nearly always have the power to expel offending foreign organizations, or scare them through raids and investigations (Katumanga 2004). They can enact regulation and laws concerning the operation of NGOs in their borders, and visibly enforce them when necessary (Edwards and Hulme 1996b, Ndegwa 1994). Governments have used these powers to restrict funding opportunities for NGOs and implement stringent limitations on their activities. The Kenyan government itself has proposed limiting funding from foreign sources (Republic of Kenya 2013). Yet, when put to the test, the idea that NGOs delegitimize government appears not to have merit. Particularly when collaborative relationships are present, NGOs have the potential to support government legitimacy.

9

Conclusion: blurring the boundaries between NGOs and the state

A comparative analysis

> *"People consider us government. They are confused about where government starts and [our NGO] stops."*
>
> (NGO worker, Machakos district, 2008)
>
> *"The government is now more of an NGO than the NGOs are!"*
>
> (NGO leader, Machakos district, 2008)

INTRODUCTION

Throughout this book, I have argued that under specific conditions, NGOs strengthen the state. Taken individually, each substantive chapter demonstrates the impact of NGOs on one of four "elements of stateness." Focusing primarily on NGOs' role in public service provision, this study shows that NGOs have supplemented a sense of governing presence within the territory; they have expanded the state's capacity to provide services; they have influenced a slow turn toward participatory governance practices; and they have boosted the legitimacy of the state. Taken together, the chapters tell a story about how the state itself is changing in response to this new phenomenon.

NGOs, however, do not simply stimulate change within public offices and agencies and among government officials. Instead, in many cases, NGOs themselves take on roles and responsibilities traditionally associated with public administration of services by public, government actors. As political scientist Walter Oyugi argues, government and NGOs have become partners in the development process in Kenya; NGOs' activities parallel and complement those of the government (2004, 48). I argue, however, that NGOs run more than analogous programs to their government counterparts. NGOs have moved away from being third-party players, and toward integration and interweaving into the de facto organizational fabric of the state in Kenya. In work comparing Kenya and Zimbabwe, others show that while NGOs are "constituted outside the state, [they] act in the public sphere" (Osodo and Matsvai 1997, 5). The line between nongovernmental and governmental organization thus blurs, as service provision decisions are made, programs are offered, and district-wide planning is undertaken jointly. Moreover, with the blurring, government performance improves. In Kenya, the performance is still poor, but progress is evident.

Should we be surprised to see such phenomena – nominally nongovernmental actors assuming government responsibilities in a developing country? Is it a sign that these states are getting weaker in the face of powerful international actors? Not at all. Political theorists since Tocqueville have described situations in which formally nonstate actors undergird weak states. Much as the churches, community organizations, women's groups, and village councils of early America took on responsibility for the education of children, the paving of roads, and the digging of wells, NGOs act in Kenya today as supplements and prompts to government. This role is evident not only in the physical provision of services, but also in patterns of governance and decision-making. In Kenya, as in the United States, "the tradition of a strong civil society bears some of the brunt of governing. Even before it became fashionable, government in the United States utilized the private sector... to help make and implement policy" (Peters and Pierre 1998, 238, citing Salamon 1981 and Kettl 1987).

In Kenya, the state became stronger because of NGOs – more capable of expressing territoriality, better able to provide services, more accountable in service provision, and more legitimate. Migdal's (2001, 22) writings on the state reinforce the possibility of this type of arrangement, stressing that the practices and actors of the state are "the practices of a heap of loosely connected parts or fragments, frequently with ill-defined boundaries between them and other groupings inside and outside the official state borders and often promoting conflicting sets of rules with one another and with 'official' law." Putnam (1993) made a similar observation about civic associations improving government performance in northern Italy.

The comparison to Tocqueville's observations is not made to indicate that developing states today should be seen as replicating the US two centuries ago. Instead, these recurring themes remind us that the organizational composition of states should not be understood in starkly bifurcated terms, in which "government = state" and "nongovernmental = outside the state." Instead, we should take heed of Migdal's (2001, 16) description of the state as more complex than a single entity. As he says, "the state, no more probably today than at any other time in its history, does not have this unity, this individuality, this rigorous functionality" (2001, 18).

In addition to the recognition of a multiplicity of possible organizational configurations of the state, however, I demonstrate in this book that the developing state has not been *undermined* by NGOs; rather, it has been *reinforced* by them. While some scholars, the news media, and politicians have portrayed NGOs as threatening the state, in fact their actions serve to bolster it. In the language of Cameroon scholar Janet Roitman (2005), NGOs reconstitute the state, creating new networks of actors deploying state technologies.[1] Or, as Callaghy, Kassimir, and Latham (2001, 7) put it, trans-boundary organizations like NGOs have become involved in shaping and constituting order and authority in various African social and political contexts.

Kenyan citizens are pragmatic about the limitations of their government, even as they hold beliefs about services a government should provide to maintain the social contract. The Kenyan government clearly understands these priorities of a state, and makes efforts to fulfill the most fundamental states services of education, healthcare, and security through public agencies, even as it leaves others to the nongovernmental actors. Providing universal free primary education, in particular, was one of the most visible programs of the Kibaki administration.[2] Likewise, in cities and towns – particularly in Nairobi – improving physical security has been a clear priority.[3] NGO representatives also mentioned feeling that these three services were primarily the responsibility of government,

---

[1] Roitman does not write about NGOs, but about other types of nonstate actors deploying state functions. She argues that regulation of trade and legitimate authority over this regulation are no longer solely in governmental hands, but rather that a multiplicity of legitimate authorities has taken shape.

[2] The program is not without its faults. Because students no longer have to pay prohibitive school fees, the cost of providing universal education in some areas of the country has been vastly overcrowded classrooms, since additional classrooms and teachers have not been provided at the same rate as new students enroll. Single classrooms can have more than 120 children (2007–29; 2007–30).

[3] That said, the capital, Nairobi, is still a city with high crime rates, and where news headlines like "Crime wave blamed on police officers" remain common (*Daily Nation*, May 26, 2005, 18).

and that their role was to complement government on lesser priorities. As one NGO worker said, "Common people understand that government . . . gives schools, hospitals, security. Nothing else. So we try to do what is overlooked by them" (2008-18). While NGOs often grumble about the way government works, they do not see their role as competing with it, but as filling gaps where public agencies do not reach.

At a larger level, the implication is that the state is and remains an important actor – only its composition has changed slightly. Contrary to claims that globalization is overwhelming the state with "races to the bottom," in which social welfare is sacrificed to the whims of global economic competition (Strange 1996), we find that the introduction of new actors and interdependencies creates new possibilities in service provision and capacity. As Weiss (1998) argues, globalization requires states to become more efficient and capable, enhancing their abilities both internally and externally. Through interpenetration of its activities with those of government, NGOs have begun to facilitate this process in Kenya.

NGOs have also become a means by which the state can conduct service provision "experiments" at little cost to public coffers. Because of the structure of their funding sources and accountability mechanisms, NGOs – often relatively well-funded vis-à-vis their government counterparts at the local level – have the flexibility and resources to attempt a variety of types of programs, projects, and service provision methods, even when their failure rates are high. Government agencies in most poor countries, especially at the local level, do not have this type of leeway in their budgets or in their programmatic decision-making. These states can make use of this feature of NGOs, allowing NGOs to bear the costs of programmatic experimentation and then adopting only their successful programs at the district, province, or national level.[4] Already, Kenyan government offices show signs of adopting NGOs' participatory methods, as well as some of their internal quality control mechanisms like service charters and employee performance appraisals.

The chapters on state legitimacy, moreover, tell us that the government has been able to benefit from the positive views citizens have of NGOs. This finding may surprise the current Uhuru Kenyatta presidential administration, which appears to believe the opposite, and has attempted to restrict NGO freedoms and funding repeatedly (ICNL 2015). It is crucial for the government to realize that the greatest influence on government legitimacy in Kenya is whether people trust their government officials

---

[4] Clark (1995, 596) makes a similar point.

and politicians. Although some African politicians blame international actors, civil society, or NGOs for their lack of popularity, the findings of Chapters 7 and 8 show that governments' own actions have the greatest impact on citizen's perceptions. The more transparently they govern, the more legitimacy they will garner.

Finally, both the relatively high legitimacy rates in the survey results and the data obtained in one-on-one interviews demonstrate that the Kenyan people are relatively forgiving or understanding of the financial and developmental difficulties of their government. In interview after interview, respondents talked about how Kenyans believe that the government has a responsibility to provide for them, but essentially accept that it is not going to do so – either because it is unwilling or unable. When NGOs provide in government's stead, people do not then blame government for slacking on its duties. Instead, they tend to be grateful that some state-like organization is trying to look out for them, particularly in rural areas among the extremely poor and uneducated.

NGOS AND THE STATE IN COMPARATIVE PERSPECTIVE

These trends are not particular to Kenya, nor to Africa. Throughout the world, scholars and practitioners have found synergistic relationships between NGOs and governments that positively affect service provision and state development. Most of these studies are academic articles focusing on one particular sector in one or a few countries. Here, I synthesize them briefly to show that NGO–state integration has been documented in the health sector as well as in education, sanitation, slum upgrading, policing, libraries, park services, and international environmental governance. Comparative evidence comes from other parts of Africa, Central, South and East Asia, the former Soviet Union, Latin America, the United States, and international governance organizations.

It is important to note that the manner and reasons for NGO integration into service provision differs across regimes. Most clearly – and in line with the findings of Chapter 3 – NGO–government interactions differ in more liberal regimes than in the corporatist (sometimes called state-corporatist or neo-corporatist) systems of Latin America, East Asia, and the former Soviet Union. In the latter group, the state bargains with or provides licensing and regulation to NGOs, unions, and other sorts of civil society organizations ostensibly to organize them, but often also in order to restrict or limit them (see Schmitter 1974, Unger and Chan 1995, Saich 2000, Heurlin 2010). Usually, the state designates particular organizations as interest group intermediaries, giving them power relative to other organizations in the system but usually weakening them relative to government. The organizations help implement policies of government and to organize others in the sector.

In Kenya, however, NGOs have not been silenced by their involvement in government. In this way, NGOs in Kenya often act like a "Trojan horse," entering government committees openly – even by invitation – only to change the government from the inside. Rather than government co-opting civil society, it is in fact slowly adopting the strategies and mechanisms promoted by civil society in its governing processes. Counter to the clear and significant setback incurred following the presidential elections of 2007, this adoption suggests a movement toward democratization and civic empowerment in Kenya, however small. This theme was addressed in detail in Chapter 6.

Africa

With respect to Kenya specifically, other scholars have conducted research that supports the conclusions of this book. In a comparison with Tanzania, for example, van Klinken (1998, 349) argues that the clear line separating NGOs and governments is "mythical," with interdependence blurring their boundaries. As I do, he describes governments subsidizing some NGOs, NGO investment in other government programs, the movement of personnel between the sectors, and the small elite world in which both types of workers intermingle (ibid.). Examining collaborative slum-upgrading programs in Nairobi's Mathare Valley, Otiso (2003) also argues that NGOs, government, and business partnerships are successful because the benefits of each sector make up for the downsides of the others. State service provision becomes stronger through the integration of nongovernmental actors. In the health sector as well, Wamai (2004, 2) makes an unusual comparison of Kenya and Finland, asserting that NGOs' contributions are larger than previously understood in both countries: not only do NGOs operate at least 20 percent of healthcare facilities, they are also "indispensable" collaborators in health policy-making within government bodies.

Looking beyond Kenya in Africa, Robinson's (2011) mixed-method cross-national study finds that alongside political will, government coordination with NGOs and other civil society organizations proved to be the most prominent factor in successfully reducing HIV prevalence rates at the national level. NGOs lent both communication channels for prevention messages, and legitimation for those messages (ibid.).

Brautigam and Segarra (2007) likewise identify increasingly collaborative NGO–government relationships over time in Gambia, which are facilitated by donor requirements and by both parties slowly coming to realize their mutual interest in working together – a very similar pattern to what I observed in Kenya. In Gambia, NGOs played key roles in the early 2000s development of Gambia's national Poverty Reduction Strategy Paper (PRSP), which led to NGO involvement in a number of other sectors in both policymaking and implementation (ibid.), despite the country's military regime.

In Tanzania, moreover, Mercer notes ways in which government officials act like NGOs and vice versa, blurring the boundaries between them (1999, 253–254). Tripp argues that another type of nonstate entity, the informal economy, has acted in much the same way as NGOs do in Kenya today. She asserts that the informal economy in the 1980s and into the 1990s in Tanzania was often seen in a negative light, but in fact kept the state from collapsing by providing a safety net for the people (Tripp 1997). This argument suggests that a variety of types of nonstate actors may play similar roles during times of strain.

Latin America

Outside of Africa, the trend repeats. NGO–government synergies have become increasingly common in Latin America. In Mexico, for example, NGOs often provide innovation in the implementation of social services, but do not have the funds to scale up their activities to the regional or local level and rely on the government to do so (Pick, Givaudan, and Reich 2008). The government, meanwhile, has been able to develop sound policies and goals, but often falls short in implementing new activities stemming from these policies (ibid.). Working together on services allows NGOs and government to combine the strengths of each, thereby improving service delivery in ways that benefit both sets of actors (ibid.). This mutualism has been evident in a variety of conditional cash transfer and other programs in health and education.

In Brazil, nongovernmental actors have joined in the governance process in multiple ways. Concerning water resource management, they have gained what Abers and Keck (2013) call "practical authority" – the ability to make and implement decisions and recognition for their role in shared governance in the sector (2006). Such governance patterns arose from attempts at decentralization, but resulted in "an unexpected amount of state building" as government and nongovernmental actors wrestled for power (Abers and Keck 2009, 290). Much as NGOs in Kenya strengthened administrative capacity by becoming intertwined with government in policymaking and implementation NGOs in Brazil did so in river-basin governance. Indeed, Abers and Keck (ibid.) tell a remarkably similar story to that of Chapters 5 and 6.

Government bureaucrats in Brazil have also discovered that working with NGOs and other civil society actors has allowed them to overcome their otherwise weak political power to effectively implement government policy on the environment (Hochstetler and Keck 2007) and on HIV/AIDS (Rich 2013). These "activist bureaucrats" mobilized nongovernmental associations to monitor implementation at the local level and to pressure politicians to follow national policy guidelines that might otherwise have been ignored in a context of fiscal decentralization (ibid.).

In Ecuador, also, NGOs and government have increasingly worked together to create policy and provide services (Brautigam and Segarra 2007), such as co-funding and co-managing health centers (Keese and Argudo 2006). Working together allows the organizations to reach more rural communities, to reduce duplication of efforts, and to better maintain activities over a long duration (ibid.). As I concluded with respect to Kenya, scholars argue that this collaboration has helped to democratize local government in Ecuador, and to strengthen civil society (ibid.). As occurred in both Kenya and South Asia, Brautigam and Segarra (2007) argue that these allied relationships grow out of donor pressure for collaboration, as well as a process of social learning in which both NGOs and governments recognize the benefits of working together.

East Asia

NGO integration into service provision in Kenya is in some ways similar and in other ways quite different from of the pattern observed in the countries of East Asia. In corporatist China, for example, despite decades of exclusionary policies, NGOs are now frequently "welcomed" into state activities – or are created explicitly by the state – so as to remove them as a civil society threat by (Heurlin 2010). Whether welcomed or created, all societal organizations need a state sponsor in order to operate in China, leading some scholars to refer to China's arrangement as "state-led civil society" (Brook and Frolic 1997). The boundary between state and society is therefore incredibly porous, if not completely intertwined.

Conflict, when it occurs, is to a large extent contained within the state (Gallagher 2004) since NGOs and other civil society organizations are so embedded in it. They are therefore appendages of the party-state (Foster 2002).

Interestingly, however, there remain some similarities between Kenyan and Chinese NGO–government interactions. For example, scholars of China have argued, as I do, that NGOs have become interwoven with the government enough that they can be studied as "new elements of the state's administrative system," used by the government to carry out its mandated tasks (Foster 2002, 42).[5]

Where integration in China reflects state control and co-optation, in Kenya, it involves mutual adjustment and cooperation. Teets (2012), however, suggests that these collaborative efforts in service provision may indeed lead to more pluralistic decision-making in China in the future. Studying government contracting to NGOs for service provision in a range of activities, she argues that this process is already expanding citizen participation in the provision and regulation of goods and services, as it also improves the quality of service provision (ibid.).

Elsewhere in East Asia, several studies have shown other variations in these trends. In corporatist Vietnam, for example, the government opened to NGOs after 1986, but, like China, required them to partner with government-sponsored organizations (Heurlin 2010). Other scholars have found less collaboration in Vietnam than in most of the countries mentioned thus far, but nonetheless observe that the Vietnamese government is eager to increase these collaborative activities (Carrard et al. 2009). Examining the water and sanitation sectors, Carrard et al. (2009) demonstrate that NGOs have contributed in small ways to policymaking and national programmatic initiatives, but find that these types of contributions are not common, perhaps due to the many requirements and restrictions placed on the organizations.

In the same study, however, these researchers find that NGOs play a primary role in sanitation service delivery in East Timor, particularly in rural areas. As in Kenya, NGOs in the country have also been involved in representing rural needs in the creation of national policies, and they have been directly training government staff to address the challenge of improving construction, operation, and maintenance of sanitation

---

[5] Foster refers specifically to business associations in an article on the embedded nature of civil society in the state in China.

facilities (ibid.). In both countries, NGOs have facilitated access to services, especially in remote and otherwise hard-to-reach areas.

Former Soviet Union

Like some parts of Latin America, China, and Vietnam, states of the former Soviet Union tend to take a corporatist approach to service provision, but with some modifications. For example, while Kazakhstan and Kyrgyzstan largely act in line with their state-centered, top-down history, both countries also show some elements of government responsiveness to NGOs, as well as improvements to health service delivery via NGO involvement. Brinkerhoff (2002) argues that NGOs are helping to improve service delivery within the public administrations of both countries, and that NGOs also have the potential to contribute to democratization and improved governance. Examining the health sector, he finds that while the government is moving in this direction, however, patterns of the past, where the state was the dominant actor throughout society, are slow to change. These states remain authoritarian, after all, and although donor support lends the organizations some autonomy, they are still creations of the government (ibid.).

Even in Russia, where the government has become extremely hostile to civil society groups and foreign-funded NGOs, studies find NGOs collaborating with government actors – even state law enforcement agencies (Taylor 2006). The result has been an improvement in police performance as well as changing norms and values of government employees in a more liberal, democratic direction (ibid.). Indeed, just as in Kenya, NGOs in Russia are helping "low-level bureaucrats better perform their core organizational tasks" (ibid., 193). Although this finding appears to be the exception to the rule in Russia, the fact that scholars have seen such collaborative and liberalizing trends in the most unlikely of places lends further credence to the argument that NGOs are having widespread liberalizing and democratizing effects on governments.

South Asia

Collaborative, synergistic efforts for service provision occur across a range of sectors in South Asia, strengthening the state. Examining these countries in comparison to one another and to Kenya, however, reveals an interesting range of variation in the form that NGO–government interactions take. In Pakistan, for example, NGOs and governments co-produce in ways similar to those discussed in Chapters 5 and 6. Specifically, NGOs and government provide joint-resourced programs in family planning, tuberculosis, and HIV/AIDS, and NGOs deliver leprosy care and other types of healthcare services on government's behalf (Palmer 2006, Ejaz, Shaikh, and Rizvi 2011). This method of integration of NGOs into healthcare in the country is understood to make the health system as a whole more efficient, equitable, and better governed, due not only to the increased funds that NGOs bring to the system, but also to NGOs' work in health education, promotion, social marketing, and advocacy (Ejaz, Shaikh, and Rizvi 2011). As in Kenya, these collaborative relationships replace earlier interactions characterized by tension and mistrust. From independence through the early 1990s, government officials frequently, if inconsistently, sought to suppress NGOs, seeing them as adversaries, not allies. Partially due to donor influence, in Pakistan as in Kenya, collaboration became the norm over the course of the 1990s and 2000s (Batley 2011).

In nearby Bangladesh, NGO–government collaboration has become common in healthcare, education, water, and sanitation (Nurul Alam 2011). For example, cogeneration activities have raised both quality and access to tuberculosis care and prevention and other health services (Zafar Ullah et al. 2006). NGO–government relations in Bangladesh, however, are more ambivalent than in Pakistan or in Kenya: the government simultaneously works to integrate NGOs into its policy while at the same time placing restrictive regulations on them (Batley 2011, Nurul Alam 2011).

In these two countries and in India, NGOs have also bolstered state education activities by providing primary education in areas not covered by the government, and by implementing "adoption" and "improvement" programs aimed at government schools (Rose 2011, 296). In India, however, NGOs play a weaker role in setting policy for service provision, as the government maintains a more dominant position (Batley 2011) than it does in places like Kenya or Pakistan.

Developed countries and the international arena

While it is easiest to generalize from Kenya's experience to other developing countries, similarities in the NGO–government dynamic also exist with developed countries, including the United States, and in the international arena. Although the United States has always favored smaller government in comparison to European states, this trend toward privatization has grown in recent years amid economic recession and the rise of the "Tea Party" faction of the Republican Party. In the early years of the 2010s, the federal and many state governments began ceding considerable responsibility to NGOs, usually referred to as nonprofit organizations. As in Kenya, the US government can no longer afford to provide many of the services it once did. For example, in response to financial crisis, the state of California closed seventy state parks in May of 2011. In response to citizen and NGO pressure, the state legislature then passed Assembly Bill 42 in September 2011, which allows nonprofits to operate state parks that would otherwise close. This legislation built on existing state code to expand the scope of NGO operations (California State Parks Foundation 2011).

Researchers have begun to write about these blurring boundaries in the governance of US libraries, fire and police departments, and park services. According to Gazley and Brudney (2007, 397), nearly 55 percent of administrative officers in the state of Georgia report collaborating with at least one nonprofit in service delivery or planning, specifically in a relationship that extended beyond a mere contractual or grant relationship. Fifty percent of nonprofits studied in the same research reported collaboration with local government (ibid.). The study concludes from these and other findings that nonprofit contributions lead to service improvements as well as higher trust in and satisfaction with government (ibid., 410).

The findings from Kenya also mirror some dynamics that Theda Skocpol (2003) describes in the United States. She asserts that American civil society has reorganized, moving away from mass mobilization toward interest group representation through nonprofit organizations. At the same time, however, reduced civil society participation by citizens has resulted in "diminished democracy" (ibid.). Putnam (2000) makes a similar argument about the United States – he argues that government performance is getting worse in the USA as civil society weakens. This finding parallels the Kenyan experience, but runs in reverse.

Finally, studies of NGOs' roles in international organizations demonstrate that NGOs also take on state-like roles at the very macro level. Raustiala (1997), for example, studies international environmental affairs. He demonstrates that the pervasiveness of NGOs in international environmental institutions reflects an expansive state, not one in retreat (Raustiala 1997, 721). NGOs have become a core player in negotiations, taking on "previously 'states-only' governance activities" (ibid.). Thus it is not only within countries, but also at the international level that NGOs have moved into state roles.

Contrasting evidence and arguments

Not all scholars of Kenya, of NGOs, or of development generally will agree with these conclusions. One of the most fervent arguments against them comes from Alex de Waal (1997), who argues that relief organizations – both donor and NGO – do more harm than good (1997). Examining countries across sub-Saharan Africa, he argues that relief efforts have weakened states, reducing the possibilities for local solutions to local problems. Pierre Englebert (2009, 2) agrees, asserting that NGOs often help to reproduce weak states in Africa by allowing governments to depend on NGOs rather than develop their own state programs and presence. Egan (1991) agrees, arguing that NGO provision of services in Mozambique allowed the government to shirk its responsibilities – while at the same time denying government agents the opportunity to learn through experience.

Several scholars have focused on the issue of state strength. Some see the growth of NGOs and civil society as emblematic of donors' ideological desire to bypass government agencies (Dietrich 2013), thereby weakening states over time (Kamat 2004). Others argue that strong donor support for NGOs combined with a weak state leads to difficulty implementing services. Examining health services in Malawi, Palmer (2006) shows that well-funded NGOs grow frustrated with the slow place and low capacity of the government agencies, eventually bypassing government systems. She queries to what extent very weak states can truly cooperate with NGOs. Still others agree that NGOs are weakening the state, but place emphasis on the already anemic government agencies' inability to grapple with the inundation of powerful, wealthy NGOs (Pfeiffer 2003). According to Pfeiffer's study of Mozambique, NGOs draw employees away from government with their higher salaries and undermine Mozambican control of health administration (ibid.).

REMAINING QUESTIONS

In this book I have attempted to demonstrate some of the mechanisms by which NGOs influence state development, yet a number of questions about the role of NGOs in the state-building process remain. Do NGOs actually facilitate equitable development or do their programs lead to social exclusion, as some scholars have asserted (Clayton 1998)? How do NGOs' effects on the state compare to other sorts of civil society groupings, such as membership organizations, lobbyists, unions, and traditional or informal associations? Can NGOs successfully reduce corruption in a state, or are they more likely to fall victim to it (Smith 2010)? What is the relationship between NGO programs and service provision and ethnic, religious or other identity politics, particularly in clientelist political economies? Related organizational questions also remain: how can the duplication of efforts common to NGOs be reduced and efficiency increased (NGOs Co-ordination Board 2009)? What dysfunction develops when NGOs consider their own organizational survival above program utility (Doyle and Patel 2008)?

Although each of these questions deserves attention, in this concluding section, I focus on what I see as the key limitations of NGOs raised at various points throughout this book. I argue that, as a whole, the impact of NGOs on state development in Kenya has been positive. Taken together, however, the implication of the limitations that follow is that NGO involvement in state development may become more problematic over time.

Lending support to authoritarian and terrorist regimes

The finding that NGOs do not undermine the legitimacy of the state may be a double-edged sword. On the positive side, the data indicate that governments should not be wary of nongovernmental organizations. Instead of restricting NGO activities and funding sources, as currently occurs in countries scattered throughout the world, governments can allow NGOs to proliferate and benefit from the goods that NGOs provide to citizens. Normatively, NGOs are "good" for the state, following this logic.

Viewed from another perspective, however, the normative position is negative. NGO service provision has the potential to provide legitimacy for states that the international community, donors, and even the NGOs themselves do not want to support. NGOs can lend legitimacy to corrupt or authoritarian states, for example, or even to terrorism-promoting governments. In authoritarian China, for example, NGOs have begun working with municipal governments to provide services (Teets 2012), which could lend credibility to the authoritarian state.

Flanigan (2008) has demonstrated a relationship between NGOs and terrorist factions in both Lebanon and Sri Lanka. In these two countries, terrorist organizations – sometimes associated with the state – deliberately use NGO service provision to gain legitimacy. Both Hezbollah and the Liberation Tigers of Tamil Eelam (LTTE, or Tamil Tigers) use nonprofit service provision as a tool to increase community acceptance, widespread favorable opinion, and active participation in the organizations (Flanigan 2008, 500). In both cases, community support has aided recruitment efforts for their respective militias. Hamas has used charity committees and other NGO-like organizational components in similar ways to recruit new members (ibid.). Flanigan argues that terrorist co-opting of NGOs and similar organizations is possible where recipients of services are poor, basic needs are unmet, and there is no alternative provider of services (2008). While these groups are insurgents and not the state, their successful use of service provision to create a "public image of a welfare 'state'" in the areas that they control proves that NGO services can also be used to create legitimacy in oppressive or brutal states. Even apolitical service-providing organizations can have this wide political impact.

Indeed, this potential for undergirding nondemocratic polities is *most* possible when NGOs are deliberately apolitical service-providing organizations. Whereas governance NGOs in Kenya have vocally espoused a number of highly contentious positions – such as supporting the International Criminal Court (ICC) indictments and trial of senior politicians in relation to the 2008 post-election violence, lobbying to reduce MPs' salaries (among the highest in the world), and pushing for real anti-corruption efforts – many service providing NGOs intentionally eschew politics and work with governments with a questionable record in political arenas.

It is thus imperative that we not assume that NGOs bolstering state legitimacy is necessarily a social good. If it is true that NGOs providing services lower popular frustration below a level where change would otherwise be demanded, NGOs might actually act in the interests of authoritarian or even terrorist regimes. Particularly where NGOs are tightly restricted to providing services rather than engaging in advocacy or civic education activities, they may not be able to provide a civil society, democratizing function. If this is the case, donors, international organizations and NGOs themselves may need to reconsider their activities in some countries of the world. They may need to reflect on the type of NGO – apolitical service providing or good governance promoting – that they support.

Different – but not necessarily better – accountability concerns

Issues of accountability are another set of limitations to NGOs' role in state development. One of the main concerns scholars have with NGOs is their relative lack of accountability to the people they claim to serve. The argument is that NGOs are accountable not to the beneficiaries of their programs, but to their international donors, who are usually both physically and cognitively distant from the situation on the ground (Ebrahim 2003; Edwards and Hulme 1996b; Batley and McLoughlin 2010; Doyle and Patel 2008). NGOs do not necessarily start operations oriented toward their donors' goals. Over time, however, resource dependence can lead to goal displacement, in which NGOs assimilate to the goals of the donors on which they rely for funds. This is problematic because even where donors have local people's best interests in mind, they are unlikely to fully understand the vagaries of context that influence outcomes in each unique place where NGOs work. Many donors, moreover, are not primarily concerned with the wellbeing of end-user beneficiaries – rather, they are concerned with their own country's political, economic, or security interests (Olsen, Carstensen, and Høyen 2003; Lewis 2003).

Ideally, in poor countries, organizations of public administration, connected to democratically elected governments, provide all needed services to their electorate. This arrangement allows for accountability through the voting process – arguably this is what occurs in most advanced industrialized countries. NGO involvement in state activities, however, undercuts such a relationship as it bypasses the quid pro quo that emerges as elected officials and citizens exchange services for support at the ballot box. In many cases, NGOs can set an agenda with little popular mandate and almost no political consequences for failure. The absence of consequences for failure is of particular concern, given that lives and livelihoods are on the line. Related to this, the uneven distribution of NGOs geographically, even if it corresponds with need for services, is not deliberately determined, and may lead to new inequities in developing countries.

In the absence of ideal conditions, however, the question becomes whether it is better for nondemocratic but generally idealistic NGOs to contribute to service provision, or whether these unelected organizations ultimately undermine the development of strong democracies. Seeing as: (a) the alternative in most developing countries would be a lesser total supply of services in an only semi-democratic state; and (b) NGOs appear to have a positive influence on the use of participatory and democratic methods within the public service, as demonstrated in Chapter 6, we have a strong argument in favor of NGO participation. It is, of course, important to acknowledge the fairly hypocritical gap in transparency and accountability of NGOs, and to create negative consequences for preventable failure and incompetency among NGOs. Yet it is equally foolish to exclude NGOs, when their absence may lead to a far worse outcome. As Abers and Keck remind us, "studies of institutional development mainly take it as a given that duly elected bodies can generate desired policy outcomes if they so choose," but this assumption may be unwarranted (2009, 291).

NGOs in the long time-horizon

Most importantly, the long-term feasibility of relying on NGO involvement in the provision of services – not only in Kenya or Africa, but also throughout the developing world – is a growing concern for policymakers and scholars. These concerns arise out of a number of fears: that NGO funding is not sustainable (Edwards and Hulme 1996b, 964) and can end or decrease arbitrarily at any time; that NGOs create greater dependency among poor countries; and that NGOs allow government inefficiency to perpetuate (Farrington, Bebbington, et al. 1993, 333). Although this book does not address the question of long-term consequences in great detail, choosing to focus on what *has* happened and *is* happening rather than predict what *might* happen in the future, I provide a few points for consideration.

Most scholars agree that the state remains central in the *longue durée*, yet the worry persists that NGOs and donors bypass already-weak governments, which does nothing to increase state capacity. Instead, ever more emasculated governments exist, with little long-term solution (Whaites 1998). Describing Tajikistan, Martin writes, "Donor agencies have a tendency to look to NGOs as the preferred partners in development initiatives, *specifically because host governments are ineffective.* Yet in doing so, no incentive is ever provided to them to promote the kind of changes which would ultimately reduce their dependency on foreign donors" (Martin 2004, 12; see also Campbell 1996 and Cannon 1996).

As a result of this bypassing tendency (Dietrich 2013), there is a concern that developing country government inefficiency can become a self-perpetuating reality (Farrington, Lewis, et al. 1993) if governments never get the funds to improve or change. NGO experts Edwards and Hulme go so far as to argue that NGO service provision acts as a palliative, preventing structural changes that are needed to improve state capacity (1996b, 964). Moreover, without a minimum level of pre-existing governance capacity, the many actors now providing services can overwhelm a weak state's ability to set standards, coordinate, monitor, and regulate all organizations involved. International financial institutions, development agencies, and donors should clearly be vigilant in pushing forward the very difficult task of increasing administrative capacity within the state over the long term.

At the same time, it is important to remember that the Kenyan government, like those of many other poor countries, currently cannot supply citizens with the full extent of services needed. NGOs are helping to do so, both by offering significant financial and physical resources and by positively encouraging participatory and transparent governance processes within the government. This said, the actual level of NGO involvement in no way matches that of government, either in the level of tangible or financial resources from donors (Organization for Economic Cooperation and Development 2013). Recall from Chapter 3 that although NGOs provide a significant level of core service provision, the government still provides a majority of services among survey respondents. Indeed, in recent years, donor agencies have returned to direct budgetary support for developing country governments (Koeberke, Stavreski, and Walliser 2006). This change has made some NGOs worry more about their finances than they did in the 1990s or early 2000s. As one informant said, "Funds of government are up – and if it continues, NGOs won't need to be there anymore" (2008–33). At the same time, such open-use general budget support from donors isn't universally granted. In Kenya, many donors cite government mismanagement as a reason to limit direct budgetary support (Hornsby 2013). Both NGOs and governments face the real issue of inconsistent and precarious donor funding situations, which makes long-term planning exceedingly difficult.

Ultimately, however, the problems of development and of service provision in Kenya are the responsibility of the Kenyan government.[6] NGOs are currently assisting with short-term development and maintenance efforts; they should not be seen as a long-term alternative to functioning public administration (Brautigam 1994, Chege 1999). At a certain point, NGOs are not able to scale up their activities – they are simply not large enough and may become overstretched if they expand further (Palmer et al. 2006). Thus, "the only alternate to state failure is the state itself" (Zaidi 1999, 259).

Nearly all scholars who believe NGOs are supporting the state emphasize that there remain important roles for *both* governmental and

---

[6] See Martin (2005) for a similar sentiment regarding NGOs' role in Tajikistan.

nongovernmental organizations, and underscore the importance of partnership between them (Obiyan 2005; Campos, Khan, and Tessendorf 2004; Clark 1995; Jelinek 2006). For example, Kenyan scholar B.M. Makau (1996, 87) argues that expansion of education in Kenya has been possible only because of partnerships between government, communities, NGOs, and private enterprises. Asian development expert Norman Uphoff agrees, stating that exclusive emphasis on the state, market, or NGOs will not suffice to develop poor countries, since the weaknesses in any one sector are compensated for by the strengths of others (1993, 607). Goren Hyden likewise writes, "Even those who do not necessarily favor the emergences of institutions independent of the state are ready to accept that government cannot do everything and that nongovernmental organizations (NGOs) are needed to help carry out public responsibilities" (1986, 72). Combined with capacity-building efforts for the government, NGOs can help to restore strength to weakened states through their activities. Such was the case in East Timor, where NGOs and donors helped restore government capacity after the breakdown of public management (Brinkerhoff 2010).

****

Beyond scholarly debates, this research has considerable practical importance for all countries experiencing the proliferation of NGOs in their territory. Using Kenya as a case study, we see how the Government of Kenya at various stages in the past has appeared quite threatened by the NGO and broader civil society community. Former president Moi called NGOs a "security threat" (US Department of State 1998), introduced restrictive monitoring, regulations and taxes for NGOs, and even deregistered some NGOs. Was this necessary? My research demonstrates that it was not. This is not to imply that NGOs are an unmitigated good; certainly not all NGOs have positive impacts and most have profound limitations. But on the whole, they buttress the state in Kenya.

At the end of the day, two things must be remembered. First, government service provision in weakly institutionalized states can improve, partially due to NGOs influence on the way services are provided and decisions are made. As one NGO leader explained, NGOs were doing their work initially because the government was not doing it, but they now complement each other. Such collaboration does not "just happen," however – government and NGO leaders have learned that collaboration requires purposeful efforts of co-construction (Soublière and Cloutier 2015). Second, government resources, despite what many NGO supporters suggest, are far greater than those of NGOs – a situation that is unlikely to change in the future. "We'd rather work without government," said one NGO leader, "but you can't. It won't make an impact without government, because they actually do most of the service provision . . . It creates more opportunities, though, working with them" (2008–44). In fact, NGOs rely on many of these government agencies. As one interviewee explained, "NGOs also *need* government. They have certain institutions enabling them to do their jobs" (2008–52). While NGO numbers could decline again in the future, the government is there to stay.

Appendix A

Programs or projects by NGO interviewed

(Machakos: roman text; Mbeere: italicized text)

AGRICULTURE

- Lobby central government to stop providing farm-related handouts, so that agro-dealer enterprises can grow. Created a voucher program with the government as an alternative.
- Fund agricultural stakeholder forums held by governments at the district level.
- Training for enterprise development in the agricultural sector, with the goal of food security, increased agricultural productivity.
- Do microcredit, ROSCA development for farm groups. The NGO guarantees these groups' loans with one of the nationwide banks.
- Microfranchise program: horticulture, poultry, dairy, and confectionary food processing.
- Income generation development through training on: crops, animals, chicken, fruit, honey, and how to market them better.
- Livelihood program: training in agriculture, livestock, and income generation.
- Private sector development: agricultural business development.
- Work to get farm inputs sold in smaller packages, so they are affordable to the "little guy."
- Food security program: training and goat-rearing program.
- Food security: training and help growing drought-tolerant crops.
- Food security program via farming, animal husbandry training, agricultural expositions.
- Provide restocking animals (goats, chickens) for food security.
- Training in agriculture and food security.

- Introduction and promotion of drought-resistant crops, specifically cassava.
- Supply non-GMO seedlings to farmers.
- Protest and lobby against the allowance of GMO seeds and produce in Kenya.
- Agro-forestry program.
- *Revitalization of cotton farming program.*
- *Linking cotton growers to ginner for better pricing.*
- *Promotion of drought-resistant crop, amaranthus, a high-protein grain crop.*
- *Promotion of beekeeping for income generation.*
- *Promotion of modern methods of beekeeping.*
- *Training farmers on: fruit farming, beekeeping, and value addition for crops.*
- *Development of fisheries, dairy goats, and pigeon peas for income generation.*
- *Capacity building on agricultural production, business development, fundraising.*
- *Provision of farming tools, food storage, agricultural marketing programs, livestock and vet services, goat keeping, and livestock upgrading.*
- *Goat-breeding program for agri-business, food security.*
- *Livelihood support and right to food program.*

EDUCATION

- Education quality improvement program in public primary schools: infrastructure improvement, provision of instructional materials, management committee training, in-service training for teachers.
- Opened a small library with a computer-training center.
- HIV/AIDS program in schools for grades 1–4, including clubs.
- HIV/AIDS training program in primary and secondary schools.
- Child sponsorship program: education, school fees, uniforms, and food.
- Child sponsorship program: support to orphans' foster families to encourage kids to stay in a home and not an orphanage: school fees, food, shelter, medical services.
- Child sponsorship program: education, school fees, uniforms, bursaries, etc.

- Orphan and Vulnerable Children (OVC) care program: money, medical support, school fees, uniforms, counseling and food.
- OVC support program: provides bursaries, uniforms, and books to public school children.
- Youth training on HIV/AIDS.
- Training to women to become tailors – they will make uniforms used in child sponsorship program.
- Youth training on self-reliance, small-scale business development.
- Hold workshops, seminars, trainings, and research for youth: goals are to get youth employment and involvement in development.
- *Computers-for-schools program, bringing computers, generators and training to secondary schools.*
- *Creation of a computer college, with low-cost computer training.*
- *Child sponsorship program: bursaries for secondary school, clothing, etc.*
- *Sponsorships for primary and secondary school students.*
- *Early child development programs: funding of teachers.*
- *School infrastructure rehabilitation, especially in primary schools and early childhood development centers.*
- *School construction and maintenance: put up a secondary school science lab, equipped classrooms, staffroom furniture, etc.*
- *Education schools and facilities program.*
- *Adult literacy program.*

ENVIRONMENT

- Capacity building in natural resource management in drought-prone areas.
- Water provision.
- Water development: service dams, tanks and deep-well surveys and boreholes.
- Training on water management.
- Drill boreholes.
- Agro-forestry program.
- Build sand dams for business development.
- *Plant trees at the village level, promoting afforestation.*
- *Seedlings and tree farm program.*
- *Tree planting, soil conservation, tree nurseries programs.*
- *Extension of government pipeline to provide water.*
- *Provision of clean water, distribution of water pipes to groups.*

GENERAL DEVELOPMENT

- Built multi-purpose community hall and two large hostels for people staying for their programs.
- Integrated development programs: training on water/sanitation, disease prevention, food security, poverty eradication, health centers.
- Training in general capacity building: working in any sector, depending on what the community asks for.
- Training on Millennium Development Goals as part of a government awareness program: included radio programming in local languages.
- Capacity building on management skills, organizational development.
- Private sector development: encouraging savings, help opening bank accounts, group-based accounts.
- Training in income generation and microcredit.
- Rural finance program.
- Microlending program based on Grameen model.
- Created microfinance groups, given low-interest loans.
- Provide revolving small loans and grants.
- Make soap, bleach and juice for income generation, and train others on it.
- *Financial assistance via loans, check-cashing and savings programs.*
- *Revolving loan program.*
- *Business management training.*
- *Training on financial service provision, creation of financial services center.*
- *Capacity building on savings, microfinance, business skills, etc.*

HEALTH

- Child sponsorship program: support to HIV/AIDS orphans' foster families to encourage kids to stay in a home and not an orphanage: school fees, food, shelter, medical services.
- Provide counseling to orphans, many of whom took care of their dying parents.
- Built two maternities/dispensaries, to be turned over to government when finished.
- Built medical clinic in a peri-rural community: staffed by one registered nurse and administrative staff.
- Health services via clinics.
- Training community-based health workers.

- Water provision for better health.
- Bring safe drinking water to community.
- Provide hygiene and disease prevention training.
- Undertake mass vaccinations campaign, mobilizing people to get vaccinated.
- Logistics and administration of blood donor program.
- Rallies and awareness campaigns to teach people about HIV/AIDS.
- Train local and religious leaders on HIV/AIDS.
- HIV and general healthcare through clinics.
- Training on health issues, such as HIV and OVCs.
- Condom distribution and training program along major highways.
- Community assistance with HIV/AIDS-affected people.
- Provision of PMTCT (prevention of mother-to-child transmission) training, drugs in clinics.
- HIV/AIDS program in schools for grades 1–4, including clubs.
- Training on providing home-based care for HIV/AIDS patients.
- Trained VCT workers (voluntary counseling and testing for HIV); opened VCTs.
- HIV/AIDS training program in primary and secondary schools.
- Support to HIV/AIDS-affected families.
- Lobbied successfully for piped water to be brought to a greater portion of the district.
- *Mosquito net program for prevention of malaria.*
- *Healthcare: treatment, lab work, children under five, family planning, VCT, antenatal, STDs, HIV management.*
- *Medicine and medical packages to dispensaries and local hospitals: given computers, chairs, medical supplies, medicines, payment of staff, provision of donkey for fetching water.*
- *Training on proper nutrition.*
- *Deworming program.*
- *Support for people living with HIV.*
- *Training of home-based caregivers for HIV/AIDS.*
- *Food donations and support to youth living with HIV.*

MARGINAL GROUPS

- Rehabilitate street children.
- Training to women to become tailors – they will make uniforms used in child sponsorship programs.

- Monitor the abuses of the rights of women and children, report to authorities and refer to helping organizations.
- Savings associations, loans for parents of at-risk children.
- Child sponsorship program: education, school fees, uniforms, food.
- Child sponsorship program: support to orphans' foster families to encourage kids to stay in a home and not an orphanage: school fees, food, shelter, medical services.
- Child sponsorship program: education, school fees, uniforms, bursaries, etc.
- OVC care program: money, medical support, school fees, uniforms, counseling and food.
- OVC community-based care and child sponsorship.
- OVC support program: provides bursaries, uniforms, books to public-school children.
- Youth training on HIV/AIDS.
- Youth training: education, vocational training, drug abuse and behavioral change, and communications.
- Youth resource center to give constructive pastimes to the youth: goal is to train youth to do tailoring, video and documentary creation.
- Youth training on self-reliance, small-scale business development.
- Hold workshops, seminars, trainings and research for youth: goals are to get youth employment and involvement in development.
- Bring youth voices to government and international agency policymakers: e.g. National Youth Policy, MGD steering committee, etc.
- Monitor/evaluate use of government youth funds.
- Enterprise development for youth: beekeeping, value addition for fruits, horticulture, vegetables, etc.
- *Feeding programs, Christmas party for orphans.*
- *Child sponsorship program: bursaries for secondary school, clothing, etc.*
- *Relief to the elderly and marginalized: blankets, clothes, food, etc.*
- *Program on women's rights and empowerment.*

OTHER

- Hold Bible study/fun camps for sponsored children.
- Road safety program, designed to reduce accident numbers.

PEACE AND GOVERNANCE

- Act as a watchdog of government; providing info to/from government.
- Monitor government spending, implementation, and use of taxes.
- Assist people in protesting government mismanagement, misuse of funds and participating in holding government accountable.
- Initiate/inspire residents' associations across the country, to be used as a tool of governance: ultimate goal is "sustained access to public services."
- Help government make policy with regard to service provision, current wastage in government provision.
- Write "service report cards" on service provision and citizens' feelings about them: have been imitated by government.
- Organization of district-level participation in national human rights program, National Action Plan (NAP) on human rights.
- Conduct civic education training on constitution and constitutionalism, nationhood and nation building, democracy, governance, peace building and human rights.
- Conduct legal and law-based civic education, teaching people about laws, their rights, and rights vis-à-vis taxes they pay, as well as fact that they do pay tax (VAT).
- Represent minority issues at the national level: goal of influencing policy on pastoralists, livestock, minorities, human rights, land reform, constitutional reform.
- Run annual "pastoralists' week" – bringing issues particular to pastoralists to light at the national level.
- *Advocacy programs.*
- *Empowerment, governance, human rights training program.*

RELIEF

- Emergency response programs.

References

Abers, Rebecca Neaera, and Margaret E. Keck. 2006. "Muddy Waters: The Political Construction of Deliberative River Basin Governance in Brazil." *International Journal of Urban and Regional Research* no. 30 (3): 601–622. doi: 10.1111/j.1468-2427.2006.00691.x.

2009. "Mobilizing the State: The Erratic Partner in Brazil's Participatory Water Policy." *Politics & Society* no. 37 (2): 289–314. doi: 10.1177/0032329209334003.

2013. *Practical Authority Agency and Institutional Change in Brazilian Water Politics.* Oxford: Oxford University Press.

AFP. 2013. "Uhuru Turned ICC Indictment to His Campaign Advantage" *Daily Nation*, March 11, 2013. http://www.nation.co.ke/News/politics/Uhuru-turned-ICC-indictment-to-his-campaign-advantage-/-/1064/1716718/-/i5wvtp/-/index.html.

Afrobarometer. 2008. *Summary of Results: Round 4 Afrobarometer Survey in Kenya, 2008.* East Lansing, MI: Michigan State University.

Allison, Graham. 1971. *Essence of Decision: Explaining the Cuban Missile Crisis.* Boston: Little Brown.

Amutabi, Maurice Nyamanga. 2006. *The NGO Factor in Africa: The Case of Arrested Development in Kenya.* New York: Routledge.

Anangwe, Amukowa. 1995. "Maintenance of Law and Order in Western Kenya." In *Service Provision under Stress in East Africa*, edited by Joseph Semboja and Ole Therkildsen, 105–120. Copenhagen: Center for Development Research.

Anderson, J. 1970. *The Struggle for the School.* London: Longman.

Ansell, Chris, and Alison Gash. 2008. "Collaborative Governance in Theory and Practice." *Journal of Public Administration Research and Theory* no. 18 (4): 543–571. doi: 10.1093/jopart/mum032.

Arriola, Leonardo R. 2013. *Multiethnic Coalitions in Africa.* New York: Cambridge University Press.

Atibil, Christiana. 2012. "Democratic Governance and Actors' Conceptualization of 'Civil Society' in Africa: State–Civil Society Relations in Ghana

243

from 1982–2000." *Voluntas: International Journal of Voluntary and Nonprofit Organizations* no. 23 (1): 43–62. doi: 10.1007/s11266-011-9242-0.

Austin, James E. 2000. "Strategic Collaboration Between Nonprofits and Business." *Nonprofit and Voluntary Sector Quarterly* no. 29 (suppl 1): 69–97. doi: 10.1177/089976400773746346.

Baggetta, Matthew. 2009. "Making Citizens: How Associations Stimulate Individual Civic Engagement Through the Development of Civic Mindfulness." Paper presented at the American Sociological Association Annual Meeting. San Francisco: CA.

Banks, Nicola, and David Hulme. 2012. *The Role of NGOs and Civil Society in Development and Poverty Reduction.* Manchester, UK: Brooks World Poverty Institute.

Banks, Nicola, David Hulme, and Michael Edwards. 2015. "NGOs, States, and Donors Revisited: Still Too Close for Comfort?" *World Development* no. 66: 707–718. doi: http://dx.doi.org/10.1016/j.worlddev.2014.09.028.

Barber, Martin, and Cameron Bowie. 2008. "How International NGOs Could Do Less Harm and More Good." *Development in Practice* no. 18 (6): 748–754. doi: 10.1080/09614520802386520.

Barkan, Joel D. 1975. *An African Dilemma: University Students, Development, and Politics in Ghana, Tanzania, and Uganda.* Nairobi: Oxford University Press.

Barkan, Joel D., Judith K. Geist, and Njunguna Ng'ethe. 2003. *Kenya in Transition.* Washington, DC: The World Bank.

Barkan, Joel D., and Michael Chege. 1989. "Decentralising the State: District Focus and the Politics of Reallocation in Kenya." *The Journal of Modern African Studies* no. 27 (3): 431–453. doi: 10.2307/161101.

Barkan, Joel D., and Frank Holmquist. 1989. "Peasant–State Relations and the Social Base of Self-Help in Kenya." *World Politics* no. 41 (3): 359–380. doi: 10.2307/2010504.

Barr, Abigail, Fafchamps Marcel, and Owens Trudy. 2005. "The Governance of Non-Governmental Organizations in Uganda." *World Development* no. 33 (4): 657–679.

Bates, Robert H. 1981. *Markets and States in Tropical Africa.* Berkeley: University of California Press.

    1989. *Beyond the Miracle of the Market.* New York: Cambridge University Press.

Batley, Richard. 2006. "Engaged or Divorced? Cross-service Findings on Government Relations with Nonstate Service-providers." *Public Administration and Development* no. 26 (3): 241–251. doi: 10.1002/pad.422.

    2011. "Structures and Strategies in Relationships Between Nongovernment Service Providers and Governments." *Public Administration and Development* no. 31 (4): 306–319. doi: 10.1002/pad.606.

Batley, Richard, and Claire McLoughlin. 2010. "Engagement with Nonstate Service Providers in Fragile States: Reconciling State-Building and Service Delivery." *Development Policy Review* no. 28 (2): 131–154. doi: 10.1111/j.1467-7679.2010.00478.x.

Bauchet, Jonathan, Cristobal Marshall, Laura Starita, Jeanette Thomas, and Anna Yalouris. 2011. "Latest Findings from Randomized Evaluations of Microfinance." In *Access to Finance Forum: Reports by CGAP and its Partners*. Washington, DC: The World Bank.

Bayart, Jean-Francois. 1993. *The State in Africa: The Politics of the Belly*. New York: Longman.

BBC News Staff. 2013. "Did the ICC help Uhuru Kenyatta win Kenyan election?" *BBC News*. March 11, 2013. http://www.bbc.com/news/world-africa-21739347.

Bebbington, Anthony. 1997. "New States, New NGOs? Crises and Transitions among Rural Development NGOs in the Andean Region." *World Development* no. 25 (11): 1755–1765.

Bebbington, Anthony, John Farrington, David J. Lewis, and Kate Wellard. 1993. *Reluctant Partners? Nongovernmental Organizations, the State and Sustainable Agricultural Development*. New York: Routledge.

Berman, Bruce J. 1998. "Ethnicity, Patronage and the African State: The Politics of Uncivil Nationalism." *African Affairs* no. 97 (388): 305–341.

Bernard, Tanguy, Stefan Dercon, Kate Orkin, and Alemayehu Seyoum Taffesse. 2014. *The Future in Mind: Aspirations and Forward-Looking Behaviour in Rural Ethiopia*. In CSAE Working Paper Series. Centre for the Study of African Economies, University of Oxford.

Besley, Timothy, and Maitreesh Ghatak. 1999. *Public–Private Partnerships for the Provisions of Public Goods: Theory and an Application to NGOs*. In Development Economics Discussion Paper Series/17. London: STICERD, London School of Economics and Political Science.

Besley, Timothy, and Maitreesh Ghatak. 2001. "Government Versus Private Ownership of Public Goods." *Quarterly Journal of Economics*, no. 116 (4): 1343–1372.

Bevir, Mark. 2006. "Governance." In *Sage Encyclopedia of Governance*, edited by Mark Bevir. Thousand Oaks, CA: Sage Publications.

Bielefeld, Wolfgang, and James C. Murdoch. 2004. "The Locations of Nonprofit Organizations and their Forprofit Counterparts: An Exploratory Analysis." *Nonprofit and Voluntary Sector Quarterly* no. 33 (2): 221–246.

Bielefeld, Wolfgang, James C. Murdoch, and Paul Waddell. 1997. "The Influence of Demographics and Distance on Nonprofit Location." *Nonprofit and Voluntary Sector Quarterly* no. 26 (2): 207–225.

Biersteker, Thomas J. 2012. "State, Sovereignty, and Territory." In *Handbook of International Relations*, edited by Walter Carlsnaes, Thomas Risse and Beth A. Simmons. London: SAGE Publications Ltd.

Blattman, Chris. 2009. "From Violence to Voting: War and Political Participation in Uganda." *American Political Science Review* no. 103 (2): 231-247. doi: http://dx.doi.org/10.1017/S0003055409090212.

Boix, Charles, and Daniel Posner. 1998. "Social Capital: Explaining its Origins and Effects on Government Performance." *British Journal of Political Science* no. 28 (4): 686–693.

Bold, Tessa, Mwangi S. Kimenyi, Germano Mwabu, Alice Ng'ang'a, and Justin Sandefur. 2012. "Interventions & Institutions: Experimental Evidence on

Scaling up Education Reforms in Kenya." Center for Global Development. Mimeo.

Boone, Catherine. 2003. *Political Topographies of the African State*. New York: Cambridge University Press.

Börzel, Tanja A., and Thomas Risse. 2010. "Governance Without a State: Can It Work?" *Regulation & Governance* no. 4 (2): 113–134. doi: 10.1111/j.1748-5991.2010.01076.x.

Botchway, Karl. 2001. "Paradox of Empowerment: Reflections on a Case Study from Northern Ghana." *World Development* no. 29 (1): 135–153. doi: http://dx.doi.org/10.1016/S0305-750X(00)00084-X.

Boulding, Carew E. 2010. "NGOs and Political Participation in Weak Democracies: Subnational Evidence on Protest and Voter Turnout from Bolivia." *The Journal of Politics* no. 72 (02): 456–468. doi: 10.1017/S0022381609990922.

   2014. *NGOs, Political Protest and Civil Society*. New York: Cambridge University Press.

Boulding, Carew E., and Clark C. Gibson. 2009. "Supporters or Challengers? The Effects of Nongovernmental Organizations on Local Politics in Bolivia." *Comparative Political Studies* no. 42: 479–500.

Branch, Daniel, and Nic Cheeseman. 2005. "Briefing: Using Opinion Polls to Evaluate Kenyan Politics, March 2004–January 2005." *African Affairs* no. 104: 415, 325–336.

Brass, Jennifer N. 2012a. "Blurring Boundaries: The Integration of NGOs into Governance in Kenya." *Governance* no. 25 (2): 209–235. doi: 10.1111/j.1468-0491.2011.01553.x.

   2012b. "Why Do NGOs Go Where They Go? Evidence from Kenya." *World Development* no. 40 (2): 387–401. doi: 10.1016/j.worlddev.2011.07.017.

Bratton, Michael. 1989a. "The Politics of Government–NGO relations in Africa." *World Development* no. 17 (4): 569–587.

   1989b. "Beyond the State: Civil Society and Associational Life in Africa." *World Politics* no. 41 (3): 407–430.

   1990. "NGOs in Africa: Can They Influence Public Policy?" *Development and Change* no. 21 (1): 87-118.

Bratton, Michael E., E. Gyimah-Boadi, and Robert Mattes. 2008. *Afrobarometer Round 4: The Quality of Democracy and Governance in 20 African Countries, 2008–2009*. Ann Arbor, MI: ICPSR.

Bratton, Michael, and Nicolas van de Walle. 1997. *Democratic Experiments in Africa: Regime Transitions in Comparative Perspective*. Cambridge: Cambridge University Press.

Brautigam, Deborah. 1994. "State, NGOs, and International Aid in The Gambia." In *The Changing Politics of Nongovernmental Organizations and African States*, edited by Eve Sandberg, 59–82. Westport, CT: Praeger.

   1996. "State Capacity and Effective Governance." In *Agenda for Africa's Economic Renewal*, edited by Ben Ndulu and Nicolas van de Walle, 81–108. Washington, DC: Overseas Development Council.

Brautigam, Deborah A., and Monique Segarra. 2007. "Difficult Partnerships: The World Bank, States, and NGOs." *Latin American Politics and Society* no. 49 (4): 149–181.

Briggs, Ryan C. 2014. "Aiding and Abetting: Project Aid and Ethnic Politics in Kenya." *World Development* no. 64: 194–205. doi: http://dx.doi.org/10.1016/j.worlddev.2014.05.027.

Brinkerhoff, Derick W. 2002. "Government–Nonprofit Partners for Health Sector Reform in Central Asia: Family Group Practice Associations in Kazakhstan and Kyrgyzstan." *Public Administration and Development* no. 22 (1): 51–61. doi: 10.1002/pad.206.

———. 2010. "Developing Capacity in Fragile States." *Public Administration and Development* no. 30 (1): 66–78. doi: 10.1002/pad.545.

Brodhead, Tim. 1987. "NGOs: In One Year, Out the Other?" *World Development* no. 15: Supplement, 1–6.

Brook, Timothy B., and Michael Frolic. 1997. *Civil Society in China*. Armonk, NY: M.E. Sharpe.

Brunt, Carol, and Willy McCourt. 2012. "Do International Nongovernmental Organizations Walk The Talk? Reconciling the 'Two Participations' In International Development." *Journal of International Development* no. 24 (5): 585–601. doi: 10.1002/jid.2851.

Bryant, Raymond L. 2001. "Explaining State–Environmental NGO Relations in the Philippines and Indonesia." *Singapore Journal of Tropical Geography* no. 22 (1): 15–37. doi: 10.1111/1467-9493.00091.

Büthe, Tim, Solomon Major, and Andre de Mello e Souza. 2012. "The Politics of Private Foreign Aid: Humanitarian Principles, Economic Development Objectives and Organizational Interests in the Allocation of Private Aid by NGOs." *International Organization* no. 66 (4): 571-607.

California State Parks Foundation. 2011. "Key Legislation to Help Keep State Parks Open Clears Legislature." http://archive.calparks.org/press/2011/key-legislation-to-help-keep-state-parks-open-clears-legislature.html (accessed April 25, 2016).

Callaghy, Thomas. 1987. "The State as Lame Leviathan: The Patrimonial Administrative State in Africa." In *The African State in Transition*, edited by Zaki Ergas. New York: St. Martin's Press.

Callaghy, Thomas M., Ronald Kassimir, and Robert Latham. 2001. "Chapter 1: Introduction: Transboundary Formations, Intervention, Order and Authority." In *Intervention and Transnationalism in Africa*, edited by Thomas M. Callaghy, Ronald Kassimir and Robert Latham, 1–20. Cambridge: Cambridge University Press.

Cammett, Melani, and Lauren MacLean. 2011. "Introduction: the Political Consequences of Non-state Social Welfare in the Global South." *Studies in Comparative International Development (SCID)* no. 46 (1): 1–21. doi: 10.1007/s12116-010-9083-7.

Campbell, Will. 1996. The Potential for Donor Mediation in NGO–State Relations: An Ethiopian Case Study. In Working papers 33. Brighton, UK: Institute of Development Studies.

Campos, Nauro F., Feisal U. Khan, and Jennifer E. Tessendorf. 2004. "From Substitution to Complementarity: Some Econometric Evidence on the Evolving NGO–State Relationship in Pakistan." *The Journal of Developing Areas* no. 37 (2): 49–72.

Cannon, Christy. 2000. NGOs and the State: A Case Study from Uganda. In *Development, NGOs, and Civil Society*, edited by J. Pearce. Oxford: Oxfam.

Cannon, Christy. 1996. "NGOs and the State: a Case-study from Uganda." *Development in Practice* no. 6 (3): 262–265.

CARE. 2011. *Horn of Africa Food Crisis* 2011 [cited September 6, 2011]. Available from http://www.care.org/emergency/Horn-of-Africa-food-poverty-crisis-Dadaab-2011/index.asp.

Carr, Edward C. 2011. *Delivering Development: Globalization's Shoreline and the Road to a Sustainable Future*. New York: Palgrave Macmillan.

Carrard, N., D. Pedi, J. Willetts, and B. Powell. 2009. "Nongovernment Organisation Engagement in the Sanitation Sector: Opportunities to Maximise Benefits." *Water Science and Technology* no. 60 (12): 3109–3119. doi: 10.2166/wst.2009.744.

Chabal, Patrick, and Jean-Pascal Daloz. 1999. *Africa Works: Disorder as Political Instrument*. Bloomington, IN: Indiana University Press.

Chambers, Robert. 1983. *Rural Development: Putting the Last First*. Harlow: Longman.

Chaudhry, Kiren. 1993. "The Myths of the Market and Common History of Late Developers." *Politics & Society* no. 21 (3): 245–274.

Cheeseman, Nic. 2008. "The Kenyan Elections of 2007: An Introduction." *Journal of Eastern African Studies* no. 2 (2): 166–184. doi: 10.1080/17531050802058286.

Chege, Sam. 1999. "Donors Shift More Aid to NGOs." *Africa Recovery* no. 13 (1): 6.

Chieni, Susan Njeri. 1997. The *Harambee* Movement in Kenya: the Role Played by Kenyans and the Government in the Provision of Education and Other Social Services. In Seventh BOLESWA Symposium. University of Swaziland, Kwaluseni.

Chikwendu, Eudora. 2004. "AIDS/HIV – When the State Fails: NGOs in Grassroots AIDS Care." *Dialectical Anthropology* no. 28 (3): 245–259. doi: 10.1007/s10624-004-3584-6.

Clark, John. 1991. *Democratizing Development: The Role of Voluntary Organizations*. West Hartford, CT: Kumarian Press.

——— 1992. "Democratising Development: NGOs and the State." *Development in Practice* no. 2 (3): 151–162. doi: 10.1080/096145249200077991.

——— 1993. "The State and the Voluntary Sector." In *Human Resources Development and Operations Policy Working Papers*. Washington, DC: The World Bank.

——— 1995. "The State, Popular Participation and the Voluntary Sector." *World Development* no. 23 (4): 593–601. doi: 10.1016/0305-750x(94)00147-q

Clayton, Andrew. 1998. "NGOs and Decentralised Government in Africa." In *INTRAC Occasional Papers Series No. 18*.

Cleaver, Frances. 2002. "Paradoxes of Participation: Questioning Participatory Approaches to Development." In *The Earthscan Reader on NGO Management*, edited by Michael Edwards and Alan Fowler, 225–240. London: Routledge.

Cleveland, Harland. 1972. *The Future Executive: A Guide for Tomorrow's Managers*. New York: Harper & Row.

Cloward, Karisa Tritz. 2011. Jack of All Trades, Master of None: Pathologies of Grassroots NGOs. Paper read at 2011 APSA Annual Meeting, at Seattle, WA.

Cook, Linda J. 2007. *Postcommunist Welfare States: Reform Politics in Russia and Eastern Europe*. New York: Cornell University Press.

Cooley, Alexander, and James Ron. 2002a. "The NGO Scramble Organizational Insecurity and the Political Economy of Transnational Action." *International Security* no. 27 (1): 5–39.

Coston, Jennifer M. 1998. "A Model and Typology of Government–NGO Relationships." *Nonprofit and Voluntary Sector Quarterly* no. 27 (3): 358–382. doi: 10.1177/0899764098273006.

Dahl, Robert. 1961. *Who Governs?* New Haven: Yale University Press.

de Waal, Alex 1997. *Famine Crimes: Politics and the Disaster Relief Industry in Africa*. Bloomington: Indiana University Press.

Deininger, Klaus, and Paul Mpuga. 2005. "Does Greater Accountability Improve the Quality of Public Service Delivery? Evidence from Uganda." *World Development* no. 33 (1): 171–191.

Desai, Raj M., and Shareen Joshi. 2011. Can the Poor Be Organized? Experimental Evidence from Self-Help Groups in Rural India. Paper Presented at the American Political Science Association Annual Meeting, Seattle.

DFID. 2008. "Working Paper Series: Capacity Building." In *DFID Research Strategy 2008–2013*. London: DFID.

Dicklitch, Susan. 1998. *The Elusive Promise of NGOs in Africa: Lessons from Uganda*. New York: Macmillan and St. Martin's Press.

Dietrich, Simone. 2013. "Bypass or Engage? Explaining Donor Delivery Tactics in Foreign Aid Allocation." *International Studies Quarterly* no. 57 (4): 698–712. doi: 10.1111/isqu.12041.

Dietrich, Simone, and Matthew S. Winters. 2015. "Foreign Aid and Government Legitimacy." *Journal of Experimental Political Science* no. 2 (2): 164–171. doi: 10.1017/XPS.2014.31.

Dill, Brian. 2009. "The Paradoxes of Community-based Participation in Dar es Salaam." *Development and Change* no. 40 (4): 717–743. doi: 10.1111/j.1467-7660.2009.01569.x.

DiMaggio, Paul, and Walter Powell. 1983. "The Iron Cage Revisited: Institutional Isomorphism and Collective Rationality in Organizational Fields." *American Sociological Review* no. 48: 147–160.

Doornbos, Martin. 1990. "The African State in Academic Debate: Retrospect and Prospect." *Journal of Modern African Studies* no. 28 (2): 179–198.

Doyle, Cathal, and Preeti Patel. 2008. "Civil Society Organisations and Global Health Initiatives: Problems of Legitimacy." *Social Science & Medicine* no. 66 (9): 1928–1938. doi: 10.1016/j.socscimed.2007.12.029.

Easton, David. 1965. *A Systems Analysis of Political Life*. New York: John Wiley & Sons.

Ebrahim, Alnoor. 2003. "Accountability in practice: Mechanisms for NGOs." *World Development* no. 31 (5): 813–829.

2005. *NGOs and Organizational Change*. New York: Cambridge University Press.

Edwards, Michael. 2000. *NGO Rights and Responsibilities: A New Deal for Global Governance*. London: Foreign Policy Centre.

Edwards, Michael, and David Hulme. 1996a. *Beyond the Magic Bullet: NGO Performance and Accountability in the Post-Cold War World*. West Hartford, CT: Kumarian Press.

Edwards, Michael, and David Hulme. 1996b. "Too Close for Comfort? The Impact of Official Aid on Nongovernmental Organizations." *World Development* no. 24 (6): 961–973.

Egan, Erica. 1991. "Relief and Rehabilitation Work in Mozambique: Institutional Capacity and NGO Executional Strategies." *Development in Practice* no. 1 (3): 174–184.

Eikenberry, Angela M., and Jodie Drapal Kluver. 2004. "The Marketization of the Nonprofit Sector: Civil Society at Risk?" *Public Administration Review* no. 64 (2): 132–140. doi: 10.1111/j.1540–6210.2004.00355.x.

Ejaz, Iram, Babar T. Shaikh, and Narjis Rizvi. 2011. "NGOs and Government Partnership for Health Systems Strengthening: A Qualitative Study Presenting Viewpoints of Government, NGOs and Donors in Pakistan." *BMC Health Services Research* no. 11 (1): 122–128. doi: 10.1186/1472–6963-11-122.

Ekeh, Peter. 1975. "Colonialism and the Two Publics in Africa: A Theoretical Statement." *Comparative Studies in Society and History* no. 17 (1): 91–112.

Enghoff, Martin, Bente Hansen, Abdi Umar, Bjorn Gildestad, Matthew Owen, and Alex Obara. 2010. In Search of Protection and Livelihoods: Socio-economic and Environmental Impacts of Dadaab Refugee Camps on Host Communities. Nairobi: Royal Danish Embassy, Republic of Kenya, and Norwegian Embassy.

Englebert, Pierre. 2000. *State Legitimacy and Development in Africa*. Boulder, CO: Lynne RiennerPublishers.

2009. *Africa: Unity, Sovereignty and Sorrow*. Boulder, CO: Lynne Rienner-Publishers.

Epstein, Gil S., and Ira N. Gang. 2006. "Contests, NGOs, and Decentralizing Aid." *Review of Development Economics* no. 10 (2): 285–296. doi: 10.1111/j.1467–9361.2006.00318.x.

Esman, Milton J., and Norman Uphoff. 1984. *Local Organizations: Intermediaries in Rural Development*. Ithaca: Cornell University Press.

Etzioni. 1965. "Organizational Control Structure." In *Handbook of Organizations*, edited by J.G. March, 650–677. Chicago: Rand McNally.

Evans, Peter. 1995. *Embedded Autonomy: States and Industrial Transformation*. Princeton, NJ: Princeton University Press.

1996. "Government Action, Social Capital and Development: Reviewing the Evidence on Synergy." *World Development* no. 24 (6): 1119–1132. doi: 10.1016/0305–750x(96)00021-6.

1997. "The Eclipse of the State? Reflections on Stateness in an Era of Globalization." *World Politics* no. 50 (1): 62–87.

Evans, Peter, Dietrich Rueschemeyer, and Theda Skocpol. 1985. *Bringing the State Back In.* Cambridge: Cambridge University Press.

Farrington, John, Anthony Bebbington, Kate Wellard, and David J. Lewis. 1993. *Reluctant Partners? NGOs, the State and Sustainable Agricultural Development.* London: Routledge.

Farrington, John, David J. Lewis, S. Satish, and Aurea Miclat-Teves (Eds.). 1993. *NGOs and the State in Asia: Rethinking Roles in Sustainable Agricultural Development.* London: Routledge.

Fearon, James D., Macartan Humphreys, and Jeremy M. Weinstein. 2011. Democratic Institutions and Collective Action Capacity: Results from a Field Experiment in Post-Conflict Liberia. Paper Presented at the American Political Science Association Annual Meeting: Seattle.

Fernando, Jude. 2011. *The Political Economy of NGOs: State Formation in Sri Lanka and Bangladesh.* London: Pluto Press.

Fernando, Jude L., and Alan W. Heston. 1997. "The Role of NGOs: Charity & Empowerment." *Annals of the American Academy of Political and Social Science* no. 554: 8–20.

Ferris, James, and Elizabeth Graddy. 1986. "Contracting Out: For What? With Whom?" *Public Administration Review* no. 46 (4): 332–344. doi: 10.2307/976307.

Finegold, Kenneth, and Theda Skocpol. 1995. *State and Party in America's New Deal.* Madison, WI: University of Wisconsin Press.

Fisher, Julie. 1998. *Non-Governments: NGOs and the Political Development of the Third World.* West Hartford, CT: Kumarian Press.

Flanigan, Shawn Teresa. 2008. "Nonprofit Service Provision by Insurgent Organizations: The Cases of Hizballah and the Tamil Tigers." *Studies in Conflict & Terrorism* no. 31 (6): 499–519. doi: 10.1080/10576100802065103.

Foster, Kenneth W. 2002. "Embedded within State Agencies: Business Associations in Yantai." *The China Journal* no. 47: 41–65.

Foucault, Michel. 1991. "Governmentality." In *The Foucault Effect: Studies in Governmentality,* edited by Graham Burchell, Colin Gordon and Peter Miller. Chicago: University of Chicago Press.

Fowler, Alan. 1991. "The Role of NGOs in Changing State–Society Relations: Perspectives from Eastern and Southern Africa." *Development Policy Review* no. 9: 53–84.

1995. "NGOs and the Globalization of Welfare: Perspectives from East Africa." In *Service Provision under Stress in East Africa,* edited by Joseph Semboja and Ole Therkildsen. London: James Currey.

Frederickson, George H. 2004. "Whatever Happened to Public Administration? Governance, Governance Everywhere." In *Working Paper QU/GOV/3/2004.* Belfast: Institute of Governance Public Policy and Social Research, Queen's University.

Freedom House. 2011. *The Authoritarian Challenge to Democracy. Freedom in the World 2011.* Washington, DC: Freedom House.

Fruttero, Anna, and Varun Gauri. 2005. "The Strategic Choices of NGOs: Location Decisions in Rural Bangladesh." *Journal of Development Studies* no. 41 (5): 759–787.

Gallagher, Mary E. 2004. China: The Limits of Civil Society in a Late Leninist State. In *Civil Society and Political Change in Asia: Expanding and Contracting Democratic Space*, edited by M. Alagappa, Stanford: Stanford University Press.

Garrison, John. 2000. *From Confrontation to Collaboration: civil society-government-World Bank relations in Brazil.* Washington, DC: World Bank.

Gazley, Beth. 2008. "Beyond the Contract: The Scope and Nature of Informal Government–Nonprofit Partnerships." *Public Administration Review* no. 68 (1): 141–154. doi: 10.1111/j.1540–6210.2007.00844.x.

Gazley, Beth, and Jeffrey L. Brudney. 2007. "The Purpose (and Perils) of Government–Nonprofit Partnership." *Nonprofit and Voluntary Sector Quarterly* no. 36 (3): 389–415. doi: 10.1177/0899764006295997.

Gerring, John. 2001. *Social Science Methodology: A Criterial Framework.* Cambridge: Cambridge University Press.

2008. "Case Selection for Case-Study Analysis: Qualitative and Quantitative Techniques." In *The Oxford Handbook of Political Methodology*, edited by Janet Box-Steffensmeier, Henry E. Brady and David Collier, 645–84. New York: Oxford University Press.

Gibson, Edward L. 2012. *Boundary Control: Subnational Authoritarianism in Federal Democracies.* Cambridge: Cambridge University Press.

Gifford, Paul. 2009. *Christianity, Politics and Public Life in Kenya.* London: Hurst & Company.

Gilley, Bruce. 2006a. "The Meaning and Measure of State Legitimacy: Results for 72 Countries." *European Journal of Political Research* no. 45: 499–525.

2006b. "The Determinants of State Legitimacy: Results for 72 Countries." *International Political Science Review* no. 27 (1): 47–71.

Goertz, Gary, and James Mahoney. 2012. *A Tale of Two Cultures: Qualitative and Quantitative Research in the Social Sciences.* Princeton, NJ: Princeton University Press.

Government of Kenya. 2007. *Vision 2030: the Popular Version.* Nairobi: Government Press.

Government of Kenya Ministry of State for the Development of Northern Kenya and Other Arid Lands. 2008. *Drought Monthly Bulletin, Mbeere District.* Nairobi: Government Printer.

Grindle, Merilee S. 1996. *Challenging the State: Crisis and Innovation in Latin America and Africa.* Cambridge: Cambridge University Press.

2004. "Good Enough Governance: Poverty Reduction and Reform in Developing Countries." *Governance* no. 17 (4): 525–548.

Grodeland, Ase Berit. 2006. "Public Perceptions of Nongovernmental Organisations in Serbia, Bosnia & Herzegovina, and Macedonia." *Communist and Post-Communist Studies* no. 39 (2): 221–246. doi: 10.1016/j.postcomstud .2006.03.002.

Grønbjerg, Kirsten A., and Laurie Paarlberg. 2001. "Community Variations in the Size and Scope of the Nonprofit Sector: Theory and Preliminary Findings." *Nonprofit and Voluntary Sector Quarterly* no. 30 (3): 684–706.

Guber, Peter. 2002. "The Impact of NGOs on State and Non-state Relations in the Middle East." *Middle East Policy* no. 9 (1): 139–148.

Gugerty, Mary Kay. 2008. "The Effectiveness of NGO Self-regulation: Theory and Evidence from Africa." *Public Administration and Development* no. 28: 105–118.

———. 2010. "The Emergence of Nonprofit Self-Regulation in Africa." *Nonprofit and Voluntary Sector Quarterly* no. 39 (6): 1087–1112.

Gugerty, Mary Kay, and Aseem Prakash. 2010. *Voluntary Regulation of NGOs and Nonprofits*. New York: Cambridge University Press.

Habib, Adam, and Rupert Taylor. 1999. "South Africa: Anti-Apartheid NGOs in Transition." *Voluntas: International Journal of Voluntary and Nonprofit Organizations* no. 10 (1): 73–82. doi: 10.2307/27927636.

Haggard, Stephen. 1990. *Pathways from the Periphery*. Ithaca: Cornell University Press.

Hancock, Graham. 1989. *Lords of Poverty: The Power, Prestige, and Corruption of the International Aid Business*. New York: Atlantic Monthly Press.

Harbeson, John W. 1994. "Civil Society and Political Renaissance in Africa." In *Civil Society and the State in Africa*, edited by John W. Harbeson, Donald Rothchild and Naomi Chazan, 1–29. Boulder, CO: Lynne Reinner Publishers.

Haugerud, Angelique. 1993. *The Culture of Politics in Modern Kenya*. New York: Cambridge University Press.

Hazlewood, Arthur. 1979. *The Economy of Kenya: The Kenyatta Era*. New York: Oxford University Press.

Hearn, Julie. 2003. "The 'Invisible' NGO: US Evangelical Missions in Kenya." *Journal of Religion in Africa* no. 32 (1): 32–60.

Heinrich, Volkhart Finn. 2001. "The Role of NGOs in Strengthening the Foundations of South African Democracy." *Voluntas: International Journal of Voluntary and Nonprofit Organizations* no. 12 (1): 1–15. doi: 10.1023/a:1011217326747.

Herbst, Jeffrey. 1996–97. "Responding to State Failure in Africa." *International Security* no. 21: 120–144.

———. 2000. *States and Power in Africa*. Princeton, NJ: Princeton University Press.

Hershey, Megan. 2013. "Explaining the Non-governmental Organization (NGO) Boom: the Case of HIV/AIDS NGOs in Kenya." *Journal of Eastern African Studies* no. 7 (4): 671–690. doi: 10.1080/17531055.2013.818776.

Herz, John H. 1968. "The Territorial State Revisited: Reflections on the Future of the Nation-state". *Polity* no. 1 (1). Palgrave Macmillan Journals: 11–34. doi: 10.2307/3233974.

Heurlin, Christopher. 2010. "Governing Civil Society: The Political Logic of NGO–State Relations Under Dictatorship." *Voluntas: International Journal of Voluntary & Nonprofit Organizations* no. 21 (2): 220–239. doi: 10.1007/s11266-009-9103-2.

Hill, Martin J.D. 1991. *The Harambee Movement in Kenya: Self-help, Development and Education Among the Kamba of Kitui District.* London: Athlone Press.

Hirschman, Albert O. 1981. *Essays in Trespassing: Economics to Politics & Beyond.* New York: Cambridge University Press.

Hochstetler, Kathryn, and Margaret E. Keck. 2007. *Greening Brazil: Environmental Activism in State and Society.* Durham, NC: Duke University Press.

Holmquist, Frank. 1979. "Class Structure, Peasant Participation, and Rural Self-help." In *Politics and Public Policy in Kenya and Tanzania,* edited by Joel D. Barkan and John J. Okumu, 129–153. New York: Praeger.

  1984. "Self-Help: The State and Peasant Leverage in Kenya." *Africa Development* no. 54 (3): 72–91.

Hornsby, Charles. 2013. *Kenya: A History Since Independence.* London: I.B. Tauris.

Hughes, Rebecca C. 2013. "'Science in the Hands of Love': British Evangelical Missionaries and Colonial Development in Africa, c. 1940–60." *The Journal of Imperial and Commonwealth History* no. 41 (5): 823–842. doi: 10.1080/03086534.2013.814255.

Human Rights Watch. 2010. "Kenya Country Summary." In *World Report 2010.* Washington, DC: Human Rights Watch.

Huntington, Samuel. 1978. *Political Order in Changing Societies.* New Haven, CT: Yale University Press.

Hyden, Goren. 1983. *No Short Cuts to Progress: African Development Management in Perspective.* Berkeley, CA: University of California Press.

  1986. "African Social Structure and Economic Development." In *Strategies for African Development,* edited by Robert J. Berg and Jennifer Seymour Whitaker. Berkeley: University of California Press.

ICNL. 1995. *Regulating Not-for-profit Organizations.* Washington, DC: International Center for Not-for-profit Law.

  2010. *NGO Law Monitor: Kenya.* International Center for Not-for-profit Law.

  2015. *NGO Law Monitor: Kenya.* International Center for Not-for-profit Law.

  2016. *NGO Law Monitor: Kenya.* International Center for Not-for-profit Law.

IDOC. 1975. "Uhuru and Harambee: Kenya in Search of Freedom and Unity." In *The Future of the Missionary Enterprise*: IDOC documentation participation project. Rome: IDOC International.

Igoe, Jim. 2003. "Scaling Up Civil Society: Donor Money, NGOs and the Pastoralist Land Rights Movement in Tanzania." *Development and Change* no. 34 (5): 863–885. doi: 10.1111/j.1467-7660.2003.00332.x.

International Crisis Group. 2013. "Kenya's 2013 Elections." In *Africa Report.* Brussels: International Crisis Group.

Jablonski, Ryan S. 2014. "How Aid Targets Votes: The Impact of Electoral Incentives on Foreign Aid Distribution." *World Politics* no. 66 (02): 293–330. doi: 10.1017/S0043887114000045.

Jackson, Robert. 1990. *Quasi-States: Sovereignty, International Relations, and the Third World.* Cambridge: Cambridge University Press.

Jackson, Robert H., and Carl G. Rosberg. 1982. "Why Africa's Weak States Persist: The Empirical and the Juridical in Statehood." *World Politics* no. 35 (1): 1–24.

1984a. "Popular Legitimacy in African Multi-Ethnic State." *Journal of Modern African Studies* no. 22 (2): 177–198.

1984b. "Personal Rule: Theory & Practice in Africa." *Contemporary Politics* no. 16 (4): 421–442.

Jacobsen, Karen. 2002. "Can Refugees Benefit the State? Refugee Resources and African Statebuilding." *Journal of Modern African Studies* no. 40 (4): 577–596.

Jammulamadaka, Nimruji. 2012. "The Needs of the Needy, or the Needs of the Donors?" *Critical Review* no. 24 (1): 37–50. doi: 10.1080/08913811.2012.684471.

Jelinek, Emilie. 2006. *A Study of NGO Relations with Government and Communities in Afghanistan*. Kabul: Agency Coordinating Body for Afghan Relief.

Jerven, Morton. 2013. *Poor Numbers: How We are Misled by African Development Statistics and What to Do About It*. Ithaca, NY: Cornell University Press.

Joassart-Marcelli, Pascale, and Alberto Giordano. 2006. "Does Local Access to Employment Services Reduce Unemployment? A GIS Analysis of One-stop Career Centers." *Policy Sciences* no. 39 (4): 335–359.

Joassart-Marcelli, Pascale, and Jennifer R. Wolch. 2003. "The Intrametropolitan Geography of Poverty and the Nonprofit Sector in Southern California." *Nonprofit and Voluntary Sector Quarterly* no. 32 (1): 70–96.

Johnson, Chalmers. 1982. *MITI and the Japanese Miracle*. Stanford: Stanford University Press.

Johnson, Martha. 2015. "Donor Requirements and Pockets of Effectiveness in Senegal's Bureaucracy" *Development Policy Review* no. 33 (6): 783–804.

Jordan, Andrew, Rudiger K.W. Wurzel, and Anthony Zito. 2005. "The Rise of 'New' Policy Instruments in Comparative Perspective: Has Governance Eclipsed Government?" *Political Studies* no. 53: 477–496.

Kaler, Amy, and Susan Cotts Watkins. 2001. "Disobedient Distributors: Street-level Bureaucrats and Would-be Patrons in Community-based Family Planning Programs in Rural Kenya." *Studies in Family Planning* no. 32 (3): 254–269.

Kamat, Sangeeta. 2004. "The Privatization of Public Interest: Theorizing NGO Discourse in a Neoliberal Era." *Review of International Political Economy* no. 11 (1): 155–176. doi: 10.1080/0969229042000179794.

Kameri-Mbote, Patricia. 2000. The Operational Environment and Constraints for NGOs in Kenya: Strategies for Good Policy and Practice. IELC Working Paper No. 2000–2. Geneva: International Environmental Law Research Centre.

Kanyinga, Karuti. 1996. "The Politics of Development Space in Kenya." In *Service Provision Under Stress in East Africa: State, NGOs & People's Organizations in Kenya, Tanzania and Uganda*, edited by Joseph Semboja and Ole Therkildsen, 70–86. Copenhagen: Centre for Development Research.

2004. "Civil Society Formations in Kenya: A Growing Role in Development and Democracy." In *Civil Society in the Third Republic*, edited by Duncan Okello. Nairobi: National Council of NGOs.

Kasa, Sjur, and Lars Otto Naess. 2005. "Financial Crisis and State–NGO Relations: The Case of Brazilian Amazonia, 1998–2000." *Society and Natural Resources* no. 18: 791–804.

Kasfir, Nelson. 1998. "The Conventional Notion of Civil Society: A Critique." *Commonwealth & Comparative Politics* no. 36 (2): 1–20. doi: 10.1080/14662049808447765.

Katumanga, Musambayi. 2004. "Civil Society and the Government: Conflict or Cooperation?" In *Civil Society in the Third Republic*, edited by Duncan Okello. Nairobi: National Council of NGOs.

Katusiimeh, Mesharch W. 2004. "Civil Society Organizations and Democratic Consolidation in Uganda." *African Journal of International Affairs* no. 7 (1): 99–116.

Keck, Margaret, and Katherine Sikkink. 1998. *Activists Beyond Borders*. Ithaca: Cornell University Press.

Keese, James, and Marco Freire Argudo. 2006. "Decentralisation and NGO–Municipal Government Collaboration in Ecuador." *Development in Practice* no. 16 (2): 114–127.

Kenya Human Rights Commission. 2013. *Countdown to the March 2013 General Elections: Interim Elections Monitoring Report*. Nairobi: KHRC.

Kenyans for Peace with Truth & Justice. 2012. *Ready or Note: An Assessment of Kenya's Preparedness for the General Election*. Nairobi: KPTJ.

Keohane, Robert. 1984. *After Hegemony: Cooperation and Discord in the World Political Economy*. Princeton, NJ: Princeton University Press.

Kerlin, Janelle A. 2006. "US Government Funding for International Nongovernment Organizations." In *Nonprofits in Focus: Urban Institute Policy Brief*. Washington, DC: The Urban Institute.

Kickert, Walter. 1997. "Public Governance in the Netherlands: An Alternative to Anglo-American 'Managerialism'." *Public Administration* no. 75 (4): 731–752.

Kidero, Jaindi. 2013. "Too Many Questions Surround the IT Systems Collapse During the Election." *Daily Nation*, March 19.

Kioko, Wanza, Laurence Muguru Mute, and S. Kichamu Akivaga. 2002. "Introduction: Nature of Discourse on Transition in Kenya." In *Building an Open Society: The Politics of Transition in Kenya*, edited by Wanza Kioko, Laurence Muguru Mute and S. Kichamu Akivaga. Nairobi: Claripress.

Kjaer, Mette, Ole Hersted Hansen, and Jens Peter Frolund Thomsen. 2002. "Conceptualizing State Capacity." DEMSTAR Research Report No. 6. Aarhus, DK: Democracy, the State and Administrative Reforms, Political Science Department, University of Aarhus.

Koch, Dirk-Jan, and Ruerd Ruben. 2008. "Spatial Clustering of NGOs: An Evolutionary Economic Geography Approach." In *Papers in Evolutionary Economic Geography*. Utrecht University.

Koeberke, Stefan, Zoran Stavreski, and Jan Walliser. 2006. *Budget Support as More Effective Aid? Recent Experiences and Emerging Lessons.* Washington, DC: The World Bank.

Kramon, Eric, and Daniel N. Posner. 2013. "Who Benefits from Distributive Politics? How the Outcome One Studies Affects the Answer One Gets." *Perspectives on Politics* no. 11 (02): 461–474. doi: 10.1017/S1537592713001035.

Lam, Wai Fung. 1996. "Institutional Design of Public Agencies and Coproduction: A Study of Irrigation Associations in Taiwan." *World Development* no. 24 (6): 1039–1054. doi: http://dx.doi.org/10.1016/0305-750X(96)00020-4.

Landau, Loren. 2002. The Humanitarian Hangover: Transformation and Transnationalization of Governmental Practice in Refugee-affected Tanzania. PhD, University of California, Berkeley.

LeBas, Adrienne. 2011. *From Protest to Parties: Party-Building and Democratization in Africa.* New York: Oxford University Press.

Leinweber, Ashley. 2011. New Hybrid Institutions: Muslim Public Schools in Post-Conflict Democratic Republic of Congo. Paper presented at the American Political Science Association Annual Meeting, Seattle.

Leonard, David K. 1991. *African Successes: Four Public Managers of Kenyan Rural Development.* Berkeley: University of California Press.

Leonard, David K., and Strauss, Scott. 2003. *Africa's Stalled Development.* Boulder, CO: Lynne Reinner Press.

Leonard, Kenneth L., and David K. Leonard. 2004. "The Political Economy of Improving Health Care for the Poor in Rural Africa: Institutional Solutions to the Principal–Agent Problem." *Journal of Development Studies* no. 40 (4): 50–77. doi: 10.1080/00220380410001673193.

Levi, Margaret, Audrey Sacks, and Tom Tyler. 2009. "Conceptualizing Legitimacy, Measuring Legitimating Beliefs." *American Behavioral Scientist* no. 53 (3): 354–375. doi: 10.1177/0002764209338797.

Levy, Brian, and Sahr John Kpundeh. 2004. *Building State Capacity in Africa: New Approaches, Emerging Lessons.* Washington, DC: World Bank Publications.

Lewis, Peter M. 1994. "Economic Statism, Private Capital, and the Dilemmas of Accumulation in Nigeria." *World Development* no. 22 (3): 437–451. doi: 10.1016/0305-750x(94)90134-1.

Lewis, Tammy L. 2003. "Environmental Aid: Driven by Recipient Need or Donor Interests?" *Social Science Quarterly* no. 84 (1): 144–161. doi: 10.1111/1540-6237.8401009-11.

Leys, Colin. 1975. *Underdevelopment in Kenya: the Political Economy of Neo-colonialism, 1964–1971.* London: Heinemann.

Lister, Sarah. 2003. "NGO Legitimacy: Technical Issue or Social Construct?" *Critique of Anthropology* no. 23 (2): 175–192.

Liston, Vanessa. 2008. "NGOs and Spatial Dimensions of Poverty in Kenya." Paper presented at the African Studies Association UK Biennial Conference. Preston, Lancashire.

MacLean, Lauren M., Jennifer N. Brass, Sanya Carley, Ashraf El-Arini, and Scott Breen. 2015. "Democracy and the Distribution of NGOs Promoting Renewable Energy in Africa." *The Journal of Development Studies* 51 (6): 725–742. doi: 10.1080/00220388.2014.989994.

MacLean, Lauren Morris. 2004. "Mediating Ethnic Conflict at the Grassroots: the Role of Local Associational Life in Shaping Political Values in Côte d'Ivoire and Ghana." *The Journal of Modern African Studies* no. 42 (04): 589–617. doi: 10.1017/S0022278X04000412.

Makau, B.M. 1996. "Dynamics of Partnership in the Provision of General Education in Kenya." In *Service Provision Under Stress in East Africa: State, NGOs & People's Organizations in Kenya, Tanzania and Uganda*, edited by Semboja, Joseph and Ole Therkildsen. Copenhagen: Centre for Development Research.

Maren, Michael. 2002. *The Road to Hell: The Ravaging Effects of Foreign Aid and International Charity*. New York: Free Press.

Martin, Jay. 2004. *Can Magic Bullets Hurt You? NGOs and Governance in a Globalised Social Welfare World. A Case Study of Tajikistan*. Australian National University Graduate Program in Public Policy, Discussion Paper No. 92.

Matthews, Jessica T. 1997. "Power Shift." *Foreign Affairs* no. 76 (1): 52–53.

Mayhew, Susannah H. 2005. "Hegemony, Politics and Ideology: the Role of Legislation in NGO-Government Relations in Asia." *The Journal of Development Studies* no. 41 (5): 727–758. doi: 10.1080/00220380500145263.

Mbithi, Philip M., and Rasmus Rasmusson. 1977. *Self Reliance in Kenya: The Case of Harambee*. Uppsala: Nordic Africa Institute.

McGann, James, and Mary Johnstone. 2006. "The Power Shift and the NGO Credibility Crisis." *The International Journal of Not-for-Profit Law* no. 8 (2): 65–77.

McLoughlin, Claire. 2011. "Factors Affecting State–Nongovernmental Organisation Relations In Service Provision: Key Themes From The Literature." *Public Administration and Development* no. 31 (4): 240–251. doi: 10.1002/pad.611.

2015. "When Does Service Delivery Improve the Legitimacy of a Fragile or Conflict-Affected State?" *Governance* no. 28 (3): 341–356. doi: 10.1111/gove.12091.

McSherry, Brendan, and Jennifer N. Brass. 2007. "The Political Economy of Pro-Poor Livestock Policy Reform in Kenya." In *IGAD-LPI Working Paper*. Addis Ababa: IGAD Livestock Policy Initiative.

Mercer, Claire. 1999. "Reconceptualizing State–Society Relations: Are NGOs 'Making a Difference'?" *Area* no. 31 (3): 247–258.

2002. "NGOs, Civil Society and Democratization: a Critical Review of the Literature." *Progress in Development Studies* no. 2 (1): 5–22.

2003. "Performing Partnership: Civil Society and the Illusions of Good Governance in Tanzania." *Political Geography* no. 22 (7): 741–763.

Meyer, Carrie. 1997. "The Political Economy of NGOs and Information." *World Development* no. 25 (7): 1127–1140.

Migdal, Joel. 1988. *Strong Societies and Weak States: State–Society Relations and State Capabilities in the Third World.* Princeton: Princeton University Press.

2001. *State in Society: Studying How States and Societies Transform and Constitute One Another.* Cambridge: Cambridge University Press.

Mkandawire, Thandika. 2001. "Thinking About Developmental States in Africa." *Cambridge Journal of Economics* no. 25: 289–313.

Moore, Barrington. 1966. *Social Origins of Dictatorship and Democracy: Lord and Peasant in the Making of the Modern World.* Boston: Beacon Press.

Moore, Sarah, Jamie Winders, Oliver Fröhling, John Paul Jones, and Susan M. Roberts. 2007. "Mapping the Grassroots: NGO Formalisation in Oaxaca, Mexico." *Journal of International Development* no. 19 (2): 223–237. doi: 10.1002/jid.1329.

Morfit, N. Simon. 2011. "'AIDS is Money': How Donor Preferences Reconfigure Local Realities." *World Development* no. 39 (1): 64–76. doi: http://dx.doi.org/10.1016/j.worlddev.2010.09.003.

Mosley, Paul, and Suleiman Abrar. 2006. "Trust, Conditionality and Aid Effectiveness." In *Budget Support as More Effective Aid? Recent Experiences and Emerging Lessons*, edited by Stefan Koeberke, Zoran Stavreski and Jan Walliser. Washington, DC: The World Bank.

Moyo, Dambisa. 2009. *Dead Aid: Why Aid Is Not Working and How There Is a Better Way for Africa.* New York: Farrar, Straus and Giroux.

Nair, Padmaja. 2011. "Evolution of the Relationship Between the State and Nongovernment Organisations: A South Asian Perspective." *Public Administration and Development* no. 31 (4): 252–261. doi: 10.1002/pad.610.

Najam, Adil. 1996. "Understanding the Third Sector: Revisiting the Prince, the Merchant, and the Citizen." *Nonprofit Management and Leadership* no. 7 (2): 203–221.

2000. "The Four C's of Government Third Sector–Government Relations." *Nonprofit Management and Leadership* no. 10 (4): 375–396. doi: 10.1002/nml.10403.

Naseemullah, Adnan. 2014. "Shades of Sovereignty: Explaining Political Order and Disorder in Pakistan's Northwest." *Studies in Comparative International Development* no. 49 (4): 501–522.

National Council of NGOs of Kenya. 2005. *Directory of NGOs in Kenya.* Nairobi: National Council of NGOs.

National Democratic Institute and Institute for Development Studies. 2011. *Nationwide Survey in Kenya.* Nairobi: Institute for Development Studies, University of Nairobi.

Natsoulas, Theodore. 1998. "The Kenyan Government and the Kikuyu Independent Schools: From Attempted Control to Suppression, 1929–1952." *The Historian* no. 60 (2): 289–306.

Ndegwa, Stephen N. 1994. "Civil Society and Political Change in Africa: The Case of Nongovernmental Organizations in Kenya." *International Journal of Comparative Sociology* no. 35(1): 19–36.

1996. *The Two Faces of Civil Society: NGOs and Politics in Africa.* Hartford, CT: Kumarian Press.

1998. "The Incomplete Transition: The Constitutional and Electoral Context in Kenya." *Africa Today* no. 45 (2): 193–211. doi: 10.2307/4187218.

Neal, Rachael. 2008. "The Importance of the State: Political Dimensions of a Nonprofit Network in Oaxaca, Mexico." *Nonprofit and Voluntary Sector Quarterly* no. 37 (3): 492–511. doi: 10.1177/0899764007310422.

Nemenoff, Erin K. 2008. "Indiscriminate or Intentional: Locations of Nonprofit Organizations in Kansas City." *Journal of Interdisciplinary Research* no. 2 (1): 101–110.

Ng'ethe, Njuguna, and Karuti Kanyinga. 1992. "The Politics of Development Space: the State and NGOs in the Delivery of Basic Services in Kenya." In *Working Papers*. Nairobi: Institute for Development Studies.

Ng'ethe, Njuguna, Winnie Mitullah, and Mutahi Ngunyi. 1990. *Nongovernmental Organizations: Local Capacity Building and Community Mobilization*. Nairobi: Institute for Development Studies.

Ng'ethe, Njuguna. 1991. *In Search of NGOs*. Nairobi: Institute for Development Studies.

NGOs Co-ordination Board. 2009. *Report on the National Validation Survey of NGOs*. Nairobi: NGOs Co-ordination Board.

Nurul Alam, S. M. 2011. "Health Service Delivery: The State of Government–Non-Government Relations in Bangladesh." *Public Administration and Development* no. 31 (4): 273–281. doi: 10.1002/pad.608.

Obiyan, A. Sat. 2005. "A Critical Examination of the State versus Non-Governmental Organizations (NGOs) in the Policy Sphere in the Global South: Will the State Die as the NGOs Thrive in Sub-Saharan Africa and Asia?" *African and Asian Studies* no. 4 (3): 301–326. doi: 10.1163/156920905774270475.

Ohmae, Kenichi. 1990. *The Borderless World*. New York: Harper & Row.

Olsen, Gorm Rye, Nils Carstensen, and Kristian Høyen. 2003. "Humanitarian Crises: What Determines the Level of Emergency Assistance? Media Coverage, Donor Interests and the Aid Business." *Disasters* no. 27 (2): 109–126. doi: 10.1111/1467-7717.00223.

Onyango, Tom. 1998. "Letters: City Lobby a Great Idea." *The Daily Nation*, June 30.

Organization for Economic Cooperation and Development. 2013. Development Database on Aid Activities. Online at http://stats.oecd.org/Index.aspx.

Osborne, David, and Ted Gaebler. 1992. *Reinventing Government: How the Entrepreneurial Spirit is Transforming the Public Sector*. Reading, MA: Addison-Wesley.

Osodo, Patrick, and Simon Matsvai. 1997. *Partners or Contractors? The Relationship Between Official Agencies and NGOs – Kenya and Zimbabwe*. Oxford, UK: INTRAC.

Ostrom, Elinor. 1996. "Crossing the Great Divide: Coproduction, Synergy, and Development." *World Development* no. 24 (6): 1073–1087. doi: 10.1016/0305-750x(96)00023-x.

Otiso, Kefa M. 2003. "State, Voluntary and Private Sector Partnerships for Slum Upgrading and Basic Service Delivery in Nairobi City, Kenya." *Cities* no. 20 (4): 221–229. doi: 10.1016/s0264-2751(03)00035-0.

Owiti, Jeremiah, Otieno Aluoka, and Adams G.R. Oloo. 2004. "Civil Society in the New Dispensation: Prospects and Challenges." In *Civil Society in the Third Republic*, edited by Duncan Okello, 71–88. Nairobi: National Council of NGOs.

Oyugi, Walter O. 1995. "Service Provision in Rural Kenya: Who Benefits?" In *Service Provision under Stress in East Africa*, edited by Joseph Semboja and Ole Therkildsen, 121–140. Copenhagen: Center for Development Research.

2004. "The Role of NGOs in Fostering Development and Good Governance at the Local Level in Africa with a Focus on Kenya." *Africa Development* no. 29 (4): 19–55.

Oyugi, W.O., P. Wanyande, and C. Obdiambo-Mbai. 2003. *The Politics of Transition in Kenya: from KANU to NARC*. Nairobi: Heinrich Boll Foundation.

Palmer, Natasha. 2006. "An Awkward Threesome – Donors, Governments and Nonstate Providers of Health in Low Income Countries." *Public Administration and Development* no. 26 (3): 231–240. doi: 10.1002/pad.421.

Palmer, Natasha, Lesley Strong, Abdul Wali, and Egbert Sondorp. 2006. "Contracting Out Health Services in Fragile States." *BMJ* no. 332 (7543): 718–721. doi: 10.1136/bmj.332.7543.718.

Parkhurst, Justin O. 2005. "The Response to HIV/AIDS and the Construction of National Legitimacy: Lessons from Uganda." *Development and Change* no. 36 (3): 571–590. doi: 10.1111/j.0012-155X.2005.00424.x.

Parsons, Talcott. 1947. *Max Weber: The Theory of Social and Economic Organization*. New York: Oxford University Press.

Patrick, Ian. 2001. "East Timor Emerging from Conflict: The Role of Local NGOs and International Assistance." *Disasters* no. 25 (1): 48–66. doi: 10.1111/1467-7717.00161.

Peck, Laura R. 2008. "Do Antipoverty Nonprofits Locate Where People Need Them? Evidence From a Spatial Analysis of Phoenix." *Nonprofit and Voluntary Sector Quarterly* no. 37 (1): 138–151.

Peters, Guy B., and Jon Pierre. 1998. "Governance Without Government? Rethinking Public Administration." *Journal of Public Administration Research and Theory* no. 8: 227–243.

Peterson, Timothy J., and Jon Van Til. 2004. "Defining Characteristics of Civil Society." *International Journal of Not-for-Profit Law* no. 6 (2).

Pfeffer, Jeffrey. 1982. *Organizations and Organization Theory*. Boston: Pitman.

Pfeiffer, James. 2003. "International NGOs and Primary Health Care in Mozambique: the Need for a New Model of Collaboration." *Social Science & Medicine* no. 56 (4): 725–738.

Pick, Susan, Martha Givaudan, and Michael R. Reich. 2008. "NGO–Government Partnerships for Scaling Up: Sexuality Education in Mexico." *Development in Practice* no. 18 (2): 164–175. doi: 10.1080/09614520801897279.

Poole, Nigel. 1994. "The NGO Sector as an Alternative Delivery System for Agricultural Public Services." *Development in Practice* no. 4 (2): 100–111. doi: 10.1080/09614524910007763.

Prewitt, Kenneth. 1971. *Education and Political Values: An East African Case Study*. Nairobi: East African Publishing House.

2010. *Education and Citizenship in East Africa, 1966–1967: Kenya Sample*. Ann Arbor, MI: Inter-university Consortium for Political and Social Research.

Prosser, A.R.G. 1969. "Community Development and its Relation to Development Planning." *Journal of Administration Overseas* no. 8 (3).

Pugachev, Alexander. nd. Collaboration Between State and Health NGOs in the Kyrgyz Republic. Bishkek: Social Research Center, American University of Central Asia.

Puplampu, Korbla P., and Wisdom J. Tettey. 2000. "State–NGO Relations in an Era of Globalisation: the Implications for Agricultural Development in Africa." *Review of African Political Economy* no. 27 (84): 251–272. doi: 10.1080/03056240008704458.

Putnam, Robert. 1993. *Making Democracy Work: Civil Traditions in Modern Italy*. Princeton: Princeton University Press.

2000. *Bowling Alone: The Collapse and Revival of American Community*. New York: Simon & Schuster.

Rahman, Sabeel. 2006. "Development, Democracy and the NGO Sector." *Journal of Developing Societies* no. 22 (4): 451–473. doi: 10.1177/0169796x06072650.

Ramanath, Ramya, and Alnoor Ebrahim. 2010. "Strategies and Tactics in NGO–Government Relations: Insights from Slum Housing in Mumbai." *Nonprofit Management and Leadership* no. 21 (1): 21–42.

Raustiala, Kal. 1997. "States, NGOs, and International Environmental Institutions." *International Studies Quarterly* no. 41 (4): 719–740. doi: 10.1111/1468-2478.00064.

Republic of Kenya. 1963. *A National Policy of Community Development*, edited by Ministry of Labor and Social Services. Nairobi: mimeo. *Statute Law (Miscellaneous Amendments) Act*. October 23.

2002. *West Pokot: District Development Plan 2002–2008*, edited by Ministry of Planning and National Development. Nairobi: Government Printer.

2008a. "Kenya Public Service Week." In *Brochure*. Nairobi: Government Press.

2008b. *Service Charter*, edited by Ministry of Livestock Development. Nairobi.

2010. *The Constitution of Kenya*. Nairobi. *Statute Law (Miscellaneous Amendments) Bill*. October 23.

Republic of Kenya Ministry of Planning and National Development. 2002a. *Butere/Mumias: District Development Plan 2002–2008*. Nairobi: Government Printer.

2002b. *Kakamega: District Development Plan 2002–2008*. Nairobi: Government Printer.

2002c. *Kisii: District Development Plan 2002–2008*. Nairobi: Government Printer.

2002d. *Kuria: District Development Plan 2002–2008*. Nairobi: Government Printer.

2002e. *Makueni: District Development Plan 2002–2008*. Nairobi: Government Printer.

2002f. *Nyandarua: District Development Plan 2002–2008*. Nairobi: Government Printer.

2002g. *Nyando: District Development Plan 2002–2008.* Nairobi: Government Printer.

2002h. *Rachuonyo: District Development Plan 2002–2008.* Nairobi: Government Printer.

Republic of Kenya – Kenya Roads Board. 2007. Website (cited October 14, 2007). Available from http://www.krb.go.ke/).

Republic of Kenya NGO Coordination Bureau. 2006. NGO Database. Nairobi: Republic of Kenya.

2011a. *Online Database Search* (cited August 29, 2011). Available from http://www.ngobureau.or.ke/.

2011b. *About Us* 2011 (cited May 25, 2011). Available from http://www.ngobureau.or.ke/.

Rhodes, R.A.W. 1994. "The Hollowing Out of the State: the Changing Nature of the Public Service in Britain." *Political Quarterly* no. 65 (2): 138–151.

1996. "The New Governance: Governance Without Government." *Political Studies* no. 44: 652–667.

2000. "Governance and Public Administration." In *Debating Governance: Authority, Steering, and Democracy,* edited by Jon Pierre, 54–90. Oxford: Oxford University Press.

Rich, Jessica A.J. 2013. "Grassroots Bureaucracy: Intergovernmental Relations and Popular Mobilization in Brazil's AIDS Policy Sector." *Latin American Politics and Society* no. 55 (2): 1–25. doi: 10.1111/j.1548-2456.2013.00191.x.

Robinson, Rachel Sullivan. 2011. "From Population to HIV: the Organizational and Structural Determinants of HIV Outcomes in Sub-Saharan Africa." *Journal of the International AIDS Society* no. 14 (Supplement 2): S6.

Rodrik, Dani. 1997. *Has Globalization Gone Too Far?* Washington, DC: Peterson Institute.

Roitman, Janet. 2005. *Fiscal Disobedience: An Anthropology of Economic Regulation in Central Africa.* Princeton, NJ: Princeton University Press.

Rosberg, Carl, and John Nottingham. 1966. *The Myth of Mau Mau: Nationalism in Kenya.* New York: Praeger.

Rose, Pauline. 2006. "Collaborating in Education for All? Experiences of Government Support for Non-state Provision of Basic Education in South Asia and Sub-Saharan Africa." *Public Administration and Development* no. 26 (3): 219–229. doi: 10.1002/pad.420.

2011. "Strategies for Engagement: Government and National Nongovernment Education Providers in South Asia." *Public Administration and Development* no. 31 (4): 294–305. doi: 10.1002/pad.607.

Rosenau, James. 2000. "Change, Complexity, and Complexity in Globalizing Space." In *Debating Governance: Authority, Steering, and Democracy,* edited by Jon Pierre, 54–90. Oxford: Oxford University Press.

Rosenau, James N., and Ernst-Otto Czempiel. 1992. *Governance without Government: Order and Change in World Politics.* Cambridge: Cambridge University Press.

Rosenberg, Alana, Kari Hartwig, and Michael Merson. 2008. "Government–NGO Collaboration and Sustainability of Orphans and Vulnerable Children

Projects in Southern Africa." *Evaluation and Program Planning* no. 31 (1): 51–60. doi: 10.1016/j.evalprogplan.2007.08.005.

Rueschemeyer, Dietrich. 2003. "Can One of a Few Cases Yield Theoretical Gains?" In *Comparative Historical Analysis in the Social Sciences*, edited by James Mahoney and Dietrich Rueschemeyer, 305–336. New York: Cambridge University Press.

Rusca, Maria, and Klaas Schwartz. 2012. "Divergent Sources of Legitimacy: A Case Study of International NGOs in the Water Services Sector in Lilongwe and Maputo." *Journal of Southern African Studies* no. 38 (3): 681–697. doi: 10.1080/03057070.2012.711106.

Sacks, Audrey. 2012. "Can Donors and Nonstate Actors Undermine Citizens' Legitimating Beliefs?" *Economic Premise* no. 95: 1–5.

Saich, Tony. 2000. "Negotiating the State: The Development of Social Organizations in China." *China Quarterly* no. 161: 124–141.

Salamon, Lester M., Helmut K. Anheier, Regina List, Stefan Toepler, and S. Wojciech Sokolowski. 1999. *Global Civil Society: Dimensions of the Nonprofit Sector*. Baltimore, MD: Johns Hopkins Center for Civil Society Studies.

Salamon, Lester. 1993. "The Global Associational Revolution: The Rise of the Third Sector on the World Scene." In *Occasional Papers No. 15*. Baltimore: Institute for Policy Studies, Johns Hopkins University.

1994. "The Rise of the Nonprofit Sector." *Foreign Affairs* no. 73 (4): 109–122.

Sandberg, Eve. 1994. *The Changing Politics of Nongovernmental Organizations and African States*. Westport: Praeger.

Sanyal, Bishwapriya. 1994. "Co-operative Autonomy: The Dialectic of State–NGOs Relationship in Developing Countries." Research Series no. 100. Geneva: International Institute for Labour Studies.

Schatzberg, Michael. 1986. "Two Faces of Kenya: The Researcher and the State." *African Studies Review* no. 29 (4): 1–15.

2001. *Political Legitimacy in Middle Africa: Father, Family, Food*. Bloomington: Indiana University Press.

Schmitter, Philippe C. 1974. "Still the Century of Corporatism?" *The Review of Politics* no. 36 (1): 85–131.

Schofer, Evan, and Wesley Longhofer. 2011. "The Structural Sources of Association." *American Journal of Sociology* no. 117 (2): 539–585. doi: 10.1086/661593.

Schuller, Mark. 2009. "Gluing Globalization: NGOs as Intermediaries in Haiti." *PoLAR: Political and Legal Anthropology Review* no. 32 (1): 84–104. doi: 10.1111/j.1555-2934.2009.01025.x.

Seay, Laura. 2010. "Substituting for the State: Civil Society Organizations & Public Goods in the Eastern D.R. Congo." Paper presented at the American Political Science Association Annual Meeting, Washington, DC.

Segarra, Monique. 1997. "Redefining the Public/Private Mix: NGOs and the Emergency Social Investment Fund in Ecuador." In *The New Politics of Inequality in Latin America: Rethinking Participation and Representation*, edited by Douglas A. Chalmers, Carlos M. Vilas, Katherine Hite, Scott B. Martin, Kerianne Piester and Monique Segarra, 489–515. New York: Oxford University Press.

Selznick, Philip. 1949. *TVA and the Grass Roots*. Berkeley: University of California Press.

Sen, Siddhartha. 1999. "Some Aspects of State–NGO Relationships in India in the Post-Independence Era." *Development and Change* no. 30 (2): 327–355. doi: 10.1111/1467-7660.00120.

Sending, Ole Jacob, and Iver B. Neumann. 2006. "Governance to Governmentality: Analyzing NGOs, States, and Power." *International Studies Quarterly* no. 50 (3): 651–672. doi: 10.1111/j.1468-2478.2006.00418.x.

Shively, W. Phillips. 1969. "'Ecological' Inference: The Use of Aggregate Data to Study Individuals." *The American Political Science Review* no. 63 (4): 1183–1196. doi: 10.2307/1955079.

Skocpol, Theda. 1979. *States and Social Revolution*. New York: Cambridge University Press.

2003. *Diminished Democracy: From Membership to Management in American Civic Life*. Norman, OK: University of Oklahoma Press.

Small, Mario Luis. 2011. "How to Conduct a Mixed Methods Study: Recent Trends in a Rapidly Growing Literature." *Annual Review of Sociology* no. 37 (1): 57–86. doi: 10.1146/annurev.soc.012809.102657.

Smith, Daniel Jordan. 2010. "Corruption, NGOs, and Development in Nigeria." *Third World Quarterly* no. 31 (2): 243–258. doi: 10.1080/01436591003711975.

Soublière, Jean-François, and Charlotte Cloutier. 2015. "Explaining Levels of Local Government Involvement in Service Delivery: The Dynamics of Cross-Sector Partnerships in Malawi." *Public Administration and Development*: n/a-n/a. doi: 10.1002/pad.1715.

Stern, Rachel E. 2013. *Environmental Litigation in China: A Study in Political Ambivalence*. New York: Cambridge University Press.

Stirrat, R. L. 2008. "Mercenaries, Missionaries and Misfits: Representations of Development Personnel." *Critique of Anthropology* no. 28 (4): 406–425.

Stoker, Gerry. 1998. "Governance as Theory: Five Propositions." *International Social Science Journal* no. 50 (155): 17–28.

Strange, Susan. 1996. *The Retreat of the State: the Diffusion of Power in the World Economy*. Cambridge: Cambridge University Press.

Suárez, David, and Jeffery H. Marshall. 2014. "Capacity in the NGO Sector: Results from a National Survey in Cambodia." *VOLUNTAS: International Journal of Voluntary and Nonprofit Organizations* no. 25 (1): 176–200. doi: 10.1007/s11266-012-9331-8.

Suchman, Mark C. 1995. "Managing Legitimacy." *Academy of Management Review* no. 20 (3): 571–610.

Sunshine, Jason, and Tom Taylor. 2003. "Moral Solidarity, Identification with the Community, and the Importance of Procedural Justice: The Police as Prototypical Representatives of a Group's Moral Values." *Social Psychology Quarterly* no. 66 (2): 153–165.

Swidler, Ann. 2007. "Syncretism and Subversion in AIDS Governance: How locals cope with Global Demands." In *AIDS and Governance*, edited by N.K. Poku et al. Surrey: Ashgate.

Swidler, Ann, and Susan Cotts Watkins. 2009. "'Teach a Man to Fish': The Doctrine of Sustainability and Its Social Consequences." *World Development* no. 37 (7): 1182–1196.

Tamarkin, M. 1978. "The Roots of Political Stability in Kenya." *African Affairs* no. 77 (308): 297–320. doi: 10.2307/721836.

Taylor, Brian D. 2006. "Law Enforcement and Civil Society in Russia." *Europe-Asia Studies* no. 58 (2): 193–213. doi: 10.2307/20451183.

Teets, Jessica. 2012. "Reforming Service Delivery in China: The Emergence of a Social Innovation Model." *Journal of Chinese Political Science* no. 17 (1): 15–32. doi: 10.1007/s11366-011-9176-9.

The National Council of NGOs. The National Council of NGOs 2005. Available from http://www.ngocouncil.org/index.asp.

Thomas-Slayter, Barbara. 1985. *Politics, Participation and Poverty: Development Through Self-Help in Kenya*. Boulder, CO: Westview Press.

Tocqueville, Alexis de. 1835. *Democracy in America*, ed. J.P. Mayer, trans. George Lawrence. 1969. New York: Harper Collins Perennial Classics.

Transparency International Kenya. 2003. "*Harambee*: the spirit of giving or reaping?" *Adili* no. 37: 1–2.

Tripp, Aili Mari. 1994. "The Impact of Crisis and Economic Reform on Tanzania's Changing Associational Life." In *The Changing Politics of Nongovernmental Organizations and African States*, edited by Eve Sandberg, 121–137. Westport, CT: Praeger.

 1997. *Changing the Rules: the Politics of Liberalization and the Urban Informal Economy in Tanzania*. Berkeley, CA: UC Press.

 2000. "Political Reform in Tanzania: The Struggle for Associational Autonomy." *Comparative Politics* no. 32 (2): 191–214. doi: 10.2307/422397.

 2001. "The Politics of Autonomy and Cooptation in Africa: The Case of the Ugandan Women's Movement." *The Journal of Modern African Studies* no. 39 (1): 101–128.

Turner, Thomas, and Crawford Young. 1985. *The Rise and Decline of the Zairian State*. Madison: University of Wisconsin Press.

US Department of State. 1998. *Kenya Report on Human Rights Practices for 1997*. Washington, DC: Bureau of Democracy, Human Rights, and Labor.

Umali-Deininger, Dina, and Lisa A. Schwartz. 1994. "Public and Private Agricultural Extension: Beyond Traditional Frontiers." In *World Bank Discussion Paper 236*. Washington, DC: World Bank.

UN Habitat. 2010. "Challenges of Municipal Finance in Africa." In *Human Settlements Finance Systems Series*. Nairobi: UN Habitat.

UNAIDS/WHO. 2004. *Kenya: Epidemiological Fact Sheet – 2004 Update*. UNAIDS and WHO.

UNDP. 2010. "The Real Wealth of Nations: Pathways to Human Development." In *Human Development Report 2010*. Palgrave: UNDP.

Unger, Jonathan, and Anita Chan. 1995. "China, Corporatism and the East Asian Model." *Australian Journal of Chinese Affairs* no. 33: 29–53.

United Nations Nongovernmental Liaison Service. *Objectives and Activities* 2011 (cited April 21, 2012). Available from http://www.un-ngls.org/spip.php?page=article_s&id_article=3136.

Uphoff, Norman. 1993. "Grassroots Organizations and NGOs in Rural Development: Opportunities with Diminishing States and Expanding Markets." *World Development* no. 21 (4): 607–622.

USAID. 1982. *Recurrent Costs: Problems in Less Developed Countries.* Washington, DC: US Agency for International Development.

Vakil, Anna C. 1997. "Confronting the Classification Problem: Toward a Taxonomy of NGOs." *World Development* no. 25 (12): 2057–2070. doi: 10.1016/s0305-750x(97)00098-3.

van de Walle, Nicolas 2001. *African Economies and the Politics of Permanent Crisis, 1979–1999: Political Economy of Institutions and Decisions.* New York: Cambridge University Press.

Van Der Heijden, Hendrik. 1987. "The Reconciliation of NGO Autonomy, Program Integrity and Operational Effectiveness with Accountability to Donors." *World Development* no. 15, Supplement 1: 103–112. doi: 10.1016/0305-750x(87)90148-3.

van Klinken, Marinus K. 1998. "Beyond the NGO–Government Divide: Network NGOs in East Africa." *Development in Practice* no. 8 (3): 349–353.

Van Ryzin, Gregg G. 2004. "Expectations, Performance, and Citizen Satisfaction with Urban Services." *Journal of Policy Analysis and Management* no. 23 (3): 433–448. doi: 10.1002/pam.20020.

Waiguru, Anne. 2002. Corruption and Patronage Politics: The Case of Harambee in Kenya. Paper read at Transparency International Workshop, Brisbane, Australia. Website www.ictregulationtoolkit.org.

Wallis, M.A.H. 1985. *Bureaucrats, Politicians and Rural Communities in Kenya,* edited by Paul Cook. Manchester: University of Manchester, Department of Administrative Studies.

Wamai, Richard G. 2004. NGO and Public Health Systems: Comparative Trends in Transforming Health Care Systems in Kenya and Finland. Presented at the International Society for Third Sector Research Biannual Meeting, Toronto.

Watkins, Susan Cotts, Ann Swidler, and Thomas Hannan. 2012. "Outsourcing Social Transformation: Development NGOs as Organizations." *Annual Review of Sociology* no. 38 (1): 285–315. doi: 10.1146/annurev-soc-071811-145516.

Weber, Max. 1919. "Politics as a Vocation." In *From Max Weber: Essays in Sociology,* edited by H. Gerth and C.W. Mills. New York: Oxford University Press.

Weiss, Linda. 1998. *The Myth of the Powerless State.* New York: Cornell University Press.

Werker, Eric, and Faisal Z. Ahmed. 2008. "What Do Nongovernmental Organizations Do?" *Journal of Economic Perspectives* no. 22 (2): 73–92. doi: 10.1257/jep.22.2.73.

Whaites, Alan. 1998. "NGOs, Civil Society and the State: Avoiding Theoretical Extremes in Real World Issues." *Development in Practice* no. 8 (3): 343–349.

White, Sarah C. 1996. "Depoliticising Development: the Uses and Abuses of Participation." *Development in Practice* no. 6 (1): 6–15.

Whittington, Keith E. 1998. "Revisiting Tocqueville's America." *American Behavioral Scientist* no. 42 (1): 21–32.

Widner, Jennifer A. 1992. *The Rise of a Party-State in Kenya: From Harambee! to Nyayo!* Berkeley: University of California Press.

1995. "States and Statelessness in Late Twentieth-Century Africa." *Daedalus* no. 124 (3): 129–153.

Wittenberg, Jason. 2007. "Peril and Promise: Multi-Method Research in Practice." *Qualitative Methods* no. 5 (1): 19–22.

Wolf, Thomas P., Carolyn Logan, and Jeremiah Owiti. 2004. A New Dawn? Popular Optimism in Kenya after the Transition. In Working Paper 33: Afrobarometer.

World Bank. 1989. *Sub-Saharan Africa: from Crisis to Sustainable Growth.* Washington, DC: The World Bank.

2005. *Capacity Building in Africa: An OED Evaluation of World Bank Support.* Washington, DC: World Bank.

Civil Society 2011 [cited November 8, 2011]. Available from http://go .worldbank.org/19WRCK3AY0.

World Development. 1987. "Supplemental Issue Covering Topics of NGOs and International World Values Survey." *World Development* no. 15.

World Resources Institute. 2003. "Awakening Civil Society." In *World Resources 2002–2004: Decisions for the Earth: Balance, Voice, and Power.* Washington, DC: World Resources Institute.

Young, Crawford. 1988. "The Colonial State and its Political Legacy." In *The Precarious Balance: State and Society in Africa*, edited by Donald Rothschild and Naomi Chazan, 59–62. Boulder, CO: Westview Press.

1994. "On the State." In *The African Colonial State in Comparative Perspective*, 13–42. New Haven, CT: Yale University Press.

2004. "The End of the Post-Colonial State in Africa? Reflections on Changing African Political Dynamics." *African Affairs* no. 103: 23–49.

Younis, Mona. 2007. "An Imperfect Process: Funding Human Rights – A Case Study." In *Ethics in Action: the Ethical Challenges of International Human Rights Nongovernmental Organizations*, edited by Daniel A. Bell and Jean-Marc Coicaud, 38–53. New York: Cambridge University Press.

Zafar Ullah, A. N., James N. Newell, Jalal Uddin Ahmed, M. K. A. Hyder, and Akramul Islam. 2006. "Government–NGO Collaboration: the Case of Tuberculosis Control in Bangladesh." *Health Policy and Planning* no. 21 (2): 143–155. doi: 10.1093/heapol/czjo14.

Zaidi, S. Akbar. 1999. "NGO Failure and the Need to Bring Back the State." *Journal of International Development* no. 11 (2): 259–271. doi: 10.1002/(sici)1099–1328(199903/04)11:2<259::aid-jid573>3.0.co;2-n.

Index

CPSIA information can be obtained at www.ICGtesting.com
Printed in the USA
LVOW11*2305250816

501863LV00008B/112/P